TONY CURTIS
THE AUTOBIOGRAPHY

Also by Barry Paris:

Louise Brooks

TONY CURTIS

T·H·E A·U·T·O·B·I·O·G·R·A·P·H·Y

TONY CURTIS
and BARRY PARIS

WILLIAM MORROW AND COMPANY, INC.

New York

Copyright © 1993 by Tony Curtis and Barry Paris

"Richard Cory" from *The Children of the Night* by Edward Arlington Robinson (New York: Charles Scribner's sons, 1897).

It is the policy of William Morrow and Company, Inc., and its imprints and affiliates, recognizing the importance of preserving what has been written, to print the books we publish on acid-free paper, and we exert our best efforts to that end.

Library of Congress Cataloging-in-Publication Data

Curtis, Tony, 1925–
    Tony Curtis: the autobiography / Tony Curtis and Barry Paris.—1st ed.
        p.   cm.
    Filmography: p.
    Includes index.
    ISBN 0-688-09759-6 (alk. paper)
    1. Curtis, Tony, 1925–   .   2. Motion picture actors and actresses—
    United States—Biography.   I. Paris, Barry.   II. Title.
    PN2287.C698A3   1993
    791.43′028′092—dc20
    [B]   93-28127
                                                                          CIP

Printed in the United States of America

First Edition

1 2 3 4 5 6 7 8 9 10

BOOK DESIGN BY MICHAEL MENDELSOHN OF MM DESIGN 2000, INC.

To my parents,
the past . . .
And to Lisa,
the future . . .

FOREWORD

Thank God for snobs. I never told Tony Curtis this, but when his autobiographical project came up, a number of my academic friends advised me to turn up my intellectual nose. Yes, his films made more money and were more successful than those of most other actors and actresses combined. But he never won an Oscar. And he never inspired a master's thesis. He was just too—too what?

Too *popular*.

That snobbery opened my eyes. I grew up with Tony Curtis. I never missed his films. I wanted to meet him, and the minute I did, I liked him. I liked his brutal, off-the-wall honesty, his flights of existential fancy, his original take on films and film history, his desire to explore the pain and truth of his own sexuality. The more I got to know him—in California, in New York, in a lot of places in between—the more I liked him.

But when it came time to sit down and start the real literary work, it struck me with a certain horror that I was severely handicapped as a film historian: I liked him *too* much. My pro-Tony bias would constantly tempt me to tamper with his story and embellish it to make him "look better." The solution, when it finally came, was not to tamper with it at all; not to pretend that I do anything other than admire Tony Curtis, his life, and his films: to let him tell his story his way, and certainly without "ghostwriting." But being pedantic and opinionated, I had certain things I wanted to say and certain colleagues of Tony's whose input I wanted to include.

We decided to integrate the voices of Tony's friends and family, and my selective film commentaries, directly into the text. With the aid of designer Michael Mendelsohn, we have set off all such sections in different type, signing and dating them for clarity. The reader may thus savor the ruminations of the interlopers or—if annoyed or distracted by them—simply skip over them and move on to Tony's narrative. It is an effort to improve upon the tired old "star biography" format: those "as told to" memoirs in which helpful hacks pass off kiss-and-tell revelations as the subject's own words.

The loftier goals of this book include film truth, sexual truth, and the resurrection of certain directors and unsung heroes of Hollywood, but most of all the celebration of an American life—Tony Curtis's—fascinating in itself, more so because it has been lived in the realm of our national fantasy-pastime, the movies. The goal of this Foreword is to affirm that everything I have to say is restricted to the insets and footnotes, and that the rest (all but a few transitions and the dates I compulsively supply) belongs wholly and authentically to Tony Curtis. There are multiple voices here, but there is no voice—on a movie sound track or the printed page—like Tony's.

Our new hybrid approach strives rather grandly to synthesize biography and autobiography. What better life to try it out on? Tony Curtis is one of the most dynamic, complex, and enduring pop-cultural figures of our time—a major player in American film for four decades. A case can now be made, from these pages, that he is also the single most candid and canny inside observer of the Hollywood era he epitomized and helped to define.

—BARRY PARIS
Pittsburgh
June 1993

ACKNOWLEDGMENTS

Many people made this book possible and shared the belief that it should be something different—and better. By their participation, they made it so.

We owe a special debt of gratitude to TC's distinguished friends and colleagues who took time to give us their recollections, notably: Nicky Blair, Tommy Culla, Charles Fabian, Joe Franklin, Janet Leigh, Jack Lemmon, Walter Matthau, Sidney Poitier, Gene Singer, and the incomparable Billy Wilder. Kirk Douglas, Burt Lancaster, Frank Sinatra, Lew Wasserman, and Dodi Fayed also deserve thanks for their key roles not in the writing but in the living of this "life."

The Curtis family itself was superb in its support, particularly Kelly Curtis and Scott Morfee, Jamie Lee Curtis and Christopher Guest, Alexandra Curtis Sargeant, Allegra Curtis, Nicholas Curtis, Benjamin Curtis, and Lisa Deutsch Curtis. Eli and Nancy Blumenfeld are an integral part of that family; Eli provided Rock of Gibraltar advice and support at every stage of the book, from beginning to end.

Another family came through too: Wyoming B. Paris I discovered "Marilyn Monroe: The Last Interview." Wyoming B. II and Nancy contributed valuable reference works. Claire Paris and Pamela Paris Loyle contributed criticism—which they do so well. Above all, Myrna Paris devoted countless hours to photographic research, fact checking, and hawk-eyed manuscript revisions.

Support troops included Jack Kaplan, S. Chad Anyan (director of the Galerie at Tatou), Peter F. Paul, Dale C. Olson, John Scotto, Phillis Drapkin (of Behind the Scenes Travel), Megan McGough Sutherland (long-distance from Egypt), Pittsburgh Mayor Sophie Masloff, and the computer services department of the St. Regis Hotel in New York City.

Invaluable research and photographic assistance was provided by always generous Leonard Maltin, John Barba, Howard Cutler, Ellen Martin, Barnet Shindlman, Beth Allen, the Academy of Motion Picture Arts and Sciences' Margaret Herrick Library, the New York Public Library at Lincoln

Center Library (Billy Rose Collection), and Ron and Howard Mandelbaum of Photofest. The pioneering biographical work of Allan Hunter (*Tony Curtis: The Man and His Movies*) and James Robert Parish (*The Swashbucklers* and *Hollywood's Great Love Teams*) were also of great value.

Those stellar agents Robert Gottlieb and Daniel Strone of the William Morris Agency were responsible for launching the project, and those long-suffering, cool-headed editors Paul Bresnick and Ben Ratliff at William Morrow and Co. for midwifing it to successful completion. The enthusiasm of our British editor, Tom Weldon of William Heinemann and Reed Consumer Books, was also heartening.

Two other participants were the ones without whom all would have been lost: Maria Ciaccia—ace researcher, transcriber, and authority on Hollywood of the fifties—and the Divine Miss Jennifer Walsh, ace personal assistant to TC, who put in endless hours on the project beyond the call of duty. Always with a smile.

To all of them, we extend deep thanks.

—TONY CURTIS AND BARRY PARIS

CONTENTS

TONY CURTIS
T·H·E A·U·T·O·B·I·O·G·R·A·P·H·Y

C·H·A·P·T·E·R O·N·E

FATHERS AND SONS

New York City was the training ground. Hollywood was a piece of cake by comparison. East Seventy-eighth and First Avenue in Manhattan was the no-man's-land where I once got the shit kicked out of me in my own neighborhood. Usually I was so fucking fast, with a running start I could leap over cars and get away from anybody if I had to. But one day I was cornered by four or five guys—the only time I ever got caught. I learned something from that. I decided it wasn't going to happen again.

When I was ten or eleven years old, this German kid named Frank Webber at Public School 82 used to bait me all the time. He just hated my guts, for some reason, and he'd yell horrible names all the time: "Lousy kike! Sheeny asshole! Jew bastard! Big-nose Hebe! You killed Our Lord!" Oh, yes, how do you do, and what's *your* name? Walking down the street in those days, you knew you were a Jew, even though you didn't quite know what that meant. *Why are they after me? What did I do?* I didn't know until much later that my counterparts were already being killed in Germany.

Even in the mid-1930s, the war was already on even in America: The soldiers were boys, and the trenches were in New York City. You didn't dare go into a neighborhood you didn't come from. You couldn't get halfway down the block before you'd be followed and, next thing you knew, a bunch of guys were hitting you with broom bats. From Seventy-eighth and First on up through the Yorkville section was Nazi land. This was the Berlin of Manhattan, the rabid German nationalist area—the war zone. I liked it. I was born to it. Those little American Aryans would beat up any Semitic-looking kid who wandered into their preserve.

15

The only thing to do was find a couple of pals and stick together, which is what we did. We collected milk bottles and old condoms for ammunition. We'd pee into them and put a few other things in them, and deposit them on the roof of an empty tenement at First and Eighty-fourth for safekeeping. We'd find them later by their smell. In those days, the Nazis had Bund marches on First Avenue from Seventy-ninth Street going north, wearing their swastikas and brown shirts and boots. On Nazi march days, we would go back to that tenement, grab the fire escape ladder, pull it down and go up with it, then climb up onto the roof. Me and my friends would hide up there and, when the moment was right, we'd take those rubbers and bottles filled with love and affection and fling them down on top of them. The Nazis had a group of guys about our age who worked the edges of the parade, and as soon as they saw things coming off the roofs, they'd run up those tenements and try to catch us.

So we had these incredible battles and rooftop chases: up and down staircases, into alleys, hiding in ashcans and under cars. We'd stand and peek over that roof when the Nazis came goose-stepping up the street. The Nazi kids would stay on one side and look up and see if they could see our heads pop up on the other side. But we were so erratic in our attacks, they were never quite sure. We'd look over that roof and then step back a few feet and twirl that charming little missile, and let it go. It would go sailing—*plop!*—hopefully, on the head of a Nazi.

Before it even hit the ground we'd be gone, down the fire escape, through the alleys, and across to the next building, ending up on good old Second Avenue. Those junior storm troopers would fan out, trying to find us, but we'd be long gone under the turnstile of the Second Avenue El, on our way downtown. We fuckin' drove them crazy. We'd walk down the street and look at each other, and we knew what we were: yes, freedom fighters—or fighters for I don't know what. We felt heroic, like Gary Cooper and the Spanish patriots in *For Whom the Bell Tolls*. We were the renegades in some larger-than-life story. It wasn't so different from seeing a movie— or, I found out later, being in one. Real and unreal at the same time. Thrilling, and then the letdown. No matter what happened during the day, I'd slink back home and go back to being Bernie Schwartz, the mild-mannered little Jewish boy, at night.

* * *

I'm more interested in that reality of my life than in what Marilyn Monroe or Barbara Stanwyck was like. I don't want to turn the people in the movie business into something they weren't, myself included. There was nothing extraordinary about those people. The only extraordinary thing about any of us was that we were thirty-five feet tall on the screen of a movie theater. That's it. We were no better or worse than anyone else, and no better or worse than that image on the screen. But because of the enormity of that image, there seems to be more meaning in it. Well, there *isn't*. Marilyn was an ordinary woman. We're all ordinary people made extraordinary by our fame, not by our personal integrity or frustrations or any other qualities that people want to give us.

I'm only interested in how I've evolved as a person. To me, Marilyn Monroe and Frank Webber from P.S. 82 are of equal importance. The kids I grew up with are as much a key to me as Kirk Douglas or Jack Lemmon. People are always hitting me with names: "What was Natalie Wood really like?" I am not impressed by great film stars or great writers or great scientists. I'm not Rona Barrett. Marilyn Monroe's idiosyncrasies don't really interest me. They were people who made some mark in something called *the movies*. It doesn't do them or me a service to judge them. In my life, I have found that I picked up as much information from that Nazi kid in New York who kicked the shit out of me because I was Jewish as I ever did from John Huston on the set of *The List of Adrian Messenger*. To me, they both had the same amount of energy. They're both equal pieces in my mosaic.

I have to say it again: We were mere mortals. Yet people thought, *God, he must be a legend. He must be something solid to be on a thirty-five-foot screen!* Actress ZaSu Pitts's mother looked at ZaSu and said, "You must be something really special, ZaSu, to be so big up there!" It blew a lot of minds. A lot of people couldn't handle it. They saw their own huge image and thought they were King Kong. They didn't know they were King Shit. They thought they were eight-hundred-pound gorillas who could sleep anywhere they wanted. But they still had the same personal madness and insecurities of the little people they always were. So did I. How could a fabulous thirty-five-foot guy like me be so fucked up? I used to get bummed out about it a lot. Some of the other guys and girls got so bummed out they ended up killing themselves.

You've got to blow the smoke out. You've got to get rid of that Madonna concept, that Rona Barrett concept, of pumping up "movie legends" with bellows: "Clint Eastwood—the new John Wayne." *Real men.* Why? Clint's an original; he's fine just the way he is. It's not Clint, it's the idiotic people in the publicity machine that do the comparing. Why do we have to stand on the shoulders of midgets to think we're better than other people? Einstein was a brilliant man, but why do I need to get on his shoulders to find some higher level of consciousness? Who needs a spinoff of him? I've got enough trouble just being a spinoff of Bernie Schwartz.

I'm not trying to be glib. I understand why people are fascinated by movie actors. How many people do we know who are truly beautiful, truly intelligent, truly poetic? If they're in our neighborhood at all, it's for maybe twenty minutes, and then they go off to Vegas or Paris or Hollywood, and we never see them again. The only place we see that kind of beauty, or think we see it, is on the screen. That was especially true in the thirties, forties, and fifties, before television and satellites took over. Marilyn Monroe was an amazingly beautiful woman with the most vulnerable-looking face. Yes, she was. But big fucking deal. She was an ordinary woman who happened to have an extraordinary body and face. Billy Wilder on the set of *Some Like It Hot* was an extraordinary man. They were all fine people, but I've got to put them in proper perspective, for myself and for anybody who takes the trouble to read this.

Film people are always changing, like everybody else. Some people's noses keep growing. (My father's nose kept growing, much to his chagrin, and I was really worried about that as a kid.) Our faces change. A cute little boy or girl grows up to be an ugly adult, or vice versa. Tough luck. That's the breaks. I'm a very privileged person, and I know that and enjoy it, and I let everybody know how joyful I am. I want to share that. I want to share my looks, my life, everything. Life's too short to worry about your savings account. Time is as big a mystery to me as it is to anybody else, and maybe this little story illustrates that:

In 1948, when I first came to Los Angeles, I rented a house on Sycamore and Franklin Avenue. It was "early California"—I don't know how else you'd describe it—a funny little house with dark shingles and wood panels on the outside, and squeaky windows with latches on them. It had a pool—not a very big pool, but a pool—and it was filthy. The drainage didn't work. The water was so dark, you had the sensation that if you jumped in, it would just bounce you right out. That's how thick and green it was, like a stopped-up stream with no irrigation.

I was going to Universal every day for acting classes, voice classes, horseback riding, and I'd take the trolley back to Hollywood, then get off and walk from La Cienega to Sycamore. One day I got home and decided I'd take a swim. I ran in, took off all my clothes and went out into that pool, so filthy and cold. I hit it on the run, sank down in the water, and then got out shivering. I went inside, took a shower, put on my shorts and tank top, came up the steps—and here I am now talking to you.

That's how quick those forty-five years went by.

I am determined to make this book different. I'm not interested in the Shelley Winters approach. There's already enough bullshit around to provide fertilizer into the twenty-first century. I want to try not to bend everything in my life to suit my own purposes, even though we all do that. Even if we're writing *The Rise and Fall of the Roman Empire,* we cannot keep out that chicken soup our mother fed us. There's no way you can write anything without leaving your own Rosetta stone imprinted all over it.

I'd like to show you New York in those Depression years of the early thirties. They're embedded in my mind as clearly as etchings, sharp and distinct. I'd like to show you Hollywood when I first saw it in the late forties, before the studios collapsed and everything about movie making changed. I'd like to show you what it was like on the inside of that business, and what it was like on the inside of *me.* I'm intrigued by what Louise Brooks said: that you can't ever know somebody unless you understand their sexual life. It's amazing and true. A lot of people are frightened by that, but I'm not one of them.

In the film *Let 'Em Have It,* some kids are all excited because they're going to see a Tony Curtis movie—but they're not as excited as *I* am when I see a Tony Curtis movie. Millions of kids wanted to be Tony Curtis. Including me.

My life is a cornucopia: all kinds of fruit and vegetables tumbling out of that horn of plenty, in no logical order. In *Citizen Kane,* remember the extraordinary construction of that opening scene? The window stays in exactly the same part of the screen with each dissolve until you're inside and those lips are saying "Rosebud," and it's never referred to again or explained until the end. I'd like to find out what my "Rosebud" is—where in the streets of New York City it lies, with slivers of it in California, too.

In more ways than one, this book is my search for that Rosebud.

There are no absolute rules, there's just somebody else's game plan. Once at Hugh Hefner's house, we started to play poker, and this one guy said, "These are the rules: Deuces are wild, and one-eyed jacks, but only if it's a third hand played, and dealt by the fourth man. The betting can only be a dollar. If you want to check and raise, you can't unless you're the player before the next player . . ." I listened to this fucker and thought, *Oh, yeah, right.* I knew what he was doing. He was trying to build into that game a way that he couldn't lose. Control. But you can't control anything.

I found that out early. My mother and father found it out even earlier. My parents, where they came from, how they were formed—that's crucial to me. I'm intrigued by Europe. When I look at a map, I obliterate where the borders are marked and I just see this vast piece of real estate where that Mongolian strain came down through a narrow little gorge and ended up in Romania or Czechoslovakia. I always felt that the best of the breed made it through that gorge and settled in Hungary.

The same thing happened in America. People got off the boats on Ellis Island and ended up in Manhattan with eight, fifteen, twenty-two cents to their name. They went as far as that change in their pocket got them: maybe New Jersey, maybe Cincinnati, maybe somewhere where a few relatives were. If you only had a nickel, you got off the boat and settled in lower Manhattan. Mid-Manhattan if you had seven cents. If you had a dime, you could end up in the Bronx.

My father was an incredibly good-looking man, as you can see from the photograph. I was about four there. My mother looked a little like Pola Negri. Of course, a little Pola Negri can go a long way. My parents and their backgrounds are still a wonderful mystery to me. A few years ago my daughter Kelly and I went to the little Hungarian town of Mátészalka—just thirty miles from the Russian border—where my father was born. We saw his house and the synagogue he attended as a boy and young man. This synagogue had been closed since the Hungarian revolution in 1956, but one old guy had the key and opened it for us. There were holes in the ceiling and birds flying around; a beautiful old place. On the wall were the names of some of our relatives who didn't survive the Holocaust. It was a very moving experience.

My father wanted to be an electrician, and his father, my grandfather,

The Schwartz family—Manuel, Helen, and their firstborn son, Bernie—on vacation in New Jersey

took him the 150 miles from Mátészalka all the way to Budapest in a buggy for his apprenticeship. But when they got there, the electrician's shop was all locked up. So instead of *schlepping* back to Mátészalka, he took him into this tailor shop next door and made him an apprentice to the tailor.

"But Papa, I want to be an electrician. Can't we wait one more day?"

"No, I have to get back, and this donkey will never make the trip twice. He's the only one I've got."

How about that for destiny? That's how his career change came about. A life determined by a lock on a door and the frail legs of a mule.

So my father came to America in 1921 and worked as a tailor. What he always *really* wanted to do was be in show business as some kind of performer, though he was never quite sure what. One day he picked up a Hungarian-American newspaper and spotted an ad that said, "Dancers wanted, one dollar an hour—ten o'clock tomorrow morning," with an address in Brooklyn. The next morning he closed up the tailor shop for the day. I remember it distinctly, watching him get ready for this audition. He put on his one good pin-striped suit, tie, vest, spats, gloves—the way he dressed was really something—and then, after announcing his Big Break in show business to us, he left for the trek to Brooklyn. He got there and walked into the building. There's a Hungarian guy sitting there.

"I understand you're looking for dancers," my father says in Hungarian.

"What can you dance?" the guy asks.

"I can dance anything."

"Can you tango?"

"Of course I can tango."

"Can you do a fox trot?"

"Yes."

"What about the bolero?"

"In my sleep."

"All right, then go in the back."

He goes in the back.

"Take off your jacket, hang it up. Take your shoes and socks off."

He takes them off. There's a big vat with grapes. They roll up his pants. A Hungarian group plays *csárdás* music; they're hiring guys to make wine! Nobody'd go if the ad said, "Grape-stampers wanted." Would you? But if it said, "Dancers wanted," they'd go. I think he actually ended up doing it; a buck an hour was a helluva lot then. And at the next show-business interview, when they asked, "What have you done?" he could say, "I'm a dancer. I dance for a living."

That was my father. I loved that man.

But my father wasn't just Manuel Schwartz and my mother wasn't just Helen Schwartz. Jon Hall and Maria Montez were my parents, too. Jon Hall was Ali Baba, and he married Maria Montez, and I was *The Son of Ali Baba*. Go see *Ali Baba and the Forty Thieves*, and you'll see my other mommy and daddy dearest—they're part of my family tree. It was 1944 when they got together in that picture, and nine years later, *The Son of Ali Baba* was born! I love the fact that I came through both those seeds. One is the Tony Curtis seed, and the other is the Bernie Schwartz seed. So I could come from anyplace. Nothing was tying me down. I could be anybody I wanted to be. People tried to label me, but I didn't care. Fuck 'em and feed 'em fish.

Movies made that possible. But how many great potential stars never

Manuel Schwartz in costume as a pre-Revolutionary French
gentleman, with a note to that effect on his shoulder, in case anyone
was in doubt

made it because there was no camera around? Four hundred years ago, that
great-looking guy somewhere in Mongolia would've made Arnold
Schwarzenegger look like *Mrs.* Schwarzenegger, but there was no camera
around. How can we believe in destiny when a little illusion machine like
a camera can determine it? What about the beautiful women that could

23

have been great singers and actresses? Why was I lucky enough to find that playground of the world where I could frolic around with Helen of Troy and play ball with Achilles?

As some little-old geography teacher in Pittsburgh once said, "We are what we are because we are *where* we are." And *when*, too. If there are now eleven million Hungarians, one hundred years ago there were maybe five million, and one hundred years before that, two million. There must have been a time when the whole Hungarian population was really just a couple of families; a few tribes that slowly grew. Hungarians think of Hungary as a kind of aristocratic country. Everybody comes out of that aristocracy, which explains why all Hungarians are so proud of their heritage. I don't know if you know or care, but Hungarian is the only non-Indo-European language in Europe; it came from Attila the Hun's boys and girls in Asia. The message is the medium, and the medium is the language. I still speak it pretty well, and whenever my Hungarian kicks in, I find I become another person. I think differently. My sense of reality changes, and my sense of who I am switches to another tempo. If you feel inadequate or unsure of yourself in one language, when you switch to another language, suddenly you're not as vulnerable. In English you lack the confidence to speak informally with a woman, but maybe in French that disappears for some reason. But if you don't know or bother to learn another language, you don't have that luxury.

My first words were Hungarian. I hardly ever heard English or even Yiddish at home; we spoke only Hungarian. Whatever Yiddish or "American" I picked up, I learned in the streets. I didn't realize I was in America till I was six or seven and started going to elementary school. I thought Mátészalka was around the corner somewhere, and I was sure that Budapest was just down the street. As a young boy in New York, I spoke with a thick Hungarian accent. That was a tough place to grow up in, in any language. There were so many sounds you heard all around you, and they all ended up in your speech.

That language hurdle was what was most difficult for my parents. They met and got married in New York (May 22, 1924) but never really learned English thoroughly, and they never stopped speaking Hungarian all their lives. It was such a rich form of expression. Every now and then, before I sleep, I hear those soft, rumbling accented words my parents and my father's friends spoke around me. I'd fall asleep at his feet while they were playing cards. Hungarian has such a lilting sound. It still mesmerizes me,

24

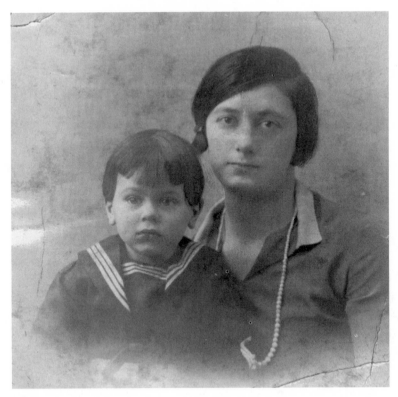

Serious serenity: Helen Schwartz holds three-year-old Bernie in New York studio portrait (1927).

which is why I still love to speak it. Whenever I'm somewhere where there's a Hungarian, he always comes up and introduces himself. I went to a restaurant-deli the other day, and sitting right next to me were some Hungarians who sounded exactly like my father and mother. We spoke, and it was like some beautiful little sliver of the past.

My parents belonged to the First Hungarian Independent Lodge. My father ended up as president of it for a while. Every summer they used to have picnics in New Brunswick, New Jersey, and in Brooklyn. I remember the goulash served on paper plates, and all the kids running around. The colors and sounds and smells of those people were fabulous. It amuses me now to think of how my children ended up with grandparents like Helen and Manny Schwartz. When Kelly and Jamie, Nicholas and Ben, and Alexandra and Allegra open up the door of their past, these Hungarian Jews come trundling out, ready to make strudel, dying to talk to you about the

Danube and all their unhappiness. Actually, most of my kids never knew them, but it must have been shocking or at least disconcerting for my wives and girlfriends to meet my parents for the first time.

"Where did *they* come from? How did he get to be the offspring of *them*?"

My earliest memory is as strange and disconnected as one of those old movie flashbacks shot through gauze: I have this image of sitting in a car—a 1922 Hupmobile four-door sedan, black with tan interior—driving in New York City, sitting next to a little girl who was crying. We were both going to get our tonsils out. I was about five, so it must've been 1930. I have no idea who the girl was or whose car it was. I just remember the city popping by the window, and that it was one of the few car rides I'd ever had.

I was born at the Flower Hospital in Manhattan on June 3, 1925. They said I was breast-fed for six months and gave it up only because I was asked to. We lived in the East Eighties for a while; then Astoria, Queens, then back to Manhattan; then the Bronx. My brother Julius was born at Woodstock Hospital in the Bronx in July 1929, but soon after that we were back in Manhattan at my father's new shop, Manuel Valet Service, on Lexington Avenue. My father kept changing shops, and we moved around a lot: Eighty-fifth and First, Seventy-fifth and Third, Sixty-second and Second.

Seventy-third and Second is the place I remember most. That was *my* street. On the corner was a huge second-hand clothing store crammed with all kinds of good stuff. All day long, people ran in and out of there, buying jackets, selling pants. I loved that area, with those push carts rattling up and down between Seventy-second and Seventy-ninth. The Second Avenue subway was above ground there, and the entrance was at our corner on Seventy-third. Right under the El stood a newsstand owned by my aunt and uncle, Albert and Ethel Klein. Ethel was my mother's half-sister. Their son, Andrew, my cousin, was a big hulking guy, who'd sit in the booth and make model airplanes and eat sandwiches. He'd let me come inside on winter days and hang out with him. He was nice to me. I'd chew gum in there and watch the world go by.

There was a restaurant called Little Czechoslovakia a few feet away. I hung out with Victor Mikus, whose family owned it. Victor used to make funny noises and had an odd habit of pushing out spit through his teeth. He fancied himself a painter, and I remember him once ridiculing one of my drawings. I never forgave him for that. I've been drawing all my life.

Tony Curtis, out of costume, as baby Bernard Schwartz: the first nude portrait (1926)

Victor became a cartoonist, but I became the painter. Life is funny, when you take it personally.

I went back to look at the old neighborhood a few months ago. My father's tailor shop, next to Little Czechoslovakia, has a FOR RENT sign in the window. I was amazed at how narrow those old buildings were. Our first-floor window was eye-level with the street. Our second-floor window was eye-level with the El. My father spent all day downstairs, pressing clothes on his steam machine and using the sewing machine. My mother took care of the front.

We lived in back of the shop. My mother and father slept in one corner; Julie and I slept together in another corner. There was a toilet in the third corner. In the other corner was the place where my mother did the cooking, and in the middle of the room was a table. That was our home— one room; living quarters for four people. How and when did my parents make love? But that was no big deal. A lot of people in those days lived ten or twelve to a room. I lived among the pipes and boilers and electrical and plumbing equipment, especially in the basement, which gave us a great place to hide and play.

My father would break his ass all winter long for us. Then every year when summer came—religiously—he would go off alone to the Catskills for two weeks and ride horses. That was his one extravagance.

The woman who owned our building was Mrs. Sapphire, who lived on the top floor. I think she liked my father, but nothing really went on between them. Maybe that's why she was always pissed off. I once went up there to deliver some clothes, and she opened the door and then slammed it shut. I just had time to see that her bed was in the middle of the room, which struck me as odd. Why did Mrs. Sapphire sleep in the middle of the room? That's a good question and a good title for a book I'll never write. I have some theories.

Anyway, one day she just decided to dispossess us. Kicked us all out on the sidewalk, literally: me, my brother Julie, the dog, my mother, my father, and all our possessions. Everything was thrown out on the street in the gutter under the Second Avenue El, including all the customers' clothes strung out on their racks. There we were on the street, with people gathered around saying, "Oh, those poor kids!" I was around eleven, and I started to cry. I felt so sorry because all those women gathered around were wailing for us. I remember my father outside, running up and down and across the street until finally he found a condemned tenement house we could live in for a while. We moved into the back of it. Within two or three hours, that became our new home. He didn't waste any time. How could he, with his wife and two kids out there weeping in the street?

So many of the buildings around there were condemned, and since nobody lived in that one, we stayed there for a long time. One night somebody tried to break in, and my father picked up the wooden slat that he used inside sleeves to press them and scared the guy off.

So you get the idea. It was a very difficult time, and that area was tough. I had to be careful where I went because I was a Jew, because I was young, and because I was handsome. It made me wiry and erratic and paranoid, which is what I still am. Always on guard. Right up the block from us were fancy apartments with lots of elegant, snappy-looking rich kids coming out, all dressed up in their wonderful clothing. And there I was, a tattered little motherfucker. The rich kids would walk away from us whenever we came near. But even then I knew I was better looking than any of them. I shouldn't say that, but that's what I thought. The juxtaposition—the fact that we lived almost right on top of each other—always amazed and amused me. Their doormen would yell, "Get the fuck away from here, you little prick!" I got so accustomed to that, whenever I walked down the street past them, I'd step down into the gutter, and then back up onto the sidewalk. I never gave anybody the chance to kick me off.

The thoroughfare around Seventy-second Street was important in my life. There was a Catholic church called St. John the Martyr at Seventy-second and Second that my Italian buddy Frank Vitucci took me into one day. He said, "Come in behind me and do exactly as I do." I said okay. We walked in the church, and the first thing he did was kneel down and bless himself right outside the door. So I knelt down on one knee and blessed myself. We got inside, he blessed himself again, and so did I. Then there was holy water. He put some on his finger and blessed himself. I dipped in too, and blessed myself. He knelt down before we went down the aisle, and I did that. Finally, we went down the aisle, got into the pew. He knelt down, he blessed himself. I knelt down, I blessed myself. Then we sat down. So I'm sitting in this hallowed place, and he looks at me and says, "Hey, did you fart?" I said, "No, should I?"

The synagogue my father took me to as a boy was Congregation B'nai Jehuda at 352 East Seventy-eighth Street. I'd go for the big holy days. My father would stand there with his tallis on and his yarmulke and his prayer-book, mumbling those ancient prayers in Hebrew, rocking back and forth. I'd stand beside him with a prayerbook saying to myself, *How the fuck do I get out of here?* He would poke me and turn the page for me to keep me up to date in the service. Our breaths would be foul because we'd been fasting so long. All those stale old men, with the women upstairs because we couldn't sit together. I'd say, "I gotta go take a leak." He'd say, "Go, go!" I'd go out and take off, if I thought I could get away with it. On normal days I could go till five or six without eating. On holy days I never could.

That condemned building we lived in still looks the same, believe it or not. In the back was a little courtyard—courtyard is really too fancy a word for it—where the women hung out all their clotheslines. Since nobody else lived there, we had access to the whole building, and I used to sneak up into those rundown, empty apartments to play. All the time I lived there, I was sure it was going to be torn down the next day or week. Little did I know they'd fix it up and, fifty years later, people would still be living in it. I wonder what that guy who "condemned" it thinks, looking down (or up) on it now.

The elevated train is long gone, but in those days my vista was that El traveling in front of the fire escapes past all those redbrick tenements. For lack of anything better to do, I'd sit on the fire escape and watch the trains go whizzing by at rush hour. I'd see the same trains and the same people every day, and after a while I started to recognize some of them. There was one funny little man in particular, with an umbrella. I'd see him every day at exactly the same time. The train would stop, and it was so close we could make eye contact. Sometimes he'd nod at me, and I'd nod back. This went on for a long time, and then one day he just disappeared and wasn't there anymore. I didn't really think anything about it until a couple of weeks later when a train came by and stopped and, all of a sudden, I noticed he was there again. I'm looking at him through my window, and I must have had a kind of surprised look on my face. He looks back at me, and I see him mouthing the words, "I've been sick!" It's like we had this *relationship*. Only in New York City.

In the heat of summertime, my brother, Julie, and I slept out on either the bottom fire escape or the one above it. Each one of those fire escapes was different, each one individual in its design. Those brownstones were only four or five stories tall because people couldn't walk up any more flights than that without having a heart attack. They were tiny and unassuming little buildings, but the people who built them had their own sense of beauty and individuality.

I went to Boy Scout meetings in a red building on Seventy-fifth Street that's still standing. It gave me a place to go in the wintertime at night. We tied knots, the usual things. I loved it. Farther down, in the middle of the block, was a great little Hungarian restaurant. The building at 305 East

Seventy-fifth had an incredible backyard area with a sort of playground place where my friends and I used to chase each other. My pal Frankie and I used to hang out there a lot because he and his family lived right next to it. I'd come over, and his mother would take Italian bread, cut it in half, put butter and garlic on it, and put it in the oven. It was fucking delicious.

One day I went to pick him up, and she says, "C'mere, Bernie, I want to show you something." She takes me by the hand and drags me down the hall from the kitchen into Frank's little bedroom. She says, "Look at this!" She pulls down the covers of his bed, and there's a big piss stain right in the middle. She said, "Look what he does!" I was not the arbiter of bed-wetting—I didn't dare tell her I was one of the kings of the bed wetters, just up the block. But there she was showing it to me, trying to embarrass him in front of the embarrassed. *Coward, take this coward's hand. . .* I felt bad for him, but Frankie took it stoically, as we all took that kind of bullshit from our mothers.

At least Frankie got to stay in the same place and wet the same bed. At one point my parents put me and Julie in an orphanage for a while. I never knew exactly why. It probably had to do with getting kicked out of one place and trying to find another one. That orphanage home was on Sixty-second Street, between First and Second, and my brother and I were there for about a month. Julie was four or five; I was eight or nine. I remember pissing in the bed a lot. They used to give us all cookies and hot chocolate made with water at six o'clock, but then they stopped and wouldn't give it to us because we pissed in the bed, or at least I did. It was grim; Oliver Twist stuff. When I saw the musical *Oliver*, it reminded me of that funny little period in my life. I'll never forget the long corridors of that place. It was bad, but not horrible. At least Julie and I were together.

Later we moved to Fox Street in the Bronx for a while, and I liked it. The Bronx was safer, which was probably why my parents moved us there, but around 1937 we went back to that same neighborhood in Manhattan, and I lived there long enough to get shaped up. A little redbrick apartment building on East Seventy-fifth was the nicest one we ever lived in. It was twenty dollars a month. My father was generating eighty, maybe one hundred dollars a month income—twenty-five bucks a week, no taxes. You could have a box lunch and go out for dinner for thirty-five cents for the whole family. I don't remember it as poverty. But I remember that the back of my heels were always bleeding. In summer, the mosquito bites on my legs were always scratched bloody. I remember having Keds and short pants

Bernie at age five and a half in Central Park

and stockings that always fell down around my ankles. I was a mean little fucker. Mean and lean. Fast and curious.

Once I took Julius to Central Park. If he was about three, I must have been seven. Why my parents let me roam around the city I'll never know, but they did. I took Julie by the hand, and we went to the park and watched them feed the seals. While we were watching, a guy got behind me, and I could feel his erection in the small of my back. I didn't know what it was, and I didn't move. I just held on to my brother, and when they finished feeding the seals, we left. I only knew that there was something odd about it. That was my introduction to the oddness of the living experience. I picked up on it. But it didn't drive me nuts or make me crazy. I just said to myself, *Stay away from feeding the seals and don't get backed up against the wall*, or, *Watch out for older guys when you go to the movies*. I was just figuring out what was safe for me. *Wary* was the word. Always aware. But I was still able to maintain a sense of joy and appreciation of being alive.

Once, a million years later, I wrote a mystical poem that I liked to a girlfriend that I didn't really like:

> Go ahead, try to make it tougher,
> try to break my balls,
> try to get me to admit
> that maybe I ain't all.
> Well, let me tell you one thing, kid,
> I've had it up and down,
> and one thing sure you'll never see
> is me when I was nine.

Nine—what a number that was to me. Nine is the last number before everything gets double-digited. I liked that number. It had a never-ending quality about it, more infinite to me than eight. When I used to feel so defenseless as a little kid, the only thing I could say was, "Yeah, I'm going to call my big brother!" But there wasn't any big brother. Or, "Fuck you, I'm going to my country estate in Southampton." But there wasn't any country estate. "Yeah, well, one thing sure you'll never see is me when I was nine!" That, somehow, made sense to me.

What was so unique about me at nine? Probably nothing. But no one will ever see or remember me as nine. What's a nine-year-old boy like? At that age, it takes forever to go through that year. Absolutely no one pays attention to you when you're nine. No one wants to know what you're thinking, or if you're hungry, or what your yearnings are. You're just nine, get the fuck outta here. You need a haircut, you have to change your underwear, you get toothaches, your legs hurt, you hate school. You want to go out and play in the afternoon. You want to go to the movies. You like knishes and root beer. You start to notice girls a little; you like to peek through windows and watch them undress. You like cars. You like to travel but not too far away, so you won't get lost. You have to be careful of certain

The Schwartz family on holiday in the Catskills (1932): Manny, Helen, Bernie, and Julie in front

guys with funny ways about them. Certain women look weird. All this goes on at nine. You don't know anything about anything. Someone says something to you about the World War; what do you know about the World War or anything else?

34

My brother Julie was nine when he got hit by a truck on First Avenue in 1938. Something happened to me, walking around there recently, when I went back to see the spot. I felt like a boy; incredibly vital and streetwise again, especially in the sense of traffic. That was where I learned it the hard way. If you survive growing up on the streets in Manhattan, there's no way you'll ever walk into a street blind again. That antenna just shoots up. Maybe it takes the death of a brother or a sister. Nothing personal about it. It just happened.

I remember Julie with great affection, though to be honest, it's hard for me to recapture exactly what he was really like. He must have been extraordinary. All I know is that I enjoyed his company and that we had a nice time together. I remember once, when he and I were in Central Park, we stood in line at a water fountain. When it was my turn, I put some in a cup and turned around and almost handed it to him, but then I drank it myself. So I was a bit cruel in my behavior with him, the way a lot of older brothers are. He was four years younger. I was his bodyguard and his mentor and his *tor*mentor as well. But we got along well. Earlier, when we were living in the Bronx, he got brushed by a car and banged up his head and his eye. About nine months later—after we'd moved back to Manhattan—he got hit by the truck. I always wondered if maybe he wanted to die; if maybe he was frustrated by his own little living experience.

First Avenue was a two-way street in those days, and Julie was there following an American Legion parade between Seventy-seventh and Seventy-eighth. I was thirteen and didn't want to be bothered with him. I was playing with my group when Julie came over and I told him, "Go play with your own fuckin' friends." He disappeared. I never saw his eyes again. I always had terrible feelings about shunning him like that. It was a Friday in September, warm and muggy. I remember vaulting over a metal banister on the sidewalk as he turned around and went down First Avenue. A little while later, I remember laughing hysterically with a couple of my friends; something struck me so funny. I swear that he got hit when I was laughing hysterically. That was the weird way I knew something was wrong.

I got home and he wasn't with me, my mother got frantic and immediately started searching the neighborhood. Somebody came up to her and said, "There was a boy hit by a truck at Seventy-eighth and First." Then the police came and picked me up and drove me to the hospital to identify him. I didn't think about it at the time, but I always wondered afterward why they took me instead of my mother or father. The only way I could tell it

Julius Schwartz on the first day of school (1937)

was Julie was because the year before, when he was drinking water at school, some kid hit his head and his front tooth snapped against the fountain and broke off. My cousin John Breiner was a dentist, and he said, "When he's older, I'll fix it for him," but he never did. In that little hospital room, Julie's head was so swollen I couldn't recognize him. But his lips were pulled back and I could see that tooth, so I knew it was him. There was nothing in that hospital room but poor little Julie and a glass of water with a straw on the side. I stayed there for a while and talked to him a little bit, even though he never answered.

Years later I read that even when you're unconscious, you are still "receiving" constantly. Your mind is still taking in information. Even if you're dead drunk or out on drugs, some logic inside of you is still operating—you're never shut down completely. When I read that, I was relieved, because I realized my brother must have heard me in that hospital room. He must have known I was there.

In a way, I didn't mind that my mother and father made me go there to identify him, even though I still wasn't a man—I wasn't bar mitzvahed yet. I didn't really blame them at the time. They couldn't come to grips with that reality. On the other hand, later, I came to resent it pretty badly. Sending a boy to do a man's job was more cruel and cowardly on my mother's part than my father's, because she always manipulated him. But he allowed it, and so they were both equally unthinking and oblivious to the elder son.

The cops brought me back home that night, and the next morning my mother and father went to the hospital themselves. Later, around noon, I was sitting on the stoop of my father's tailor shop, underneath the El, when I saw my mother running across the street, screaming, "Julie's dead! Julie's dead!" That's how I found out. It was a Saturday. The truck driver was drunk, and people said, "It's a shame your brother died, because if he'd lived, he'd have gotten a big settlement." My parents never got a dime from anybody after my brother's death, not that it would have made a difference. Julie was just another victim. I've kept his cap and schoolbooks for fifty years, because that's all I had left of him.

At the time, I went down to the East River and asked God to let me see him just one more time. If He would just let me do that, I promised I would always be a good boy, from that day on, and that I'd never ever tell anybody about it. It would be our secret. But He didn't. I just remember Julie lying there in his coffin in the funeral parlor. Some diluted blood seeped out on the pillow, and they had to turn it over.

C·H·A·P·T·E·R T·W·O

THE BOY WARS

Even now, I haven't fully come to grips with those years and how they affected my thinking, my sense of myself, and my universe; I'm not sure I ever will. On those harsh New York streets, trying to stay alive myself, I lost a brother. I became irascible, irritable, more wary than ever. I just wanted to maintain myself. Every tooth in my mouth was decayed. I'd get some free dental work from my cousin John or at the Guggenheim Clinic now and then, but I was really like an animal: well-mannered, but still an animal, always on the run. My growing up was uncontrolled.

I used to skim up and down those streets like crazy. I'd dart in and out of those pushcarts on Second and Third avenues, speed-running, and then jump on the back of a trolley. I hitched trolleys anywhere I wanted to go. I was a great hitcher. No one else did it as gracefully or elegantly as I did. I never got on when it was stopped. I'd wait for that trolley car to pick up almost to full speed while my buddies would watch. I'd start on the sidewalk under the El. We'd see the trolley coming from the corner. The guys would poke each other and say, "Watch Bernie!" I'd be in the middle of the street like Fred Biletnikoff, the Oakland Raiders split end who'd stand on the line getting ready and when they'd snap that ball, he'd run. That's how I used to get ready, too. You would have no idea what was in my mind. That trolley would go screaming by at fifteen to twenty miles an hour, and I'd take off, run alongside of it and grab that window bar. The speed would slap me up against it. I'd hold on, and people calmly reading their papers on their way home from work would jump. All of a sudden this crazy little blue-eyed kid is staring at them like a fly splattered on a windshield. There were no mistakes. You couldn't make mistakes. I never thought of it as anything other than just physically expressing myself. I was an excellent athlete. I could go up and down fire escapes without batting an eye, which turned out to be a great help to me later in the movies. Our tenement house was a little higher than the one next door. In between, in back, there was an empty lot maybe twenty feet wide. Since I was the crazy athlete of the neighborhood, my friends used to come to our apartment for the major stunts. We'd take the mattress off my bed and up onto the roof of the building across from that empty lot. Then I'd get up on the edge of my roof and sit there for about ninety minutes, trying to screw up my courage to leap from one roof to the other. It was downhill, but little did I know that jumping downhill was just as dangerous as jumping level, especially if you were running.

One day, when I finally did it, that speed or velocity or whatever the fuck it was ricocheted me off the mattress and into the side of the building. I cracked some ribs and banged up one side of my head hard.

Pretty soon after that I got hit with a baseball bat by some guy who was chasing me. He swung it and got me as I was running. It wasn't a direct hit, and I kept on running, but the left side of my head had some damage, and I'm still pretty much deaf in one ear from it. Between those two things, I had a lot of trouble at the time. I must have had a concussion. For weeks and weeks, I was sick and couldn't sleep right. I couldn't hear properly and I couldn't see right. My mother knew something was wrong, and I caught hell for it. But then it slowly disappeared.

It was like we were in training for combat. And we were. A good example was ring-a-levio-kokoko. This was a game we played in the streets from the time I was seven or eight up until I was about fourteen. It was a late-afternoon summer game, especially for August when the weather was warm and sweet and uninterrupted, and the late afternoons would go on forever. There was no school, of course. It was a game of great dexterity and stamina, and only us mean, lean Jewish kids—and maybe a few lean, mean Catholic kids too—could play it. You had to be lean and mean.

We played it on a block-long street, dodging behind and between cars, running from sewer to gutter, or walking right down the middle of the street like Gary Cooper in *High Noon*. There were four or five guys on each team. One side was the pursuer and the other was the pursued. First you took a piece of chalk and made a little square jail at the upper end of the block. The jail never changed; that piece of real estate was set for both sides.

39

If you were caught by being tagged, you had to go and stand in that box—but only when it looked as if you could be freed by one of your surviving comrades. You waited for liberation. Liberation was quite an experience, because the enemy never diminished. The enemy was always four or five guys. The heroes started out with that same number, but you knew you were going to diminish down to one. The game could go on all night long if you kept freeing your buddies, which made the other team very angry. But you could only escape and be liberated if that one remaining hero could avoid being captured and run up and put his foot inside the jail square and say, "Ring-a-levio-kokoko, ring-a-levio-kokoko, ring-a-levio-kokoko, three times!" Those were the magic words, and they are embedded in my mind forever. You had to say "three times!" at the end of it, or it didn't work.

So you would run down the street and wait for the other guys to come after you. You had nothing to do but dodge and hide until they caught you or some of your men, and as soon as one man was caught and put in jail, all the other guys decided how they were going to liberate him—who was going to be a decoy while the others finessed their way around the parked cars, which became the natural obstacles, and the moving cars as well. As the traffic changed, so did the game. You would time your moves so that when the light changed and cars came screaming up the street, you'd run behind them. If you were fast enough, you could jump onto the back of a car and hold onto it and let it take you close enough to the jail.

The reason I'm detailing this game is because it became a metaphor for life. There were no holds barred. You could do *anything*. I liked it for that. I learned a lot about living from that game. Years later, a lot of magazine writers used to call me "street smart," but that expression sucks. It doesn't begin to tell the story. But this game gives you a sense of what it was like to be raised in a city. You could never see a kid in Kansas playing a game like this. They didn't have those kinds of natural boundaries, those canyons of tenements running up and down. Even if the sun was out, you didn't see the sun except for certain hours of the day. Your street got the sun for a little while, then it went over to the next block. It only shone in your street from 12:00 to 12:30 and then it went to the next street. If you were smart you could have four hours of it by going from neighborhood to neighborhood at just the right time. But those other neighborhoods didn't want you around because they knew you'd already gotten your sun for the day.

To be oar not to be? TC at fourteen in the Catskills

So you had to repeat "Ring-a-levio-kokoko!" three times, including the words "three times," real fast, before the prisoners could break away. It took about six seconds to say it all, and you had trouble holding on that long to a guy who was struggling. With rare exceptions, I was always the last guy. No one could get me. I mean, I was *fast*. But the game was exhausting physically, and you didn't want to run up and free each guy individually, so you waited until the jail filled up a little bit. I was always the speedster, the conniver. I loved to drag out the end of the game until everybody else had been captured. I loved that tension. My mother would yell, "*Ber-nie!*" and I'd yell back, "*Ma, please, I'm in the middle of the game!*" While that game was going, you didn't have family, you didn't have friends, you didn't have school, you didn't have religion—you were just *in that game,* a magnificent New York City street game. You'd have fans watching—neighbors sitting up on the fire escapes just before dusk, watching. They knew what was going on. If you didn't know the game, you wouldn't know what to watch for. It became an extraordinary ritual.

Those moments were as important to me as anything in my life. Around then, at age twelve, I wrote a poem one day when I was still in bed trying to recuperate from the jump and the baseball bat. I stuck it away and saved it in a little notebook:

A stifled soul but cries for grief
because of thoughts of nonbelief.
And yet, if it would just take heed,
look about, forget its need,
a soul could watch the world flit by
and one's remorse would be a sigh.

I wasn't even bar mitzvahed yet. I was just a fucked-up kid running around New York, wanting to stay alive. A mean, angry, neurotic little Jewish boy writing a poem to nobody.

When the bar mitzvah finally came in 1938, my father engaged some musicians to play at our house that night. By ten o'clock, all the relatives and guests had left. But my father had paid them to play till midnight, and by God, they were going to play till midnight! By that time I was done poring over the gifts I'd gotten, and I had the radio on real soft, listening to *The Shadow*. My mother was cleaning up the dishes in the kitchen. But my father made those poor musicians—two violinists and a cymbalist—play till midnight. He sat there in an upholstered chair in the corner of the room while the three of them kept on playing in front of him. I still see him so clearly, sitting there with his hair combed flat, his little mustache carefully trimmed, his tie and tiepin and spats, a glass of wine in his hand—a bold feudal lord, finishing off his evening thoughts and thinking of his dead son as much as his live one.

A man named Paul Schwartz (no relation) took an interest in me and helped set me straight, at least in some ways. He was a nice man with one short foot and a receding chin. He wasn't a truant officer, as some of the movie magazines said later. He was director of the Henry Street Settlement House, which ran the summer camp I went to on a lake in Peekskill, New York. I was around eleven. You gave them five cents a week during the school year, and by the end of spring you had enough money to go away for two weeks at this camp. I spent two seasons up there. There were cows and horses and cowshit and horseshit and raspberry bushes and apple trees and bullshit. I got poison ivy on my balls and had to lie in the infirmary with calamine lotion all over me. It was worse than the curse of the vampires. By the time those two weeks were up, I couldn't wait to get the fuck out of there.

Across the lake was a Nazi bund summer camp that flew the German swastika and the American flag. These fucking Nazis would attack us and say things like, "You know what a Jew is? A Jew is a nigger turned inside out!" I could never forget that. They were all skinheaded, and they'd go out in their canoes and come over to our camp, which was for poor children from those lower-class neighborhoods in New York. There were a lot of black and Jewish kids there, and the Nazis loved that. They'd come over at night and throw stink bombs. They would take bottles and make Molotov cocktails to try to start fires in our camp. It was another battlefield in the same war going on back in Manhattan. Throwing the piss-bombs down from the roofs was just one part of it.

Let me tell you a little more about the boy wars I went through in New York City. Not the Boer wars. The B-o-y wars. My brother, Julius, was a boy soldier who died early. We didn't have haircuts, we didn't have uniforms, we didn't get any subsistence pay, and no money was sent home to our parents, but it was a fucking war. The adults didn't fight it; the kids had to fight it. Like Vietnam, you were fighting a war even though you had no idea what it was about.

Milt Singer and I were the only two Jewish guys in P.S. 82, which was on First Avenue between Seventy-second and Seventy-first streets. The main Hungarian-Jewish neighborhood was a few blocks away, and those kids went to another school. We were kind of gypsies, living wherever my father would open up a tailor store. So I don't know how I got assigned to P.S. 82, but I did, and it was predominantly German, Austrian, Czech, and some Italian. It would have made any Jewish kid more paranoid, and that's exactly what it did to me.

That Nazi kid Frank Webber gave me trouble all the time. We'd line up outside to go to class, and as we'd walk up First Avenue he'd push or knock me into the street, hoping I would get hit by a car. I never could understand why. That hate and those awful words; all that stuff they hit us Jewish boys with. He kept it up for a long time, until one day I just went berserk during a school assembly. He kept it up and kept it up until it just got overwhelming. I don't remember exactly what provoked me. He was bigger than I was, but I leapt on his back like a monkey. I just grabbed him around the neck, and started punching him on the head as hard as I could and held him tight around the neck until he fell and almost fainted. It took a bunch of guys to tear me off his back.

So they took me to Mr. Rescol, the acting principal of the school, and sat me in his office. He was a pretty nice man. "I can appreciate how you feel and what went on," he said to me, "but you can't solve it that way." He seemed to understand. But I didn't know what he was referring to. I didn't know anything about anything. All I knew was that this guy was trying to kill me. So that's why Frank Webber was always an important image in my brain. When the war was over, and I came back from the navy, I used to go down in that neighborhood looking for him, hoping I'd find him somewhere. I wasn't sure what I would do to him, but I would have hurt him if I could have.

Milton Gene Singer: "Bernie and I met in P.S. 82 in Yorkville when we were about twelve. We were just a few months apart in age, and we went through grades six, seven, and eight together, as I recall. It was a small public school, maybe four hundred students, and there couldn't have been more than four Jews in the whole school. To be a Jew at that time in Yorkville was akin to being in Munich. I had grown up in Detroit and didn't know anything about Jewish things. My parents were not at all religious, and I'd never been to a synagogue in my life. So we moved to New York, and there I am in Yorkville, and the kids picked up immediately that I must be Jewish, which meant they'd start to pick on you. I never was any taller than five feet nine inches, and I was never one to look for a fight, but when somebody said something about Jews, it would kindle something in me. Of course, if the guy was too big, I left him alone. They were only kids, and they didn't know *why* they hated us, but Jews were the thing to hate. We were fair game for them.

"Bernie had trouble with a guy named Webber, my problem was a guy named Knute Heinz. 'Dirty Jew!' he'd yell. I'd say, 'What?' He'd say, 'Meet me at three o'clock.' I'd get there early and try to look tough, so sometimes he'd say, 'The hell with it, I'm backing off from this guy.' Bernie would tell me, 'So and so called me a dirty kike.' Sometimes he'd handle it himself. Sometimes I'd say, 'I'll take care of that.' I wasn't any bigger than he was; maybe a little more gutsy or stupid. I'd get in fistfights, and I don't recall that I lost any, because I avoided the guys I knew could take me.

"Bernie and I went all over together. 'Where you going?' he'd ask me. I didn't know. 'Come on back to my father's tailor shop.' Mr. Schwartz was a very nice, unassuming man. Always working.

44

Mrs. Schwartz had a real strong sense of *Yiddishkeit*. I knew his brother too. We talked about family things and being poor. We'd go out and walk and walk, usually up and down First Avenue, and pretty soon one thing became very clear to me: Whenever we passed people, I'd turn a little and hear them all saying, 'Look at that good-looking kid!' For a while I was so flattered, I thought, *'Gee, isn't that nice.'* But then it dawned on me, the compliments weren't for me. It was always Bernie Schwartz they were talking about. That amazing face. I'd say, 'Bernie, don't stand next to me and make me look like a rag.' Blue eyes, beautiful skin, pitch-black hair, lean build; he was so gorgeous, it stopped people in their tracks. I always felt a little bit proud just to be seen with him."

—GENE SINGER TO B.P. , October 13, 1992

Like any other war, there were truces. You couldn't fight all the time. You knew being a Jew had something to do with the way you looked. So you tried to become nondescript. I didn't want to be black, I didn't want to be white, I didn't want to be Jewish, I didn't want to be *anything*. I was fascinated by that Nazi boy-war zone and drawn inexorably to it. Unless somebody recognized me from school, I passed as anything. I could be Italian, German, French—anything. I could walk through like a UN representative, only better. They got shot at. I got through. I could look like I was one of the guys in the neighborhood. I would change my slouch and walk a different way, depending on where I was. If I was in an Italian neighborhood, I would give my body a certain twist; in a German neighborhood, something a little more stiff. Different modes. That's where my first acting lessons were, but they weren't acting lessons, they were survival lessons. They came in handy later on in the movie business, which was as rough and as mean as those streets.

The truces never lasted too long. In those Manhattan neighborhoods then, a lot of tenement houses were torn down, leaving empty lots with remnants of brick foundations. It looked like the trenches of World War I, and we used to have our own wars there with rocks and slingshots and BB guns—lots of ricochet shots. They were thrilling experiences. We'd meet after school, two groups of kids on either side looking at each other over walls.

The parents were always above it all. They'd speak politely to each other

45

The Boy Scout troop from P.S. 82: Bernie Schwartz standing, second from right

during the day, but their sons would fight each other in the afternoon and at night, hyped up from the poison they fed them. Years later when I was in Russia showing *Some Like It Hot*, I met a man named Zhukov, who was head of the Soviet film industry. He loved me and my wife, whoever she was then, and he invited me to his dacha, and we had a great dinner. Afterward he said, "Well, back to the wars." I said, "What do you mean by that?" He explained that in Russian history during the internal wars between cities, the battles began precisely at dawn and went on to some precise hour of the afternoon. Then in the evening one general would send the other a polite note: "Please join me, Alexei, for dinner tonight; some wine, some wenches." The answer would come back, "Thank you, Nikolai, I would love to."

That night, the white flag would go up, and the one general would cross the valley to where the other general was. "Ah, how are you, dear Nikolai?" "Quite well, Alexei, I haven't seen you since the old days." They talked and they drank and they fucked and then they embraced and said, "Well, back to the wars." The general went back just before dawn, got onto his hill, the other one went to his hill, and when the sun came up, the two sides began to kill each other again. And that's pretty much how it was for us during those boy wars in New York.

In running and jumping over the roofs, the unevenness of the buildings was a real challenge: You had to leap over one, climb up the other, climb down another, then swing off onto a fire escape. If the street looked clear, we'd come down the steps, if not, we'd stay up on the roof. You'd drop down from the bigger buildings onto the smaller ones. You could come off a roof and onto a window ledge or fire escape, then up the fire escape and onto another roof. There was no thought of falling. I would climb off and shimmy across that empty space, always with my eye on the sparrow, the ledge, anything I could grab a hold of. All I needed was a handle. A handle of money, a handle for saving your life; it's all the same. Some people didn't have strong handles, so they did it by getting good grades in school, or in subtler ways. To a lot of people, chasing a pair of aces is just as profound as chasing Socrates, and so is chasing a pair of Jews.

There were hundreds, maybe thousands, of those bund marchers and Nazi kids, and we didn't really know what they were doing or what *we* were doing. We just knew we hated the way those motherfuckers treated us. My "gangs" were really just little groups of guys I hung out with. You had to do that if you walked the streets. We didn't bump people off or anything like that. Once we stole a case of Cokes. That was about the worst thing we ever did. Most of the time we just hung out with each other for protection.

My pal Frank was one of the kids who filled up those rubbers with piss, and I could never quite figure it out. Frankie had no business being with us. He was an Italian, but he looked more Jewish than the rest of us, and he was the toughest motherfucker on the block. He and I never thought about "ethnic background" as such. We just knew we weren't welcome in certain areas, and that's what we found so attractive about going there. We couldn't believe they would shove us out. After the war I went back looking for him and couldn't find him. I heard that he died—I'm not sure how—because he'd somehow gotten in trouble, if not with the Mob, then with some other Italians. He probably became a runner. That's what kids in those neighborhoods ended up doing. Frankie was very sweet and giving. But once crossed, forget it. He never forgave nothin'.

My father had a lot of Italian friends too, because where we lived, around Seventy-third between First and Third, was an ethnic conglomeration of Italians, Czechs, Catholics, Hungarians, and Jews. My father admired the way a lot of those natty, older Italian men dressed. He dressed like that too—very chic, despite his poverty—and he always held on to his theatrical ambitions. I saw him once in a theater when I was very young, about four years old. I remember sitting next to my mother in the balcony of some theater in New Jersey, looking down. I distinctly remember seeing him on stage, gesturing. He played the violin (self-taught), and he had been an amateur actor in Budapest, but his poor command of English made it impossible for him to work as an actor in New York.

So he had to be a tailor and live in that tiny little apartment with three other people. In the front, the length of it, was the tailor store with a counter and all the equipment. All the clothing that was being tailored, cleaned, or pressed hung from one wall. We lived in the back. One day when he finished work, my father went straight into the bathroom, washed up, and took out this blue pin-striped suit that he'd made for himself. He got all dressed up; white and black Cuban-heeled shoes, tab collar with a pin, dark-blue tie, and double-breasted vest jacket. Then he reached up on top of the bureau and took down a violin case, took out the violin, tuned it up, went to the window that looked out onto the back courtyard—the same courtyard that all the other apartments looked out onto, dingy and dark, with everybody's clotheslines—and played Hungarian songs. That was my father. All dressed up impeccably. He was going nowhere. He just got dressed up to play his violin.

He seemed pretty mellow that time, but not always. Once I caught him under the stairwell of that tenement house that we were dispossessed from later, with a big kitchen knife in his hand. He must have been drunk or strung out. Frustrated and destroyed. There he was, under the stairwell with a knife in his hand. He wasn't threatening anybody. No one else was around. It looked like he was going to plunge it in himself. I never understood what passion or what drama drove him to that, but there he was. He must have been terribly depressed, a young man in his mid-thirties feeling he'd come to the end of his life unfulfilled, going nowhere except under the stairs in a Manhattan tenement. Stuck in that miserable, fucking city—cold in the winter, hot in the summer—with a wife and two sons. All those dreams he'd had as a boy in Hungary; then coming to America and never getting beyond Manhattan. He should have left us and gotten on a bus to California or as far as it would take him. But all their lives my mother and father could never break that European spell. Even in New York, they still lived in a European environment with their fellow Hungarians. That was my father's dilemma. He just went from one little tailor shop in Hungary to another one in Manhattan.

But there were many things I loved about my father. The thing that intrigued me most about him hit me when I was about fifteen. Until then I

Amateur violinist Manuel Schwartz in the late 1930s

thought of him as just a Hungarian orthodox Jew, a tailor in New York City—interesting style and personality, kind of laid-back, never really verbalizing his feelings. I'm like that, too—I verbalize a lot, but not my feelings. But high up on his left arm he had a tattoo that was like a coat of arms. On the bottom, it said, Knowledge Is Power. It was in English, so he must have had it done after he came to America. I was always fascinated by that expression on his arm. I took it literally, without really knowing what it meant. But I knew it didn't just mean school knowledge, and over the years it made me a voracious observer of everything. In a really positive way, that was the legacy my father handed me, "Knowledge Is Power." Why this Hungarian gentleman would put this below his left shoulder in English is a mystery and a mitzvah to me. It could have said "Go fuck yourself," but it didn't.

My mother, on the other hand, was an aggressive, ambitious woman. She found herself tied down by this inappropriate marriage. Her husband was not providing enough opportunities. He wasn't a dreamer. He never said, "Let's close this down and start something bigger," which is what she always wanted to hear. My mother once caught him with an Irish girl. How she caught him, I don't know, but she found out he was fucking an Irish girl. One day she ran across her, and this woman said to my mother, "Don't hold your breath for a nickel's worth." What does that mean? It's breathtaking. This good-looking Irish lass looking at this good-looking Hungarian lass, both immigrant girls, the same age, big tits, voluptuous—and both of them wind up with this good-looking, mysterious, odd, dark-skinned man. I dream of that relationship and what it must have been in my father's life. How lucky he was to have had that little lass. He was not a frivolous man, but he was obviously trying to escape from my mother.

So was I, after Julie was killed. She was erratic in her behavior, quite brutal. There were many beatings. She'd get a maniacal look on her face when she was slapping me. Today we'd call it child abuse. In those days a parent would do it to a child and nobody would say boo. It stemmed from her background. Her own mother was a twenty-year-old girl from a small village at the time she married my grandfather, who was then about sixty-five years old. His first wife had died, and he was a very violent, jealous man. My mother told me he once locked her mother out of the house for some offense, and her mother cried outside all night long, "Let me in, let me in!" My mother and her sister Olga had been farmed out by their father when they were five and six years old to work in strangers' homes as servants, scrubbing floors.

That was the environment my mother came out of, and she was full of all that anguish and anger, which never let up. In her later years, I thought maybe she would be happy about my success in the movies, but not really. She reveled in it to some extent; she became a charter member of the Hollywood Mothers Club. Imagine, my mom hung out with Gary Cooper's mom! She must have gotten a kick out of that. But at heart, she was envious of my success, and she was always so lame in her feelings. Quite neurotic.

50

In 1940, when I was fifteen, my parents had Robert. As a young boy his erratic behavior wasn't too noticeable, but when Bobby was around six it got progressively worse. She tried to keep him in school, and he did learn to read and write, but that was about the extent of it. Every now and then I read in the paper that they've discovered a new chemical that helps schizophrenia. Maybe, maybe not. But there was nothing around to help it then. My brother Bobby's disease was the same as my mother's, and we all suffered the "fringe benefits." That sliver of schizophrenia runs in the family. I have little flares of it myself. All mankind does. Nobody completely escapes that sense of inability to deal with themselves. Bobby was institutionalized most of his life because of it, and my mother could never come to grips with that or with herself.

She was Helen Jekyll and Mama Hyde, maiden name Klein, born between Hungary and Czechoslovakia, raised in Hungary, came to America in 1922. She was short but well proportioned, five feet five inches, vivacious, charming, despondent, funny, mean, and intelligent. Her voice was beautiful. I remember resting in her lap as a child as she sang sweet Hungarian melodies just for me. I loved her so then. She gave me what mothers were expected to give their firstborn: full breasts and warmth and loving. Yet she was driven by demons. What happened?

As time went on, she seemed to sour as her milk did. Life seemed to become unendurable to her. She began to lose the humor and curiosity that had made her different and appealing. Life seemed to become a disappointing chore.

In her twenties and thirties, she was able to maintain some control over her life, but she could lose her temper at will and let those demons out for a few moments. Those moments were a horror for me. She would beat me, her face contorted, her body rigid, her arms flailing at me like windmill arms aimed at my head and face, while I held up my arms and screamed for mercy. I wanted to protect the only gift I felt God had given me then, and that was my good looks. *Nobody* was going to take that away from me, for that made me different, and I would not let anybody disfigure me. Certainly not my mother; hot-tempered, lusty, and angry. She was angry at men. All men. Her father had beaten and abused her mother in the old country. By the age of four she'd seen and experienced all the ugliness of a man and woman's relationship, and grew to hate their idle pleasures. Whenever men and women were kind and pleasant with each other, she knew it was a sham just to impress their children and friends, when in reality they

51

Mother and sons (baby Bobby in carriage) in front of Manuel Schwartz's tailor shop on Second Avenue (1940)

despised each other. My mother never forgave my father, or me, or my brothers, or any man she ever had anything to do with. She suffered terribly from this hate, and from the guilt and remorse of it.

I didn't understand this, but I felt it. There wasn't a real family life. Maybe there was in a way, but—well, everybody's got a fucking excuse for their problems, and it's usually because they didn't have a good, happy home life. You know what? *Nobody* has a good, happy home life. There's no such animal. Rich, poor, famous, infamous—it doesn't exist. I look back on mine as having escaped—as having come out of it alive. Again, it was about *survival.* If you didn't get hit by a truck or fall off a roof or end up in jail as a drunk or a thief, you felt like you'd made it. Did those experiences strengthen me? Yes and no—but not really.

The truth is, getting beat up by my mother didn't help me one way or another.

*   *   *

The miracle happened to me was when I was about eight, and we were living in the Bronx on Fox Street. I was lying in bed, and the sheets caught me around the waist and rubbed up against me. I felt this incredible sensation in my groin: this overwhelming, extraordinary sensation, which was quite mysterious to me. Since I didn't think anyone else in the world had ever had this feeling, I didn't dare share it with anybody. There was no way I was going to tell anybody about it. I didn't want to blow it, if you'll excuse the expression. That first thrill was so personal. It was all *mine;* my feeling. I remember thinking it was something so special, I had to keep it quiet because I didn't want the other guys—and certainly not my parents—to know about it. The way I saw it, God had touched me with a miracle. Obviously, he liked me and wanted me to have this gift and wasn't giving it to anybody else. How else could I explain it? I had no idea what this incredible, fulfilling thing was. I thought maybe God was giving me this gift because I'd been nice to my brother for a couple of days, and if I kept my mouth shut, no one would ever know about it. I tried it again a few nights later, and found that it worked. There was no other word but *miracle* to describe it.

Later, I realized that the miracle wasn't the sensation in my penis itself. The miracle was where you could put it and what you were searching for. For a man, it's the never-ending search. It defies morals, mores, ethnic background—everything. That incredible miracle of sensation is the only one that all men and all women are created equal for. A man works in the mines and comes home into his kitchen at the end of a day, all sweaty and dirty, and there is Ethel, preparing his dinner—and it hits him. It hits Ethel too. They have the same sensation that the Sultan has with his harem. The universal equalizer. It defies all logic, and that's what I always liked about it. Whatever experience you have that day, even if it's just in your dreams, will contribute to that ejaculation. You come quickly or slowly, depending on what kind of a day you've had. That explosion is how you release yourself. If you're poor, it is the only really calming experience that you have in your life. Calming but incredibly exciting at the same time.

So I started looking at women. It was the lusty-looking ones, breasty and voluptuous in the hips, that I found most fascinating, maybe because my mother was built like that. From that time on, sex was always part of my living. I never looked at it as salacious or devious or frightening. I just knew I had to keep my mouth shut about it, like I kept my mouth shut about being a Jew. It was something you didn't discuss. Those illusive, lusty images in my brain were a composite of every woman's body that I saw. I was—I am—a heterosexual. What excited me about a woman was her breasts, her buttocks, her legs, her thighs—everything: the way she smelled, the way her hair stuck to her neck when it was a little damp, the turn of her lips, the look in her eye when she saw no one but me. Suddenly I found women and everything about them thrilling. My sexual life, because I kept it hidden, was convoluted. I found myself masturbating a lot, but it didn't take me long to figure out that the pleasure I got from that was nothing compared with girls.

I remember sitting in a movie theater on Seventy-seventh Street once. I couldn't have been more than ten or eleven, and there was a girl sitting next to me, and we were holding hands. Our hands got sweaty and hot, but we wouldn't let go, and I came in my pants. It was such an exhilarating experience—just holding her hand! Then there was this girl named "Cockeyed Annie." She had one bad eye, and she let guys touch her bosom. Cockeyed Annie took care of all us young boys on First Avenue. She'd let us rub up against her buttocks. She'd do one little wiggle, and that was the end of it. High as a kite on the Fourth of July. Fireworks! "Next." She could do ten guys before the traffic signal changed—that's how quick we came. She should have been in the *Guinness Book of Records*. For all I know, maybe she is—I haven't checked it lately.

That was my sex life as a kid growing up, never quite understanding it yet knowing the wonderful feeling it gave me. But it always had to be associated with a woman. A couple of times I found men were attracted to me, and I thought about it. I wondered what that kind of relationship might be. But I never experienced it. It wasn't something that interested me. I remember when I was about twelve some guy grabbed my dick in a movie theater. I sat there for a few minutes, but I was really uncomfortable, and the look on this man's face was so bizarre that I pulled away. All I knew was that if a girl had done it, it would've felt different.

To me there was a kind of logic to it, and still is: Some like it hard, some like it soft. Simple as that. I don't think of it as philosophical or genetic, I just know it's simple. Some like it hard and some like it soft, and you have a choice. Soft is feminine, hard is masculine, or vice versa. Some men are soft and some women are hard, but it's no big deal either way. Sex was never a major dilemma for me. I always knew what I wanted, and I always wanted

54

to get it. I had a hard-on all the time when I was a kid. I couldn't keep my hard-on *off*. I was sitting on the train one day coming home with my books from school, and I saw this guy and girl smooching. They were rubbing each other, and when I saw her put her hand on his dick, *I* came!

My sexual needs were very, very intense. Always. And I never expressed them to my parents. I never brought a girl home. I never wanted to share that miracle with my family, even later when I found out I wasn't the only one who knew about it. There was no point. There were never any sexual discussions in the house. My mother never said, "Why don't you date a nice girl?" I never heard that from her at all. Once or twice she caught me alone or found the sheets unusually stiff and gave me a kind of a stern look. But when she'd go away, I'd look in the mirror. I was so special looking, I told myself, "Even if some of the other guys talk about it, this is my special feeling. Nobody else feels it the way I do. I know my father and mother don't. Look how mean they look." If everybody felt that way, there'd be laughter in the streets and dancing in Central Park. Why would everybody run around looking so fucking unhappy if they could have that ejaculation?

I knew my father could never have experienced it, because he was almost never happy—in spite of his Irish girl—and because we were so broke most of the time, and he was always so worried about money and his responsibilities and how he was going to feed us and keep a roof over our heads. Once when he was working for Shapiro & Sons downtown in the garment district, he came home and discovered he'd lost a week's salary, twenty dollars, through a hole in his pocket. He rushed out of the house and I chased after him as he was looking frantically in the streets and gutters, with me running behind him. To this day, whenever I'm in New York City, I always find myself looking in the gutter.

Maybe that twenty-dollar bill of my father's is my Rosebud. A few years ago I was walking up Sixty-second between Lexington and Madison, and I was looking in the gutter and thinking of the days when I used to shoot marbles there. Magnificent marbles, all different colors! We'd get those yellow wood cheese boxes and cut little holes in them, just wide enough for a marble to get through. You'd move back ten feet or so, hunker down, and shoot a marble. If it got into that hole, the other guy had to give you five or ten of his marbles, but that hole was always whittled down so small that your marble could just barely get in, if it could get in at all. That was the scam we played on each other. So forty years later when I was living with my friend Gordon Butler in New York, trying to recover from drugs, I was walking up the same street, East Sixty-second between Lexington and Madison, and there in the gutter was a marble—a yellow agee. It stopped me cold. I've still got it somewhere. I've got marbles all over the place. Maybe marbles are my Rosebuds.

These are the odd things that have happened for me; not mystical, but improbable. We all have that, or some element of that, in our lives. We mistake it sometimes for religion or mysticism. It's not. It's chance. It's just an incredible combination of chance. It's how Lee Harvey Oswald killed Jack Kennedy. All those peculiar little details just came together somehow. How did that motherfucker pick that one window, of all windows, and why did that motorcade move at just the right time and speed? Not "fate." Chance.

Those are the kinds of unlikely grace notes that seem to connect one thing to the next in my life.

FUCK 'EM, FEED 'EM FISH

The other miracle was one I knew didn't exist just for me: the movies. It wasn't just the place where Cockeyed Annie and I could do the nasty. It was that whole other world—all kinds of worlds—I could escape to. I was born almost at the same time that sound movies were born. I first remember seeing something called *High Wires*, which was a Saturday-afternoon serial about stuntmen. I was about five years old. And of course I remember going to see the Buck Rogers and Flash Gordon serials and the Westerns.

When you're a kid, you don't know you're going to grow up. You just look at big people, and you don't believe it's going to happen to you. They say, "When you grow up . . . " and you say, "What the fuck does that mean?" It has no reality. What has reality is the fact that you're in a street in New York City, cold and shivering, and you go home, and your mother makes you a bowl of coffee with matzos and sugar and milk in it. That wonderful kind of porridge had reality. So did potato latkes and playing in the streets with your pals and the toothaches you got from eating too much candy. Other than that, you're not quite sure who you are or what you are, and a lot of the time you're not very happy about that, or anything else.

Then all of a sudden you go into a building. It's dark. It's got thirty-five-foot-high black-and-white images of people doing the most incredible things you've ever seen. What an extraordinary environment. For an hour or two in that warm, different planet, whatever problems I had faded away. It was as calm and reassuring as a church. It was almost always open for business. You could go in and sit down quietly in the dark, and all that anguish that was going on around you outside disappeared. I could sob if I wanted, or I could just be quiet and look up at that screen. Those experiences were very intoxicating and important for me. Now and then I thought that maybe someday I would like to bounce around up on that screen too.

The Charge of the Light Brigade was the most important movie to me when I was a kid. What a picture! I watched it over and over at Loews Seventy-second Street, glued to my seat up in the loge and forgetting everything around me. I had no sense of my body at all; just of perceiving those images on the screen and the thunder of all those sounds. The way Errol Flynn sacrificed his life for his brother, who was in love with that girl. I can still see it today in my head, the one brother knocking out the other and taking his place. It fucking brought tears to my eyes, that sacrifice. Maybe because it was around the time I lost my own brother.

The Adventures of Robin Hood, too, was a fabulous picture I loved so much. It was the first color movie I ever saw. Flynn's insouciance, his daring; it was so appealing. I could picture him walking into any pool hall in Manhattan and just taking over. He was in a movie once where he ate an onion. I went out and bought an onion and tried to eat it. Another time, in *Captain Blood*, he tore a chicken apart. I started eating like that. I loved Errol Flynn. He was lean and mean and strong.

I met him when I first got to Hollywood, at a big evening affair in his honor. We talked for a while, and he was so nice to me. He was forty-nine years old and bloated. He died at fifty, very unhappy and alone. Really alone. Like Marilyn. At that party, I held back because I didn't want people to think I was sucking up to him and because I didn't want to get a brush-off. I was always afraid of "Get the fuck out of here, kid, you bother me," which is what a lot of people out there would say. So I stayed back. But as he was talking to some other people, he looked up, caught my eye, and smiled, which made me feel more comfortable. The interchange I had with Errol was more silent than verbal, but later that night he tapped me on the back, a nice little move, and said, "You're the new guy? You're going to do great."

Was he a Nazi? A lot of people seem to think so. I have no way of knowing. Where are the facts? It was easy to bum rap people in those days: He's a fag. She's a dyke. He's a pig. She's a lousy lay. He's got a son stuck away somewhere. He doesn't want anyone to know he's married. All that shit. I learned something fast out there: If it's the second phone call or the third or the fourth, you can't believe anything you hear. It's only the first phone call that maybe tells you the truth. As soon as you turn around and tell somebody else, you embellish it, and from then on you can't trust it. I'll

58

"I'll believe Errol Flynn was a Nazi the day somebody shows me a picture of him and Hitler having tea." Instead, he's having tea with TC in Hollywood (1959).

believe Errol Flynn was a Nazi the day somebody shows me a picture of him and Hitler having tea.

Gene Singer: "When it was time to leave P.S. 82, we were all making out our applications for high school. There was a variety you could apply to. I remember very vividly that Bernie came over to my desk one day and said, 'What school did you put down that you want to go to?' I said, 'Seward Park High School.' He said, 'That's all the way downtown. I put down Vocational High School in Manhattan.' I said, 'Why?' He said, 'It's near.' I said, 'Well, I'm going to Seward Park because they've got Jews.' He said, 'Gee, maybe I'll change and go with you,' and that's what he did. He got a pencil and erased *Vocational*, and he went with me to Seward Park High School on Grand Street on the Lower East Side.

"The ethnic breakdown at Seward Park, like most of New York, was mainly Italians, Jews, some blacks, and 'other,' with a student body of about three thousand kids in all. It was a big, square block building. We were the class of 'Forty-five, I think, but we never finished. Bernie and I didn't get to see as much of each other as we had in our public-school days because in high school everybody had different schedules and changed classes and then took different buses home. He always seemed to lean toward the arty things, and it went beyond just his drawings. I specifically remember the day at Seward Park when he came over to me and said, 'I want to be an actor. How do I get to be an actor?' I replied, 'I have no idea.' But I thought about it, and a couple of days later I got back to him and told him I was a member of the YMHA, the Young Men's Hebrew Association at Ninety-second Street and Lexington Avenue, and that they had an art department and an acting department there. I gave him the name of the lady who was in charge and said, 'Go see her. It won't cost anything, and you can go from there.' And that's what he did. Years later he told me that was his first formal or informal exposure to the acting art.

"Overall, looking back and recalling him as a high-school kid, I would describe Tony Curtis as Tony Curtis. He never seemed like a Bernie Schwartz. It just didn't quite fit. His whole persona was 'Tony Curtis' even then."

—GENE SINGER TO B.P., October 13, 1992

In my junior-high years, my father kept moving his shop, and I kept moving from school to school. Every time I'd go into a new one, I'd go through the same hassle:

"What's your name?"

"Schwartz. Bernard Schwartz."

"Oh, yeah—Jewish . . ."

That kind of thing. Before I mentioned my name, I could pass as Italian, German, French, whatever. As soon as I said my name: that pigeonhole and that prejudice. I just didn't want to get hassled anymore. I'd been hassled all my life, and I wanted to go somewhere that might spare me that experience. Seward Park was out of the way, on the tip of Manhattan, but

60

the atmosphere was much better. Once I got established there, I liked it. When I was about fifteen I also joined a little theater group at the 92nd Street Y Playhouse that put on plays. We did one called *Thunder Rock*, in which I played a lighthouse-keeper's retarded son.

Those high-school days are very hazy in my mind. I paid no attention to school. All I did was barely learn how to write and read. I remember once, at the end of a spelling examination, the English teacher looked up at me and said, "Schwartz, come here." I went up. She said, "You got every word wrong." I nodded. Then she said, "And not only did you get every word wrong, you even misspelled your name!" I forgot to put the *t* in Schwartz. So I not only got a zero, I got a *minus* zero for fucking up my own name. I'll never forget that.

Another time with an arithmetic examination, I didn't have a clue. I just wrote down any random numbers that popped into my head. It turned out that one of them was right. "Multiply 4,932 by 9,687"; something like that. I looked at all those fucking numbers and just put down some huge number underneath. It was the only one I got right, by accident. That amazed me.

I never imagined for a minute becoming a doctor or lawyer or engineer. Are you kidding? I was still that neurotic, nervous, irritable boy surviving from day to day. I just grabbed whatever I could. I felt that learning how to read and write was all I really needed out of school, especially with a war going on. I didn't know what education was all about. Neither did a lot of other guys who came out of neighborhoods like mine. It wasn't real life. But by then we knew what the war was about. *That* was real.

We were living in the Bronx when I went off to the war and into the navy in 1943. I loved my navy career. They treated me like my family should have. I was just seventeen when I went in, and I didn't realize they wouldn't send you into action overseas until you were eighteen. They kept shifting me from one training school to another. I thought it was because I was so intelligent. It wasn't. It was because I was under age.

At boot camp in Buffalo, my platoon drew Chief Gunner's Mate Schneider as our drill instructor and tormentor and patron saint for eight weeks. The obstacle course was the most grueling thing for everybody. It took six minutes, full out, to complete. But thanks to New York and the boy wars and ring-a-levio-kokoko, I was ready for it. The first time I ran it, it took me five minutes and thirty-five seconds, and I eventually shaved that down to just under five minutes, which I think was a record at the base then. I know I ended up ranking in the top five. That made no impression on Schneider, who kept goading me and everybody else. But I just kept myself together and didn't allow anyone to undo me the way I saw other guys being undone.

About three weeks into boot camp, I was eating dinner in the mess hall when a kid named Alfred, who was sitting about five seats away, just went ape-shit. The sergeant got on him about something, and he suddenly screamed, "Get off me! Get off me!" and started pulling at his blouse as if some animal was crawling inside of him. Everybody around him froze and hoped Alfred would calm down. But he just kept getting louder and going more berserk, and then he picked up a knife from the table and started slashing out at people around him. Everybody tumbled away from the table and ran. Schneider finally pinned him to the ground, but he kept struggling. The drill instructor yelled, "Schwartz, gimme a hand with this guy!" I took hold of Alfred's feet and promptly got kicked in the balls. Eventually Alfred spent his energy and calmed down. His chest was heaving and he was gasping for air, but we picked him up and hustled him across the parade grounds to the infirmary, where some orderlies grabbed him and gave him a shot. When I left, Alfred was sitting in a chair, glassy-eyed and docile. I remember walking back to the mess hall behind Schneider and thinking that, for the first time, I felt like a soldier, marching behind that hard-nosed son of a bitch. After that I felt like there was nothing I couldn't do. To tell the truth, I loved those eight weeks. Everything was a new test or a new experience.

From boot camp, they sent me to signal school in Champaign, Illinois. I got my rank as third-class signalman, the equivalent of a sergeant in the army. Then I said I wanted to be in submarines, and the next thing I know I'm shipped out to sub school in New London, Connecticut. After that, they sent us by train—five fucking days in a cattle car—from New London to San Diego. What a train trip that was. There were times when it went so slow, you could get out and walk alongside of it, which we did. Now and then it would stop at some little town, and we'd go into a diner and try to meet one of the waitresses, invite her aboard the train. Sometimes the girl would stay on and go with us for a hundred miles or so. I don't know how many of the guys fucked her. All I know is, I never did.

At that point I still hadn't made love with a woman. The closest I came was in Illinois at signal school, being rubbed up against in my dark-blue sailor suit by a girl named Peggy. We went out one night and started fooling around, and then I took her home. I couldn't take her into the house because her parents were there, so we necked outside. It was freezing cold and I came in my pants. I think a lot of guys know this experience, which is not exactly pleasant: ejaculating in your skin-tight trousers in the winter while you're shivering, and then saying good night and having to walk home stiff-legged. But that's what happened. A lot of my early sexual experiences happened inside my trousers.

One of my first real times with a woman was a few months later at a whorehouse in Panama City, where we had weekend shore leave. A friend of mine named Jack had been talking about it a long time, saying the first place we'd go was this whorehouse he'd heard about. So we did. I went in and asked about the price and came out and said, "Jack, they want six bucks a hit. And I come quick." He said, "Me too." So I said, "Let's go to the bathroom and jerk off first." He said, "Great." We went in and jerked off, and then went into the whorehouse and got the girls and *still* came in about ten seconds. That's what sailors on leave were like then.

I was assigned to the U.S.S. *Proteus*, a sub tender, and for a while to a relief crew on the U.S.S. *Dragonette*, which meant we cleaned the ship and got it ready for sea. I was sent to Guam, which is where I got injured. We were cleaning the outside of the submarine, standing on scaffolding like the kind they use to clean windows in skyscrapers. As you finished one level, you'd pull the ropes, and the scaffold would go up or down. But the sides of the submarine were bowed, so it was tricky. We were only kids and not too adept at lowering and rigging. At one point, the scaffolding came away from the side of the ship and slammed me on my back. I was in the ship's infirmary for four days, but I was young and got over it. Later, in the movies, I did all my own stunts, and I would occasionally have back pain. But other than that, I was lucky and didn't have too many repercussions from it.

I was on board the *Proteus* at the signing of the peace treaty in Tokyo Bay. I watched it from about a mile away. It was a momentous experience. All the ships in the bay were brought to attention and flew their flags, and we all lined up on deck while that signing went on. I saw Douglas MacArthur and both delegations through a pair of binoculars.

Bernard Schwartz in his U.S. Navy uniform (1943)

After that I was stationed for a while longer in Guam, which had a lot
of Japanese soldiers on it after we secured the island and turned it into a
submarine relief base. Between patrols out at sea we lived on the beach in
Quonset huts. Outside that area was a baseball field, and every ten feet there

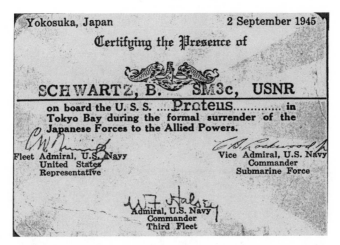

Yokosuka, Japan   2 September 1945

Certifying the Presence of

SCHWARTZ, B.   SM3c,   USNR

on board the U. S. S. .....Proteus............ in
Tokyo Bay during the formal surrender of the
Japanese Forces to the Allied Powers.

Fleet Admiral, U.S. Navy   Vice Admiral, U.S. Navy
    United States   Commander
    Representative   Submarine Force

Admiral, U.S. Navy
Commander
Third Fleet

Official certification, signed by Admirals Halsey and Nimitz, of
Signalman Bernard Schwartz's presence aboard the U.S.S. *Proteus*
during the surrender of Japan, September 2, 1945

was a post with a light on it. At night those lights went on over the barbed
wire, because the Japanese soldiers used to try to infiltrate the base and get
food. They'd do anything to get it. Every now and then, a Japanese soldier
would dress up in a sailor's uniform stolen from the clothesline, put on a
white hat and stand in line for food. Shore patrol would grab him and pull
him out.

Once some guys were playing softball, and someone hit the ball over
the fence. When one of the sailors went to get it, he was stabbed to death.
After that the marines that patrolled the area were always on alert, from
dusk to dawn. One night I heard a lot of firing, and I ran out with a couple of the other guys to the baseball field, where the fence was. A marine
threw a hand grenade. It landed and blew up, and we ran a little bit closer
and watched him go over to the fence and pull off a Japanese soldier—or
what used to be a soldier—by the foot. There was no head on him.

In a lot of ways, that's what the navy was to me: shocking, surging,
energetic, questioning, fucked up. It was about a human being who
was looking for some answers. I still don't know any, I'm just looking. But
in the navy, everybody knew exactly where he stood right from the
beginning, and if anybody didn't like it, fuck 'em and feed 'em fish. That
term came out of the navy. Some crews arrived for food, and an officer on

Signalman Schwartz with shipmate Rube Goldberg on Guam (1945)

an inspection told the chef, "You've got to make them some decent food. We need steaks, potatoes, that kind of thing." And this chef listened to him quietly and then he said, "Fuck 'em, feed 'em fish," because that's all they had in Guam.

That became my motto: "Fuck 'em, feed 'em fish." That was my bumper sticker for life!

I never had any interest, involvement, or experience on the West Side at all. I'd hit Broadway every now and then, but there was so much action on the East Side, I never needed or was comfortable on the other half. Even now it doesn't seem quite "right" to me. There's something peculiar about the West Side.

66

I was sixteen when I saw my first Broadway shows. I'd sneak in during the first-act intermission, but I usually found the musicals boring. I saw Orson Welles in *Around the World in Eighty Days* right after the war, and that was an explosive experience. But I don't really recall any other major drama event in my life until I saw Marlon Brando in *A Streetcar Named Desire* in 1947. When I saw *Streetcar*, I sensed that some revolution would happen in acting. He revitalized the whole profession. It was an amazing performance. Little did I know that when I got out to Hollywood, we'd live together for four months, renting a house on Barham Boulevard, while Marlon was doing *The Men* at Warner Bros. and I was just starting out at Universal. But that was down the line.

When I left the navy, I went back to my parents' place on Stebbins Avenue in the Bronx and got into the Dramatic Workshop of the New School as a full-time day student, using the GI Bill to give me an education in any subject I wanted. I was stunned when I found out I could take up acting. Erwin Piscator was head of the workshop, which was located at the President Theater on Forty-eighth Street. Walter Matthau, Harry Belafonte, Bea Arthur, Michael Gazzo, and Joe Sargent were students there too. We all

On a quadruple date just after the war: Bernie—as always—at the wheel

67

Bernard Schwartz (far right) and friends in Jimmy Ryan's, a New York City nightclub, New Year's Eve, 1946

auditioned, got up and acted our guts out. The teachers sat there saying, "You got the job. Next!" We thought we were great Shakespeareans. We didn't know they *had* to accept us because we were veterans. You couldn't be turned down. The government paid your tuition and gave you sixty-five dollars a month, a lot of money in 1946. Subways were a dime. You could have lunch for fifteen cents. You could get beautiful jackets for eighteen, twenty dollars. So all my money went for clothes.

When that first workshop semester was over, I thought I knew a lot about acting and I took a job with the Stanley Wolf Players, which was a non-Equity stock company. They sent little plays up to the Borscht Belt in the Catskills. We did *This Too Shall Pass* and *The Jazz Singer*—cut-down versions—after dinner, for an hour of theater. We worked outside of the kitchen or wherever they could set up. I got ten dollars a week.

While I was doing those plays up in the Catskills, I was seen by a guy named Oscar Ostroff from the Yiddish theater in Chicago. He offered me a job, and so I went there, to the Douglas Park Theatre. They did skits, scenes, tap dances, songs—sort of Yiddish vaudeville. The MC would shout out the intro:

"Jenny Goldstein—dance for us!"

"Menachem—sing for us!"

Bernie Schwartz, for some reason, had to become "B. White." Every time I stepped onstage, the audience would applaud—they expected me to *do* something. Everybody had a specialty but me. I just did the slice-of-life scenes. In one of them, l came home with a dime because I'd shined some guy's shoes. The mother said, "My son will never work!" The father said, "Go out and get a job!" I said, "Ich woll bessig gestorben!" ["I'd rather die!"]

It was rough. Thirty-seven Jewish mothers were around, bum-rapping you on and off the stage. There was a girl named Henrietta Jacobson, and they kept telling me, "Nu, Bernie, *marry* hah!" She was a nice girl, but all I could think of was the title of that Jewish porn film, *Debbie Does Nothing*.

I couldn't handle it. So I left Chicago early and went back to the Dramatic Workshop in the winter of 1947. A few months later, I was doing *Golden Boy* at the Cherry Lane Theater. I was Joe Bonaparte, the kid who played the fiddle and wanted to be a boxer. They had barely gotten it together—they needed a weekend play. Another one of my acting school productions was *The Prince Who Learned Everything Out of Books*. I was a clown hired by the king to teach the prince about life.

Walter Matthau: "It's the Dramatic Workshop of the New School for Social Research. We called it the Neurotic Workshop of Sexual Research. A lot of sexual research went on there. That's why people become actors, they want to get fucked from here to China.

"Everyone thought Bea Arthur was my sister. She later said she hated me because I never made a pass at her. Harry Belafonte didn't like me because I told him to stick to singing and forget about acting, and he took that as an insult. Talk about pretty. Tony Curtis and Harry Belafonte. Two of the great beauties. How could I compete with them?

"I worked with Piscator, and so did Tony. Piscator was ostensibly very pompous. He didn't quite know how to present himself as the teacher of American would-be actors. In World War I, in the middle of a bombardment his sergeant said to him, 'What did you do in civilian life?' He said, 'I was an actor,' and he felt so humiliated that he wanted desperately to give the acting racket a good name, like the religious racket had. If a man is a priest or a rabbi, he's proud of his calling. Piscator wanted theater to be like that. Sometimes it is, and most of the time, it's not. Mostly, it's Madonna.

"But Piscator's real goal in life, I think, was to have a play without actors, just turntables and a projection machine, the director, all kinds of backdrops. But not actors. Actors asked questions. They weren't respectful.

"Anyway, Tony and I did Shakespeare together. In fact, I think we both were vying for the officer in *Twelfth Night* [Act v, Scene 1]:

> Orsino, this is that Antonio
> That took the Phoenix and her fraught from Candy . . .
> Here in the streets, desperate of shame and state,
> In private brabble did we apprehend him.

"I recall that Tony came over to me and said, 'Hey, Walter, what does that mean, '*took the Phoenix and her fraught*'? I said, 'I haven't the slightest idea what that means, and you shouldn't worry about it either, because you're going to be a movie star.'"
—WALTER MATTHAU TO B.P., June 16, 1993

I really was the least likely to make it. No one had much faith in me. But *I* did! The school was kind of laid back—a few classes, a few plays. And then out of nowhere, during *Golden Boy*, an agent named Joyce Selznick saw me and liked me. (She always said she was related to David O., but she wasn't.) I went up to her office, where it turned out she worked for the Max Richards Agency. I remember walking up to her desk, and she looked up at me and just stopped what she was doing. She introduced me around to a lot of other people.

I met her on a Monday. That Wednesday I'm out playing stickball in the Bronx, and my mother screams, *"Bernie! Bernie!"* That was another thing I loved about New York: mothers yelling *"Harry-y-y!" "Billy-y-y!"* out the window. My mother was not a flighty woman. She wouldn't yell for me like that if it wasn't important. I ran up. "Yeah, Mom?" She says, "Someone from Universal called." I ran to the phone and called them back. A nice woman

Bernard Schwartz and unidentified co-star clowning in the play *The Prince Who Learned Everything Out of Books* (1947)

named Miss Landau, Bob Goldstein's secretary, said, "There's a plane ticket to California for you."

I left that weekend, just before my twenty-third birthday, in the late spring of 1948. On the plane there was a guy with a herringbone coat, mustache, cigar, hat, gloves, spats. I was sure he was a gangster:

"Hey, kid, where you going?"

"I'm going to Hollywood."

"What for?"

"I'm an actor, under contract at Universal."

"Did you see any other studio?"

"Well, at Warner Bros. everybody wants to get out of their contract. Olivia de Havilland sued them to break hers but Jack Warner wouldn't let her. And if you go to 20th Century-Fox, it's the Schenck Brothers, and they're looking for Tarzan. If you go to MGM, they want musical stars. Columbia, I'm not sure what they want. But Universal . . ."

So this guy listened to me, and when we got off the plane, he said, "Do you want a ride into town?" I look and see this limo—this was obviously a heavy dude, but he never told me his name. We go to his home first, he gets out and tells the chauffeur to take me where I want to go. Then he adds, "My name is Jack Warner. If they ever drop you at Universal, come and see me at Warner Bros., and I'll change your name to Tyrone Goldfarb."

Magnificent! So Jack Warner was the first movie mogul I ever met. Every now and then I'd get a call from him. I wasn't a troublemaker. I was very New Yorkish and handsome, and Jack loved me. "Look at that good-looking Jewish kid!" he'd say. Louis B. Mayer felt the same way. Harry Cohn at Columbia wanted to adopt me. He was so pissed off that I was under contract to Universal. All those guys were nice to me.

The big word in Hollywood was *fate*. Destiny, Tarot cards, psychics, readings, kismet. When you met somebody, it was "meant to be." I was never a Tarot reader, but I always found the Tarot cards themselves appealing. So mysterious. Death isn't death, for instance—it has nothing to do with death. The Tarot cards are not unlike Magritte paintings: They don't tell you as much as you think they should, and what they do tell you has nothing to do with what you think they mean. To look at the Magritte painting of a fireplace and a locomotive coming out of it—those incredible Magritte concepts. Tarot practices what Magritte preached: symbolism in the form of surrealism. Destiny and fate are big parts of both.

Hollywood in the summer of '48 was one of the great times and places, chasing that kismet all the time. One of the first things I did was to learn how to drive and buy a convertible—not necessarily in that order. I never drove a car in my life until I got out to California. Where would you learn to drive in New York City? I hitched trolley cars anywhere I wanted to go. So in L.A. there was a used-car dealer called Sailor Jack's where I bought a dark-green 1935 Chevy convertible, with green upholstery and a torn top, six cylinders, and stick shift, for $212. The odometer was stuck at 183,000 miles. Sailor Jack told me it was a cherry, and I believed him. In fact, the only thing cherry in that neighborhood was me. A week later I was teaching myself to drive on the Universal back lot, top down, showing off to all the girls who were under contract—blowing kisses to them, like I was in a parade. A horse wrangler was out teaching the girls to ride, and I got so caught up watching them that my foot slipped off the clutch, and I slammed into the barn. With hay flying, I came to an abrupt stop. The girls laughed, and the wrangler smiled and said, "You want a horse?"

"Only if it's got automatic transmission," I said.

After that I got a Buick convertible, pale green, Dynaflow drive, whitewall tires, and next a maroon Mercury convertible in which I almost killed myself. I didn't know how to take the turns, and I was still learning to use a stick. Then came the motorcycle. I got a Harley that was a harbinger of the future. I wore a T-shirt and jeans and hopped on my bike, which I'd had about eight days, and started tooling down to Malibu on the Pacific Coast Highway. Everything was going nicely when, for some reason, I found myself tumbling through the air. I remember thinking, *How the fuck did I get up here?* There was no bike under me. The next thing I knew, I hit something, bounced off something, slid, and wound up lying in the gutter. I didn't feel hurt. I didn't feel anything. All of a sudden, I turn my head a little bit and see my motorcycle tumbling in the air, wheels spinning, about eight feet from me. The back wheel hits the ground and, because it's still in gear, spins the bike even further. This crazy bike with a mind of its own is flying around and crashing into the fucking mountain on the side of the Pacific Coast Highway near the beach, into a retaining wall. I look around. My jeans are torn a little, and I bruised my ass, but that was it. Not a scratch on this *punim* of mine. I knelt down and blessed myself instantly, hoping God wouldn't know I was Jewish. That was just seven months after I came out to California. I looked at that bike, lying there dying and said, "I'll never get on that fucker again." I had it repaired for two hundred dollars and then got rid of it immediately. Never got on a bike again.

One of the things I did instead was get into swimming. I was born in New York City and never saw an ocean, but my father and I used to paddle around in the East River—with the turds floating by—and later I learned to swim in the lake in Central Park where the rowboats are. Other kids would dive in there, and the tourists would throw money in, and the boys would swim down to the bottom to retrieve it. I hardly ever left the steps, though I made it look like I did. But one time somebody threw what looked like a fifty-cent piece, and I went beyond where I could stand. I started to flail and drown but finally I got the edge of those steps and pulled myself up. Close call. From then on I learned it properly.

Now in California, I began to take long swims all alone, and it was the greatest therapy I ever knew.

CHAPTER FOUR

ALL YOU WANT IS A TIP

 The first movie bit I ever did was in a robbery story called *Criss Cross* (1949), which Robert Siodmak directed.* It starred Yvonne de Carlo, the Arabian Nights temptress from *Salome* and *Scheherazade*. She was one of the biggest sex symbols of the day.

I'd been under contract just a very short time, and I was on the main street at Universal one day, when a guy with a German accent comes up to me and says, "My name is Siodmak. I do this film here called *Criss Cross*. I need someone to dance with Yvonne de Carlo. Can you dance?" I said, "Yeah, sure I can dance." The music was called "Brazilian Rhapsody." I didn't know how to dance at all, but from my waist up I could wiggle a little.

So they put me in a light blue suit (one of my own), and I reported that day to the set of *Criss Cross*. I was introduced to Yvonne de Carlo and Burt Lancaster, a thrilling experience. Burt had already starred in one or two movies, and was on the fast-track rise. We became really wonderful friends. The same with Yvonne. She is one of the loveliest women I've ever known in films; sweet, very generous in her feelings, magnificent body, beautiful actress. I've always cared for her. She's always in my dreams. She and Burt both made me feel like they wanted to see me make a success. I was on-screen for only two minutes, but something about that footage—my looks, my suit, that Brazilian dance—struck a nerve. Universal got a load

---

*Robert Siodmak (1900–1973) was an acclaimed German director whose first film, *Menschen am Sonntag* (1929) (*People on Sunday*), also marked the beginning of Billy Wilder's and Fred Zinnemann's careers. Siodmak fled the Nazis, and by 1940 was in Hollywood, where he made a string of dark psychological thrillers for Universal that in many ways were more "Germanic" than his German films, including Burt Lancaster's stunning debut, *The Killers* (1946), based on an Ernest Hemingway story.

of letters about the new unbilled guy, and like all the studios, it paid attention to letters.

A few weeks later I was on the corner of Sunset and Laurel one morning and decided I'd go into Schwab's, which had a pharmacy, sundries, Hollywood trade papers, and a counter where you could sit and read them over coffee and toast. Next to me was an old extra named Sam Bagley, chomping on a big cigar, having his breakfast there. He told me about a casting call at Universal for a hoodlum movie called *City Across the River*. I was under contract there and knew I already had a part in it, but for some reason I didn't mention that to Sam. A couple days later I saw him at the studio. "Sam," I said, "I got that part." He smiled and said, "You're welcome, kid. You owe me one." For years after that I made sure that Sam Bagley had a bit part in almost every movie I made. I don't quite know why.

You're welcome, Sam.

I have odd memories of that *City Across the River* experience. I recall that Josh Shelley got paid $600 a week, and he carried the money in a little leather bag around his neck. I never saw that in my life before. I was stunned by a guy carrying cash around like that. In those days, a hotel room cost $20. Six hundred dollars was a fucking fortune. But mostly I remember that Maxwell Shane, the director, out of orneriness and stupidity, wouldn't let me have the lead. Peter Fernandez and Al Ramsen got the big parts, even though they didn't go near that New York accent. And there I was, all through that picture, talking like the perfect New York kid I was. I was the only one out of that group of guys that made it. Dick Jaeckel worked again, but the rest of them went down The Toilet of No Return. I sneaked into a theater to see for myself if what people were telling me was true—that at the end of the movie, when they introduced "Anthony Curtis as Mitch," women screamed for me. It was true.

City Across the River (1949) was produced and directed by Maxwell Shane from Irving Shulman's topical hit novel *The Amboy Dukes*. Its unorthodox opening did away with credits entirely. Instead the cast was introduced one by one at the end, and a very cool "Anthony Curtis" stole the curtain call from fellow juvenile delinquents Jaeckel, Ramsen, Shelley, Fernandez, and their "dames," Sue England and Barbara Whiting.

At the outset, columnist Drew Pearson (in a rare film appearance) intones a prologue: "The city where juvenile crime seems to be is the city across the river, but don't kid yourself. Though this is Brooklyn, it could be your city, or any other large city where slum conditions take their toll in juvenile delinquency. For the next eighty-nine minutes, you're a kid named Frankie Cusack going down a confused road toward gangsterdom—toward murder."

Frankie (Fernandez) is a good kid at heart who spends nights out with his gang, the Dukes, as much to escape his carping mother (Thelma Ritter) as anything. "Buy a house? What with?" she harangues his father. "For four years we were on relief. You walked around like a dog because you couldn't support your family . . ."

TC as Mitch is one of the Dukes, which we'd know anyway from his duck's-ass hairstyle. When a local hood assigns the gang to rough up a restaurant owner, he goes along with the pack and draws our attention by being the handsomest of the lot. At Vocational High School, a teacher catches one of the hoods making a

The Amboy Dukes gang in *City Across the River* (1949): Micky Knox, Joshua Shelley, Anthony Curtis, Richard Jaeckel, Peter Fernandez, and Al Ramsen

zip gun. "The Dukes ain't a gang, we're a *club*!" says Fernandez. "You guys make me sick, always trying to reform us."

Soon enough, the Dukes' "Happy Times Billiards" hangout is the scene of a rumble: "What's the big idea lettin' these spics in here?" It is the first use of the word in a major Hollywood film. In the ensuing brawl, brawny TC beats up and humiliates every "spic" in sight.

During the next day's anarchy at Vo Tech, the Dukes are kicked out of school. "They're a pack of wild animals," says the teacher who suspends them. "Sometimes I think the only answer is to clear out all the people and drop an atom bomb on the whole slum." In a scuffle after school, to the atmospheric screech of a jigsaw, the teacher is shot.

TC reenters for a surprisingly moving scene in which he tries to console Shelley over the loss of his girl to Fernandez. It is Shelley's scene, but Curtis steals it. He then disappears but finally gets another moment to shine toward the end at the Dukes' "Benefit Dance," during which he pimps his own girl. There the "sex-crazed" jazz adds to the ambiance and leads to a climactic rooftop chase that closes the picture, with Drew Pearson's somber moral:

"Frankie—he'll serve his time, and perhaps with time will come hope. . . . But what about all the other Frankies? That's the challenge to all of us."

The Dead End Kids and the Bowery Boys had made movies with a similar message—squalor produces delinquency—in the late thirties and the forties, but this one predated *Rebel Without a Cause* by six years. Action, script, and characterizations are all fairly crude in *City Across the River*, whose "Brooklyn" setting was really the Universal backlot in California. (The New York exterior consisted of stock footage.) But the movie earned back far more than its tiny $120,000 budget, while TC—in the first of his many sexy white T-shirts on-screen—stood out strikingly. He wasn't the only one who wondered why he wasn't the star delinquent. A lot of critics and fans asked the same question. The answer: Universal had simply gambled on the wrong "unknown."

—B.P.

Michael Gordon was directing *The Lady Gambles* (1949), with Barbara Stanwyck, about a compulsive gambler.* I was a bellhop who had to deliver a letter to Stanwyck. But on the day I went down on the set dressed as this bellboy, I had a sty. My eye was swollen so badly, I went to Gordon and said, "Sir—my eye." He said, "Kid, you're better looking with one eye than most other guys with two, so don't worry about it." That put me at ease.

In my one big scene, when Barbara Stanwyck opened the door, the camera would come in for a half-shot, and I'd hand her the letter. My line was, "It looks like it followed you halfway across the country." We rehearsed it once or twice. Then they had to readjust the lights, so I walked behind the set. I was waiting in the back, looking up from behind at this set propped up by supports that looked like those crutches Salvador Dali used to paint. It was so quiet and eerie back there. I loved that part of a stage set. It was wonderful, like the end of the world. You could just inhabit that space like a womb, waiting to make your entrance. I'm mumbling to myself: "It *looks* like it followed you halfway across the country." "It looks like it followed you halfway across the *country.*" I kept emphasizing different words, trying to find the right one. I tried every conceivable way to say that fucking line.

All of a sudden, Michael Gordon comes around the back of the set. He was a handsome, wonderful-looking man. He must have heard me rehearsing this line, or maybe he just sensed what I was going through. He pauses for a few seconds, then he walks up to me and says, "All you want is a tip." Then he turned around and walked away.

All I want is a tip? A fucking light went on in my brain. So when Stanwyck opened the door, I said, "It looks like it followed you halfway across the country," and I don't know how I said it, but I must have said it right. With that, she gave me a dollar tip.

It was the best direction I ever got in a movie. No director can ever top what Michael Gordon told me. To this day, when I go to work in a movie, all I want is a tip: I want somebody to think I'm just a little bit better than what's expected of me. That's the way I've tried to live my life too.

I always felt fortunate to have had that as my first real piece of direction, even though I didn't really get much chance to use it in my next picture,

* Michael Gordon (1909–1993) was a Yale-trained stage actor and director who turned to films in 1940. Shortly after *The Lady Gambles,* he had his biggest hit with *Cyrano de Bergerac* (1950) but then ran afoul of the House Un-American Activities Committee's Red witch-hunt. Blacklisted for almost a decade, he came back for *Pillow Talk* (1959) and other later successes.

Johnny Stool Pigeon (1949). It was a dope-smuggling thing directed by William Castle, and it starred Dan Duryea and Shelley Winters. I was a deaf-mute killer. All I really remember about it is a shot where I had to lie in a coffin. They were bringing drugs across the border in a coffin, and when they opened it up, they found me.

Before the scene they told me, "Tony, we can't do this shot without giving you an injection first so you'll lie still and your eyes won't twitch." I said, "Look, my eyes aren't going to twitch. You don't need to give me any shot." I was so nervous, but I got in the coffin to prove it. They opened the thing up, and there I was, twitching. "See, Tony, you can't do it!" They brought in this huge hypodermic needle, and I said, "No, don't!" Then they broke up, and I finally figured out it was a gag.

One of the few people who took an interest in me in those days was Donald O'Connor, a guy I liked very much. I had a bit with him in that first *Francis* talking-mule movie (1950), which made three million bucks! I got to know Donald really well. He was so friendly and open, and he made it easy for me when I was still new and needed the encouragement. Arthur Lubin was a wonderful director, and I enjoyed doing that movie for a couple of reasons—one of which was ZaSu Pitts. God, was she funny. I loved her. I was working with the woman who made *Greed* with Erich von Stroheim when she was eighteen.

Everybody used to joke about what a great lay she was when she was young. I would look at this woman and try to project some sexy creature into her, but it was beyond me. She was considered a great lover in her youth, but with a name and personality like that —"ZaSu, I love you!"—I just couldn't see how it worked. Once or twice after *Francis*, I met ZaSu in the commissary, and she was always exactly what she seemed on the screen. She loved my looks. "Oh, Tony, you're so handsome!" I never saw a lot of her, but when I did, she would draw me out. We always had some funny little repartee. She was never quite as funny as she looked, but what a great character she created. It was a thrill for me to be able to know people like that, to touch them and to have them touch me.

I had a seven-year contract with renewal options every six months. The first four months I made $75 a week, but I had to join the Screen Actors Guild, so they deducted $120 a month, I think, from my salary. So with taxes and loans, I took home about $32. I lived in a place called the Sycamore House for about $60 a month, room and board, communal kitchen. Then I moved to a place on Sierra Bonita in Hollywood that

Howard Duff and Burt Lancaster knew about. I loved them and their Irish kind of humor. Once while I was at the studio, they took all my stuff out of my room and changed the lock. I came home, and the key didn't work— no one seemed to know who the fuck I was. The manager opened it up and I looked in—and it wasn't my apartment! I was going crazy until I went to the studio and saw Burt laughing. Once he sent me off to get a left-handed can of film. I was naïve, but that stupid I wasn't. I said, "Okay," went to the studio, got an empty can of film, brought it back to Burt in my right hand, and told him they just ran out of left-handed ones.

ZaSu Pitts in classic form, shortly before *Francis* (1950)

That room-changing story was all over the lot, and after that everybody looked for ways to fuck around with me. To tell you the truth, I didn't mind. In some ways, I loved it. I was the kid mascot. Once on the *Francis* movie they were making me up, and it took a lot longer than usual. When they finally finished, I looked in a mirror: I had lipstick and mascara on. I said, "What is this?" The makeup guy said, "Well, you're so handsome, they wanted you a little different." So I went on the set that way, and everybody looked and said, "What the fuck is it with him?" Arthur Lubin said, "What's this?"

I said, "That's what they did in makeup."

"Who did it?"

"Frank Westmore."

"Get him down here," Lubin said. He wasn't amused.

Another time, they set me up with a new "starlet" who turned out to be a four-dollar hooker, but she was a great lay and we fucked our brains out. A couple days later, I went to the gym and Burt and some other guys were sitting in the steam room talking about her. One of them says, "You know, Harry Ray got a dose from her." They'd soaked my towel with eucalyptus oil and it was pressing against my dick, and while they're talking, I started to feel a sensation and was sure I'd caught a dose.

I was a perfect foil for this shit. But really, I was alone. I had nobody out there. Joyce Selznick "found" me and was supposed to be my agent, but I never saw her again. Someone should have helped me get started, but no one advised me about anything. They just handed me that contract and I signed it. There was no guidance of any kind. I could have used a manager or someone who could have taken me through that process. The whole direction of my career might have been different. I only started doing really well when I found Lew Wasserman in 1950. He was at the height of his ability—an extraordinary man.

In the meantime, Universal had me take fencing and riding lessons, and I gave kissing lessons. I was the unofficial kissing instructor; I'd go up to a new beauty who'd just been given a contract and say, "I've been assigned by Universal to teach you how to kiss." One way or another, they'd all end up being my pupils. A lot of other guys in town who got beautiful kisses can thank me for them. One of my "students" was Yvette Dugay, and she was excellent. She made the next Francis sequel, *Francis Covers the Big Town*, 1953, and then pretty much disappeared. I'm sorry to say I never had an affair with her.

We also had a dance class where a teacher showed you how to move with grace and style. And then there was my accent: Miss Fogler was her name, and speech was her game. She was the voice and elocution coach at MGM in 1949 when Bob Palmer, Universal's head of talent, delicately let me know that my New York accent had to go and that Miss Fogler, renowned speech arbiter and coach of the stars, could help me. So in my pale-green Buick Riviera convertible with Dynaflow Drive, I drove to the MGM studios in Culver City to meet Miss Fogler, who immediately popped six marbles in my mouth, and I promptly swallowed one. She told me to repeat "The rain in Spain falls mainly on the plain." This went on for two hours. When I got back to Universal and ran across Palmer in the commissary, he asked me how it went. I said, "Poifect. I don't come from Toity-toid Street anymore." And that was the end of Miss Fogler.

At the studio's urging I made a stab or two at the Method School of acting, which was becoming popular in New York and, to some extent, in Los Angeles. They called it "sense memory." You had to recall the feeling of an icebox, or the exact sensation you had when you held a glass ball in your hand or felt the fabric of your tie. It was valid enough for some young actors, because it gave them something to do. But the truth is, acting was the only profession people *thought about* a lot and *did* very little.

I didn't like the Lee Strasberg school of acting or anything connected with it. One night I went to a lecture at The Actor's Studio on Sunset, and they used me as an example of what movie acting was about, or not about. I sat there stunned. I hadn't even made a name for myself and already they were saying, "That kid out at Universal just stands there and thinks he's acting."

I was really pissed off, but I went back one more time to watch. Maybe I was missing something. I wasn't. That whole Strasberg school was created by the idiosyncrasies and genius of one man, Marlon Brando. From *him*, not Strasberg, came the likes of James Dean and Paul Newman and Monty Clift and John Cassavetes. It was a mind fuck: Go off in your head somewhere to find some other reality for what you were doing, regardless of what the script intended.

Universal had its own version of that. In the few classes I went to, there were six people besides the teacher, Abner Biberman, who was vain and pompous and secretly waiting for his own big break. He was hoping they'd name a school of acting after him. He was a former actor—he'd played Eduardo Ciannelli's son in *Gunga Din*—who ended up the acting coach at Universal until he got kicked out for playing around with one of the girls under contract. (Marilyn Monroe was one of his students.) He gave me and everybody a hard time. He assigned us scenes to do from one-act plays, two-act plays, the newspaper—anything. He didn't give a shit; he wasn't the one who had to do it. He'd just come in and look solemn and give you a critique. How he reacted depended on whether he'd been able to screw that starlet the night before. And these poor kids were subjected to his whims and fancies. I never took to it. They called it The Biberman Approach, but I called it The Biberman Bullshit.

There were a lot of acting schools around, all looking to make money by teaching you something that could only come naturally from inside: You needed confidence, calmness, intelligence, and an uncluttered mind to record and store away all the pieces of information. The useful thing about acting schools was that they made it possible for actors to hang around with each other and exchange job tips.

The only person who really strongly influenced my acting was Sophie Rosenstein—a big talent, an acting coach at Universal, and a very fine woman. I really enjoyed her company and the essence she gave. Sophie coached me in a monologue from *All You Need Is One Good Break*, by Arnie Manoff, which was performed for the internal lot. The acting department put on repertory evenings to show off the talent on the stage that was built originally for *Phantom of the Opera*, the Lon Chaney silent film. John Berry directed it. My character's name was Mo Rothman, whose goal in life was to open up a chain of pharmacies. I've remembered that little scene all my life, and the way Sophie Rosenstein helped me. Rock Hudson used to say she was ugly and beautiful at the same time—ugly but magnificent. Gig Young loved her and married her and stayed married to her till she died of cancer.

The fan mags wrote all kinds of crap, but there was no competition between me and Rock Hudson. When they signed me, they put under contract three or four guys that looked not unlike me. When Rock joined them, they took on a couple of guys who looked like Rock. They did it so in case Rock or I got obstreperous, they could wave somebody in front of you. Rock and I had the sweetest relationship and the best times. We hung out together. The first movie we were both in was *I Was a Shoplifter* (1950), and after that we were always running across each other at the studio. There was never any rivalry or envy because we were never really in the same character category. Later, some of our movies had certain similarities, but they never conflicted.

I was always fond of Rock, and of the other guys too. Jeff Chandler was the best of men—charming, elusive, somewhat cynical, introspective. He was badly married, but being a very honorable man, he made it work as long as he could. Jeff Hunter was always cool and friendly. John Derek was a fine guy, handsome as could be, and always kind. We all hung out together and got along nicely. We would meet at Schwab's at night, then a club, have a few drinks, pick up any girl we wanted. There was no animosity or envy, or if there was, nobody showed it. We were all under contract at Twentieth, Columbia, MGM, Universal, which made us the elite. Everybody was looking to be put under contract.

Yes, we were the elite, but what fascinates me is not the ones who made it as much as the ones who didn't; all those unsung heroes who fell by the wayside, like John and Bill Hudson (who were twins), Brett Halsey, Bobby Hoy, George Nader, and Richard Long, who was married to Suzan Ball, a beautiful, dark-haired girl with a magnificent figure.

Universal put Suzan under contract in 1950, two years after me, and I took her out for a while. We'd go for drives down to the beach and talk about what we would do if we achieved success in the movies. We both

TC's snapshot of Rock Hudson at home (1950)

wanted to be movie stars in the most intense way. She told me she wanted to bring her mother out, buy a house in the valley, travel, have a great career. She was cast as a dancer in a Jeff Chandler movie called *East of Sumatra*, but she fell during one of the rehearsals and injured her knee. A few months later they diagnosed the pain in that leg as cancer. They had to amputate her leg, and a year later she was dead at twenty-two. Suzan Ball—a kind of tragic child-figure in my life. I often think about her.

Susan Cabot was another lost soul from those days. She was going with Prince Hussein, the future king of Jordan, until he found out she was Jewish. She also went with Rock Hudson, which shows you how smart she

84

was. She was so tiny, four feet eleven inches, and wore these incredible high heels. Her son killed her with a weightlifting bar in 1986, claiming she'd driven him to it.

Karen Kupcinet was another one. She was the daughter of Irv Kupcinet, the Chicago columnist, and she came to Hollywood to get into movies. She was a dimply little girl—cute, but never going to make it. She lived just off Sunset in a little house near the Strip. She was murdered there, and in all these years, they've never found out who killed her.

Joyce Holden was a beautiful blonde, and I took her out now and then when she was under contract to Universal. She left the movies, converted, and went to work for the Jehovah's Witnesses. Peggy Dow's star almost rose, but then she married a rich Tulsa oil man, Walter Helmerich III, and had five sons. That was the end of *that* career. Sue England was a beauty who disappeared, except for some TV work later. They arranged for me to go out with Ann Blyth for a time, and then Wanda Hendrix, who was married to Audie Murphy. After she and Audie separated, I, like a fool, called Wanda and started taking her out—the Congressional Medal winner's ex-wife—I

TC and Sue England on the Universal lot (1949)

85

wasn't only stupid, I was *dumb*. He was the war hero of America, who'd blow your fucking head off quicker than he'd look at you. My brain was in my dick. She was a lovely woman, but I had to avoid Audie for months. There were others: Anita Ekberg at Universal; Barbara Lawrence and Coleen Gray at 20th Century-Fox; Lucille Barkley, whose one claim to fame was making *Bedtime for Bonzo* with Ronnie Reagan; Barbara Whiting and her sister Margaret, the singer. The Whiting family adopted me when I first came out.

These were the women I went out with. All Hungarians are crazy about women, you know, and I knew all those beautiful girls. They were the ones I spent time with, though there was nothing really serious with any of them.

When I first got to California, they sent me to take some photographs with Eddie Esterbrook, using the MGM backlot for the shots. We worked for about an hour, and then I roamed around that incredible studio watching pictures being shot and people going back and forth. I ended up in the commissary for a glass of milk and a piece of apple pie, and found this sweet-looking girl sitting next to me. She looked familiar, but I wasn't sure who she was, so I said hi, she said hi, and we started to talk. I was flirting a little and enjoying her company, and before I left I said, "I'm new in California. My name is Bernie Schwartz." She said, "My name is Judy Garland."

Judy was a woman of infinite grace; a woman and a child at the same time. I don't think she really had a childhood. She got into show business with her family, the Gumm Sisters, and was on the road from the time she was a little girl, then ended up at MGM at the age of thirteen. She was under constant stress. She was never really happy in her marriages or as a person. She was only happy when she worked—when she sang and danced. In 1951 I met her again with Janet Leigh, who was a good friend of hers, and we went to a party where I couldn't take my eyes off her. She was so gracious and kind to everybody around her. Yet I always felt a sadness in her, something unreconciled and never as fulfilling as it should have been for her.

In a way, that was true for all of us. Rock Hudson, R. J. Wagner, Natalie Wood, had started a few years earlier. Jimmy Dean was at Warner Bros. Marlon got there a year before us. We socialized with each other, took out our dates, met at social clubs without having to carry membership cards. We finished work and at the end of the day couldn't wait to get in our cars, go home, clean up, then hit the clubs: Morocco, Ciro's, Mocambo, Lucy's,

and the Club Gala, where Spago's restaurant is now. All-night madness—
we didn't know there was a tomorrow. Now we do.

The Mocambo was on Sunset Boulevard in the middle of the Strip. It
had a bar, a dining room, and a dance floor with a small stage, and along
one long wall were cages with yellow canaries. We'd go there on weekends
for an evening on the town, and I was always intrigued how those canaries
were able to survive in that smoke-filled, noisy club. One night I found out.
I happened to look over when one of the canaries toppled off its perch and
fell to the bottom of the cage, dead. A waiter standing nearby just whipped
out a fishnet from his pocket, opened the cage, and scooped it up. Another
waiter came up instantly and replaced the poor dead canary with a live one.
Nobody noticed it but me. So that was the mystery of the dead yellow canary: Some make it in Hollywood, and some don't.

About a year after I got to California, in 1949, I met Marilyn Monroe
for the first time. She was still trying to get a contract at Universal, or anywhere else. When she'd walk down the street, everybody would look at her.
She was wearing see-through blouses then, which was shocking in those
days—a fantastic-looking woman. Rufus LeMaire was the head of the casting department, and he'd talked to her two or three times, but nothing
seemed to come of it. People were being signed all over the place, but for
some reason they skipped over Marilyn. One day I was sitting in the commissary at a table next to Rufus and some of his friends, and they were talking about contract players. I overheard Rufus say, "Did you see that Monroe
girl out there?" One of the other guys said, "Yes, did you like her?" And Rufus said, "No, she's a little too trashy for me."

I wonder whatever happened to Rufus LeMaire.*

One day Marilyn and I went into Schwab's drugstore. I drove her from
the studio because she wanted to buy some makeup, and I was going to get
the trade papers. I can still see her primping in front of the mirror at
Schwab's soda fountain. Later on all the adulation and the fan clubs weren't
so difficult for me to handle, the way they were for her. I'd had that all my
life, even before I got into movies; in school, in the neighborhoods where
I lived, always a lot of furor. Everybody liked the way I looked, including
myself. When I got into the movies, it happened there too, only larger. It

---

* TC's question is rhetorical, but to answer it briefly: LeMaire was originally a Broadway producer who chased women obsessively and formed his own low-class, copycat version of
the *Ziegfeld Follies* called *LeMaire's Affairs* before moving to Hollywood to work as head
of casting for a variety of studios.

TC, a bit on the stiff side, in an early Universal wardrobe test (1949)

sounds egotistical, but what the fuck: I was used to it, even though I was still just Bernie Schwartz from the Bronx. Not long ago I came across a letter I wrote to my parents from California in December, 1949, just before they came out:

Dear folks: This morning a big special delivery package came. I opened it and found the most beautiful coat I ever saw. Dad and Mom, I love you both very much. You don't know how much I love the coat. It fits like I had it made just for me. I know I've been a little hard and difficult once in a while, when I was home, and I know I caused both of you a lot of worry. But listen, dolls, one of these days all the past will be like a memory and we'll all be together here in California. I spoke to Mr. Manny Spock, the guy who runs the Universal tailoring and wardrobe department, and told him about you, Dad, and he said that when you come out, he'll send you to the union out here. He's a big mucka in the woman's tailoring line. I also spoke to Orrie Kelly, who is the dress designer and he'll want to talk to you also. Then maybe you'll be able to come out here sooner. . . . This is a good chance for it. I'll close now and love to Bobby. It's a great coat and I love it and I love you all. Merry Christmas.

My father never really took me up on that. I brought them out, but nothing ever came of it for him. For my mother, on the other hand, it was a little

The Schwartz family relocates to Hollywood: Helen, TC, Bobby, and Manny (1950)

different: ZaSu Pitts, Patsy Kelly, and my mom, Mrs. Schwartz, became kind of a team! Patsy Kelly got to be an especially good friend of my mother's. What a combo those two were: like the Kellys and the Cohens. My mother and Patsy were about the same age. My mother was very gregarious, and Patsy found somebody very friendly in her. I would see them together having lunch now and then with ZaSu; a very amusing group. My mother joined the Matri Stellarum Club (Mothers of the Stars) and showed up once on Groucho Marx's *You Bet Your Life* TV show. She had a pretty good time with it.

But from then on I had the burden of my mother and father and brother. Bobby was just two or three years old when I went into the navy, so I wasn't around when he was growing up, and I hardly knew him. I went to war, and when I came back, I had a little brother. That fifteen years between us was a huge gap. I spent time with him, but I didn't have any patience or desire to get to know him. I went to acting school right away, and then I came to California. I'd just barely gotten established when out schlepped my parents and my brother: "Take care of us." So there I was, supporting everybody. I had to do that for a lot of years when I was first in the movies.

I am easily distracted, and when I was on a set or having a personal problem, it was very hard for me to concentrate. My mother was fucking me up, my brother was going from mental institution to mental institution, I was afraid my girlfriends were screwing around on me—whatever. No matter what, I had to come on the set and do that work, and every time that phone would ring, I'd have to run off. That was the unfortunate way I did my business. Later I started using a lot of substances, because that was the only way I thought I could get through the day.

My mother wanted me to get Bobby in the movies, and those days were hell with her. She really thought he could be in films, and at one point I did get Universal to take some test photos of him. I can't believe they actually agreed to that, but they did. She was always badgering me to do that as if it was some debt that I'd assumed. What debt did I have to her? She was vindictive and cruel when I was a boy. But somehow Bobby became my responsibility. He was on my shoulders, which was very taxing and stressful emotionally. I tried to deal with it the best I could, but all I really cared about then was how tight my pants were and how big my billing was. That hasn't changed much, come to think of it. I was just trying to learn the business and do what I was told.

Around that time, Universal sent me to Chicago on tour for a picture. I made an appearance at a theater, and while I was there I met a beau-

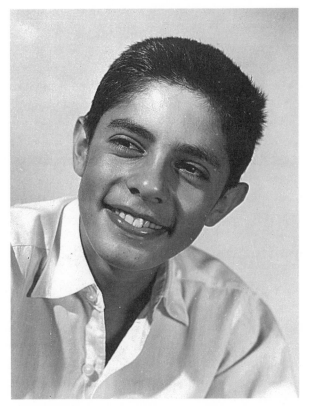

Mama insisted on it: Robert Schwartz's official Universal publicity photo (1955)

tiful girl who worked in the Universal distributing office, and I asked her if she'd go out with me after I finished the tour that day. She said yes, so we had dinner, and I took her up to the hotel room. We necked on the couch and got semi-undressed, and she started to go down on me. About the fourth stroke, she stopped and looked up at me and said, "If my mother could only see me now!" I said, "Darling, it's not polite to talk with your mouth full." It was one of those moments that stick with you for life.

In the movie profession, a lot of girls would give you anything to get an introduction to a director or a studio. It still goes on. It's a bargaining chip. Everybody loves pussy, including a lot of women. There's nothing wrong with it; it's nature. And that knowledge made it just a little bit easier to function. If you knew that, you knew everything, or almost everything. In my case, I had a problem with premature ejaculation. That affected my life. So I had to repeat a lot. To a large extent, that's how success was judged, especially by the men in the business.

In 1948, when I went out to California, I didn't really have the time or the inclination to say good-bye to anyone. I just went out there, got that bit in *Criss Cross* and things started happening for me. Four months later I was back in New York City for the first time since I'd left, doing promotion for *City Across the River.* They gave me a suite at the Sherry-Netherland Hotel and the longest black limousine you ever saw—*huge* automobile. I told the driver to take me up to the Bronx to show off for all my buddies. "Look at that car! Hey, Bernie, ya doing great!" All that good stuff. Then we came back into Manhattan, and I thought I'd take a run by the old Dramatic Workshop, maybe see some of my pals and show off there too. So I said to the driver, "Take me to the President Theater."

It was a miserable, rainy late afternoon, but he drives me down Forty-eighth Street, and who do I see out front, standing under the marquee, but Walter Matthau. He's got a long, heavy coat on and looks as grumpy as he's ever looked in his life. In fact, he doesn't look any different or any grumpier now than he did then. He's got this coat pulled up around his neck and a racing form sticking out of one pocket, and he's looking out at this cold, miserable world he's got to live in. He hates it. I'm getting this reading as I'm sitting in my limo, warm and comfy, looking at this poor guy on the sidewalk staring into the gutter and saying to himself, "What's ever going to happen for me? Nothin'." You could see that on his face.

So I say to the driver, "See that guy standing under the awning? Drive up to him as slowly as possible, and when we're alongside of him, stop." He says okay, so we drive up, and I see Walter watching this limousine come rolling up, and it stops right where he's standing. I roll the window down, I look at him, and I say, "I fucked Yvonne de Carlo!"

Then I just rolled that window back up and told the driver to get the hell out of there.

C·H·A·P·T·E·R F·I·V·E

TONY OF THE MOVIES

A guy goes to see a doctor and says to the nurse, "My name is Bernard Schwartz." It will be a few minutes, she says. Finally the doctor comes out and says, "How can I help you, Mr. Schwartz?" He says, "Well, Doctor, all my life, I've been unhappy as a man. It just doesn't fit me. I don't like the vibrations I get. I have this incredible desire to dress like a woman—to *be* a woman. I'd love it if a guy took me out for dinner and a ride in a car. I'd love to wear makeup and earrings—the whole thing."

The doctor says, "Well, how can I help you, Mr. Schwartz?" He says, "I thought maybe you could recommend a doctor who could give me a sex change." The doctor says, "Wait a minute, Mr. Schwartz. Before you go any further, let me tell you it's not possible. You don't want to do it. They'll just mutilate you, cut off sections of your anatomy and then give you some hormones, and it'll never work. Believe me when I tell you."

He says, "But, Doctor—"

"Please, Mr. Schwartz, believe me. Go home, find some way to adjust. If you're alone, and you want to dress up like a girl, who's going to stop you? You live alone? Fine. Then just do it. Save yourself a fortune, and a lot of trouble."

The guy leaves. A year later the nurse says, "Doctor, there's a Miss Bernice Schwartz to see you." In walks this beautiful, voluptuous, dark-haired, big-titted, long-legged woman in three-inch heels. She says, "You don't remember me, do you?" He says, "No, I don't." She says, "We met about a year ago. I was Bernard Schwartz then. Now I'm Bernice Schwartz."

The doctor says, "Bernie! Bernice? No, it's not possible! This is fantastic!" She says, "You told me it couldn't work, but I went to Sweden. I found this charming clinic. They examined me, they did everything. Would you like to examine me?" She gets up in the stirrups. "Look, I can even bear children."

The doctor says, "This is the most extraordinary sex-change operation I've ever seen in my life. Congratulations. But listen, I have to ask you: Don't you ever have any desire to be a man?" She says, "Never. I love being a woman. I never regret a thing, except . . ."

"Yes?"

"Well," she says, "occasionally—not very often, but every now and then—I get this tremendous urge to lay *t'fillin*."*

I often felt like that myself, with all my own split personalities. I cannot be anything less than all the different characters in my movies. All those people I played on the screen have rubbed off on me, they're all inside of me, from the Son of Ali Baba to Sidney Falco in *Sweet Smell of Success*. You've heard of people who have channels and 20 personalities? I've got 120—the ones I've been in all those movies, and I can't forget them. You can't forget being under Marilyn Monroe, or sitting on a horse, dressed in armor, with a camera car racing along ahead of you. No one could. I was the one Marilyn Monroe tried to seduce, rubbing her pussy against my face to drive me crazy. What is it, ejaculations in films don't count?

I took Kirk Douglas's eye out in one movie, Kirk killed me in another one. I'm the only guy that ever took a girl away from Frank Sinatra in a movie. I'm the only guy that ever took *two* girls away from Jack Lemmon. I'm the only guy that knocked Burt Lancaster on his ass. I'm the only son of Yul Brynner that he ever killed. I'm the son of Ali Baba with a scimitar on my waist, and this beautiful girl walks in dressed in silk and chiffon, and she kisses me, and I kiss her, and I pour some wine out of a ram's horn, and we make love—that was a reality for me. Not *reality* itself, but *a* reality. I've been in a hundred films, and if each one has thirty scenes, I've had maybe three thousand of those realities. For me, they were all reality and sometimes they get mixed up, and that's what I like about it. In my life, the fantasy has sometimes overwhelmed the reality, and vice versa. Once you step in a room, you soil it—not the verb, but the noun: You bring a little

---

*Barry Paris says I have to explain that to lay *t'fillin* is the religious ritual of wrapping the leather straps around your left arm as you recite the Torah, with the little box resting under your left arm, close to your heart. It's the butchest thing an Orthodox Jewish man can do. You can't get any butcher than that.

94

of your own soil. My soil was Manhattan and the Bronx, and the studio wasn't quite sure what to do about it. Neither was I.

When I started in movies, I knew I'd have to change my name, and I went through a whole basketful of them—every conceivable kind of name. Steven John, John Stevens . . . One of my Hungarian ancestors' names was Kertész, so I thought maybe I'd anglicize it to Curtis.* First Jimmy Curtis. Then Johnny Curtis. Finally I hit on Anthony Curtis, and it eventually got shortened to Tony. There was one particular incident that pushed me toward that:

I was in New York after I'd made my first few films as Anthony Curtis, and this pretty girl on a street corner looked at me, did a little double take, and said, "Tony of the movies!" I loved that, and from then on I thought it would be best to be called Tony. But I didn't really tell anybody about it yet; I just went around telling myself, "My name is Tony Curtis, Tony Curtis, Tony Curtis," until I decided I liked the way it sounded. Not long after that I was at a cocktail party with Janet Leigh, and there was Cary Grant, my idol. Janet said, "Come on, we'll go over and meet him." So I went over to him and I was so nervous, I said, "Hi, my name is . . . Bernie Schwartz."

I was still feeling my way around and getting to know the cast of characters out there. For a while it was cowboy movies. The first one was *Winchester 73*, in which I got tenth billing as a cavalryman and Rock Hudson got sixth as an Indian chief. But who's counting? Universal put all of us new guys in those movies—like throwing a kid in a swimming pool to make him figure out how to swim—and we did the best we could.

The stars of *Winchester* were Jimmy Stewart and Shelley Winters. She tells everybody she "made" me, but I remember her as being pretty irascible and mean. Anthony Mann, the director, I didn't know well, but I liked his expansiveness and his sense of the outdoors. The cameraman was William Daniels, who gave every shot the most wonderful atmosphere and composition. He filmed all of the great Garbo movies, but I didn't realize that until later. He was very old at that time, and, unfortunately, I didn't get to know him. I just didn't know then who all these men were and how important their backgrounds were.

---

*Hungarian director Mihaly Kertész thought along similar lines. In America, as Michael Curtiz, he made a few dozen of Hollywood's finest films, including *Casablanca* (1943).

Winchester 73 (1950), directed by Anthony Mann, was the Ultimate Western (like *Colt 45* of the same year, only much better) in which the gun itself is the star—in this case, the fabled Winchester rifle, "the gun that won the West." The 1873 model is so perfect that President Ulysses S. Grant and Buffalo Bill both own one, we learn from Sheriff Wyatt Earp (Will Geer) of Dodge City.

In honor of the 1876 centennial, Geer announces that Dodge is holding a shootin' contest, the winner of which will get the precious edition on display in the town square. "Real pretty," says James Stewart, as he and all the other men gather around to admire and fondle the clearly Freudian penis substitute. Stewart wins it fair and square over his longtime enemy Dutch Henry Brown (Stephen McNally), but Dutch steals the prize, and the rest of the film concerns Stewart's efforts to recapture it.

The love interest and token woman of the cast is Shelley Winters, who has the retrospectively ironic name of Miss Manners, with whom Stewart gradually (*very* gradually) falls in love. They are an unlikely pair indeed.

The script itself, by Robert L. Richards and Borden Chase, from a story by Stuart N. Lake, cleverly employs the rifle as a device to connect multiple situations. The subplot is that the Indians want guns too. Hence, the bare-chested and rather self-conscious Rock Hudson as Young Bull, whose speech is not quite consistent. To the white smugglers who try to cheat him, he says, "They are not the guns of which we spoke." A few moments later, after such fastidious English, he spies the Winchester and grunts, "This is gun I want!"

The Indians, led by Rock, are soon chasing Winters and her fiancé, Charles Drake. He goes "crazy yella" and tries to abandon her, but at the last minute they stumble into the safety of a U.S. Cavalry camp. Handsome young TC is among the soldiers around the campfire that night. "Pretty, isn't she?" he whispers to a companion.

That was 50 percent of his two lines in the movie, which was made during the pre–Native American awareness era of film:

TC in action in his first Western, *Winchester '73* (1950)

These Indians have no redeeming social values and certainly no scruples toward any white women they capture. Stewart gives Winters a six-gun and tells her to save the last bullet. "I understand about the last one," she says. "A girl never knows when she might need a bullet."

The Winchester changes hands a few more times, and then Dan Duryea as Waco Johnny Dean—a crazy outlaw with a maniacal laugh—kills Drake and kidnaps Shelley. Stewart and his old nemesis McNally turn out to be brothers. ("The old man sired two sons, and one was no good—never was. Dutch shot him in the back!") That, of course, calls for a final, fraternal shootout in the rocky hills.

Critic Leonard Maltin calls it "an exceptional Western, beautifully photographed by Daniels. First rate in every way, this landmark film was largely responsible for renewed popularity of Westerns in the 1950s."

—B.P.

I did two more Westerns pretty fast after that, both of them with Audie Murphy.* On top of being a great World War II hero, Audie was a great Western star. Nobody could outdraw him. One day he said, "Let's play drop the handkerchief." I didn't know what that was, but Audie explained it: The two rivals stood holding the ends of a big bandana between their teeth. The first one that dropped the handkerchief could reach for his gun. Audie never dropped the handkerchief first; he always waited for the other guy, and he still beat everybody.

What I didn't know was that some of the guns had blanks in them and some didn't. I thought we were just fooling around with empty guns, but he had two guns—an empty one in his holster and one with a blank in it behind his back. When I dropped my end of the handkerchief, he pressed the one gun into my belly and fired the other one behind his back. I heard the shot, smelled the gunpowder, looked down, and saw smoke rising. Then I fainted. They carried me into one of the makeup rooms to bring me around. Everybody got a big fuckin' laugh out of it. Audie apologized for years, and we became friends later, sort of, but I never really liked him after that.

Kansas Raiders was shot in Canab, Utah. Before that, the only relationship I'd ever had with a horse was with one that pulled an ice wagon in New York City, and once, with a girl who *looked* like a horse, but that's another story. There I was in Utah, sitting on this twelve-hundred-pound animal, and we had to gallop in and out. I had no idea what to do about a horse. I kept looking for the gearshift and the brakes and something to hold on to, while this thing just trotted around doing exactly what it wanted. Everybody thought it was funny except me. During one of the takes, this horse bucked, I fell off, and it just took off. The wrangler started after the horse, and I heard somebody say to him, "Is Tony all right?" His answer was, "Forget him. We can get all the actors we want. We only have four horses."

So much for cowboy films. After that, Universal moved me immediately into the swashbucklers. They did it with me, they did it with Rock, they did it with anybody who was under contract to them, because that

---

Sierra (1950), directed by Alfred E. Green, and *Kansas Raiders* (1950), directed by Ray Enright. *Sierra*'s cast was on hand at its June 1950 premiere in San Francisco, and was introduced one by one. When "Anthony Curtis" was called, the predominantly female audience went wild. TC was pushed onto the stage and just stood there until the shouting subsided. "I couldn't understand it," he told a reporter afterward with his usual candor. "I knew I wasn't getting it because of my acting. I hadn't done any. Then I realized that people can like you just because of your looks and personality."

was the only kind of movie they really knew how to do well—swashbucklers modeled on the Jon Hall and Maria Montez pictures. They were geared for that. They had the sets and costumes built from much earlier, for the Sabu movies, so it was a natural offshoot of those.

For a short time in those days, I roomed in the same house on Barham Boulevard with Marlon Brando. He was doing *A Streetcar Named Desire* and I was doing *The Prince Who Was a Thief*. Later I said, "Marlon, I wonder what would've happened if you'd turned left down Barham Boulevard and gone to Universal to be the son of Ali Baba, and I'd turned right and become Stanley Kowalski?"

Marlon said, "Then *I'd* have been stuck with 'Yondah lies the castle of my faddah,' and *you'd* have been yelling 'Stel-l-a-a!'"

Cary Grant used to talk about "A Streetcar Named Success": People were always getting on and falling off, he said, and he mentioned it on a photo he signed for me: "May your trip be a long and enduring one." He knew "Success" was the streetcar I wanted to get on. If I had ever played in anything like *The Men* or *Streetcar* in those days, my "look" and my career would have been different. But Universal stuck me in bloomers and a turban instead. They were setting me up for ridicule, but the funny thing is, I was more successful in some ways than Marlon. My career had a bigger flash burn.

Son of Ali Baba was the movie in which I had to stand at the top of a hill and tell Piper Laurie, "Yonder lies the castle of my father, the caliph." It came out, "Yondah lies the castle of my faddah," and I never heard the end of it. Forty years later my friend Hugh Hefner quoted it back to me: "Yondah lies me faddah's castle." I said, "Hef, I never said that. And even if I did, whose fault was it that they constructed the line that way, to start a sentence out with *yonder*? They wrote it, and I got stuck with it." Hef said, "Don't tell people that, Tony. It's a legendary story about you and Hollywood, whether it's true or not."

I've thought about that a lot, and I think I understand what he means. But I'm still sensitive about coming out of New York and being Jewish, and all the mockery of that line sounded to me like a putdown not just of New Yorkers but of Jews. British actors could get away with coming in and playing Roman generals or anything else, but if an American played the same kind of part, he got rapped because he sounded like he came from New York or Boston or some other recognizable place.

To me, "Yondah lies the castle of my faddah"—that mockery—was a lot like the words *kike, nigger,* and *fag*. It signified a putdown, an inability to accept the differences or the logic of other people. I didn't like it then, and I still don't like it. I didn't like the idea that New Yorkers, in particular, were denigrated by high-toned English assholes, you'll excuse the vernacular.

───────────── ─•─ ─────────────

Janet Leigh on the furor over TC's accent: "Neither Tony nor I had the benefit of an English accent. I came from Stockton, California, and he came from New York. But Tony took a lot more heat than I did. We kept our projects separate and didn't talk much about what approach to take to a role. He never asked help from me with his accent, but he was a good actor, and he worked on it with Sophie Rosenstein. He didn't take it lightly. When he read those things, it had to bother him. It would bother anybody, especially somebody as sensitive and intense as he was. If you're Olivier and born in London, you speak one way. If you're Curtis and born in New York, it's another way. To have it singled out must have been painful, but he never complained about it to me."

The Prince Who Was a Thief (1951) was based on a Theodore Dreiser story and directed by the highly respected Rudolph Maté. TC speaks of the "tit-and-sand" movies; others call them the "cutlass-and-kisses" or the "boobs-and-beefcake" genre—a Hollywood mainstay for years, and not just at Universal. Columbia hoped John Derek might be the next Errol Flynn in *Rogues of Sherwood Forest* (1950) and *Mask of the Avenger* (1951). At Fox, R. J. Wagner made *Prince Valiant* (1954) and Jeffrey Hunter did *Princess of the Nile* (1954). Even the more mature Jeff Chandler was assigned *Flame of Araby* (1951). The swashbucklers were a training ground; as soon as the studio felt the actors were ready, they were moved into other films.

Nobody at Universal expected *The Prince Who Was a Thief* to be anything more than low-budget (under one million dollars) escapist fare. The studio was thus amazed when it became a box-office hit and TC hailed as the successor to Douglas Fairbanks. He had insisted on doing his own stunts and had honed his swordsmanship with master Ralph Faulkner, who said: "His sense of timing is remarkable and his muscular coordination per-

100

fect. His eagerness to learn was beyond restraint and . . . carried him beyond the point of safety." In addition to TC's athleticism, audiences also liked Maté's tongue-in-cheek direction. *Time* called it "touched with humor and quite free of pretensions. It should delight youngsters without irritating grown-ups who go along for the air conditioning."

On a nationwide publicity tour, girls tore at TC's clothes wherever he went. As a result, a studio costumer did him the favor of designing "break-away" coats

TC in *The Prince Who Was a Thief* (1951)

whose buttons and sleeves and lapels came off easily when grabbed and provided souvenirs at less trauma to the wearer.

Back at Universal, the fan mail poured in. TC and Laurie became overnight teen idols and were quickly reteamed for *Son of Ali Baba* (1952), directed by Kurt Neumann. That film showcased even more of his athletic skills, with the same good box-office results.

—B.P.

Piper and I made four pictures together, but it was always bullshit about a romance. We never had one. We went out together a few times, and we necked once or twice, but that was it. She was "the flower-eating girl," which resulted from studio publicity about the fact that Piper Laurie ate flowers. I later found out that some flowers are very eatable, and that there was a certain series of beautiful yellow and red flowers that were delicious. I ate some in Honolulu. Piper knew what she was doing. But it wasn't really a health or diet thing, it was publicity. Some women bared their breasts.

Mamie Van Doren wore dresses that clung to her derriere. Marilyn wore see-through blouses. You had to find some gimmick. So Piper ate flowers. They tried to hype a romance between us, but I was doing pretty well on my own then, and when I found myself on the road with Piper, I resented it. They'd send us out on tour as Bernie Schwartz from the Bronx and Rosetta Jacobs from Detroit.* But the response on those tours was overwhelmingly in my favor, and I was selfish. I didn't want to share my career or be paired up with anybody, certainly not someone who wasn't of my own choosing. It looked as if we were a duo, when, in fact, we weren't. I didn't like that, and I don't think Piper did either.

Besides that, Piper was with Leonard Goldstein then. The Goldsteins were twin brothers. Bob brought me out to California, and Leonard was the producer who put me and Piper in *The Prince Who Was a Thief*. Piper and I were both at the same early stage of our careers, and hers was less successful than mine. She was a lovely, very appealing, beautiful young woman, but I wasn't interested in any relationship at the time. There was a lot of pressure on us from the studio, and there was some stress between us, but I tried to maintain good relations with her. It ended abruptly when we stopped making pictures together. Piper and I didn't end up friends, but we also didn't end up enemies. I always tried not to end up enemies with anybody.

The first TC fan club was started in 1950 by John H. Smith, whose mimeographed fan mag was called *Curtis-ly Yours*. It offered pictures, buttons and stamps of "Anthony," and some nitty-gritty interviews: "I was out with a girl the other night," TC told Smith. "A glamor queen. You know, had her name in lights and the world in the palm of her hands. She turned to me and with her best grade B dramatic school diction said, 'Let's go slumming downtown. It's fun to see the way other people live.' I saw red. I said to her, 'Listen, honey, I used to live in a street that other peo-

---

* Piper Laurie was just seventeen when she signed at Universal. She made *Prince* just a year later, and *The Son of Ali Baba* the next year. The other two TC-Laurie low-budget hits were *No Room for the Groom* (1952) and *Johnny Dark* (1954). In one Jewish neighborhood in Brooklyn, they were proudly billed on the marquee as "Bernard Schwartz and Rosetta Jacobs." Laurie retired after *The Hustler* (1961) and made a comeback as Sissy Spacek's mother in *Carrie* (1976), earning Oscar nominations for both pictures.

ple went slumming in. It might make me homesick. I'll take you home instead.' "

—B.P.

The fascinating thing to me, in retrospect, is that I came into movies right as the studio system was disintegrating. TV was just beginning to become popular and widespread, and the studios were already starting to fall apart and lose their battle against TV when I got there. The *General Electric Theater* program concept was taking off, and the studio moguls were all very neurotic about it. I had to take out girls who'd won win-a-date-with-Tony contests in *Photoplay* or *Modern Screen*, where they'd photograph us for the movie magazines. I would pick the girl up at her home, and if there was a television set in her living room, the photographer would cover it with a cloth and put a flower pot on it: No acknowledgment of television was allowed. It was to be avoided like the plague.

If the movie industry had embraced and adjusted to TV then, instead of thirty years later, things would have been different, and better for the movies. Cable television could have been an extension of the picture business in the fifties. But the studios weren't that smart. They were afraid, and they made the mistake of listening to the theater owners, who screamed bloody murder and resisted. The film industry itself was the big loser. That was the tragedy.

Bill Goetz and Leo Spitz were the executives who ran Universal, and sometimes I would hear their strategy discussions against TV. Bill was a gregarious man with a wonderful art collection. His wife, Edie, was L. B. Mayer's daughter. They were good friends to me and often invited me out to their house. One weekend Mayer himself was there, and they were talking about "the TV problem." There was concern. L.B. went on a tirade about the idea that there weren't enough "family" pictures being made to compete with television. On top of that, he said, low-ball, violent pictures like *The Killers* were hurting the movies' image with people in Middle America, wherever that was.

Some people were glad the studios were disintegrating, because they hated the moguls, Harry Cohn in particular. I always liked Harry, myself. One day I got an inside look at the way he operated. He liked to see me, and I'd stop by now and then, just to talk. One day my friend Dean Shen-

dal and I are in his office at Columbia, sitting there talking, and
Harry's buzzer rings. He says to
the secretary, "Well, send her in."
And in walks this beautiful girl,
maybe twenty years old, just a
magnificent young woman in a
beautiful silk summer dress. This
dress would've looked great even
on the hippopotamus in *Fanta-
sia*. On her, it was breathtaking.
She takes a look around, ner-
vously, and says, "Harry, I have to
talk to you." He says, "So talk."
She looks at us and says, "Harry,
I'd rather not talk in front of these
gentlemen." He says, "Anything
you've got to say, you can say in
front of them." She takes a deep

TC's official "signed" fan club picture

breath and says, "Harry, I can't go on this way. You promised to take care
of me, put me in a movie. It's been eight months now, it just can't keep on
like this. You have to do something, or I'm going to have to call your
wife. . . ."

That was her big mistake. He looked at her, picked up the telephone,
dialed the number, held out the phone to her, and said, "Tell her yourself."

She turned around, and I can never forget the terrible look of distress
and unhappiness on that beautiful face. She just slowly walked out. I was
completely stunned. But after a silence, Dean had the nerve to ask, "Harry,
was that really your wife?" Harry Cohn just looked him straight in the eye
and said, "You'll never know."

The truth is, I was only barely aware of all the high-level studio politics and skullduggery. I was only really tuned in to my own career, going
from one picture to another. Time goes fast when you're having a good time.
Those first three years were all telescoped. Lew Wasserman's principle was
to put me in movies that I didn't have to carry by myself. I always shared
the load with other people, and I don't think in the history of movies any
actor worked with as many major players and directors as I did and had
good relations with all of them.

104

Rudolph Maté was a good example. Hardly anybody knew he was a great cameraman in Europe before he came here and decided to become a director.* Rudy and I got along great because we spoke Hungarian to each other. They called him "Night-and-Day Rudy Maté" because he loved to keep shooting and shooting at night. He had a great flair with the camera—an ethereal gift for visualizing—but he didn't have much sense of gut-bucket living, and he wasn't very good with choice of material. The movies he directed were always a little airy. He wanted success, and so he made any picture they gave him.

The production meeting is what makes or breaks a director, and in those meetings they'd ask Rudy, "How big a party sequence are you planning?" Rudy'd say, "Twenty or thirty people." They'd say, "Let's use eight or ten and make it more intimate." By cutting it down to eight, you change the whole impact, and all of a sudden the movie changes too, but it's a lot cheaper. Instead of saying, "No, it's got to be twenty—I want that wildness in it," Rudy would say, "Okay, make it smaller." Whereas, a guy like Stanley Kubrick would say, "Fuck you! And just for that, instead of twenty, now I want *eighty*!" And in Kubrick's movie you'd notice that party, and it would make a difference.

I was a pretty face, but I wasn't *just* a pretty face. I watched every fucking thing those guys did. Everything. I understood a lot about them and their backgrounds and what they represented and what they wanted and how they were getting even with people who thought they weren't going anywhere.

Blake Edwards and Dick Quine, for example, were tight—best friends, in fact—and I was good friends with both of them.† One day Quine told me, "The definition of success is to be doing better than your best friend." That was basic for him and for Blake. The object of their striving was to do better than each other, which gave me a real insight into those guys.

I was still learning, especially about directors. *No Room for the Groom* (1952) was made by Douglas Sirk, who came from Denmark. Everybody

---

* Polish-born Rudolph Maté (1898–1964) entered films in Budapest in 1919 as an assistant to Alexander Korda and worked in Vienna, Berlin, and Paris as cinematographer for the likes of Carl Dreyer, G. W. Pabst, Fritz Lang, and Rene Clair. He came to Hollywood in 1935 and began directing in 1947. Maté directed no fewer than four of TC's early films: *The Prince Who Was a Thief* (1951), *The Black Shield of Falworth* (1954), *Forbidden* (1953), and *The Rawhide Years* (1956).

† TC made three films under Quine's direction: *So This Is Paris* (1954), *Sex and the Single Girl* (1964), and *Paris When It Sizzles* (1964), and four with Edwards: *Mister Cory* (1957), *The Perfect Furlough* (1958), *Operation Petticoat* (1959), and *The Great Race* (1965).

carried on later about what a great "cult" director he was, but I didn't find him so intriguing, and neither did Piper Laurie. Universal had a tendency to pick up certain down-on-their-luck "prestige" directors in Europe for cheap, and hope they'd come through with a couple of good pictures for the studio. But Sirk was cold and aloof and unsympathetic toward the younger actors, and he didn't impress me at all.

On the other hand, I thought Joseph Pevney was a really fine man. He was married to Mitzi Green. Before becoming a director, he was an excellent actor himself. He worked with Bogart and Julie Garfield in a lot of those early Warner Bros. movies, always playing the brother or the "other" fella. He was an excellent director in many ways, but on *Flesh and Fury* (1952) he was like Rudy Maté; he did everything the studio said. "We only want four extras," they'd say to him. Joe would hire four extras. He hurt his directing career by not demanding the quality of production he really needed. He couldn't stand up and say, "I'm not going to shoot it that way. I'm going to shoot it the way I want it." He was a very good in-house director at Universal but never was able to punch out of there into anything else. But Joe was always really nice with me and wonderful to work with. He made things agreeable and creative for the actor, and I liked him a lot.

Flesh and Fury was a boxing movie, and I'll never forget being in that ring with a guy who kept working me over and smashing me to a pulp during the rehearsals. I was getting madder and madder. When it came time for the take, he was a couple inches closer than he should have been, and I saw my opening and knocked him flat on his ass. We all rushed up and bent over him. He looked up at me and said, "Kid, is that as hard as you can hit?"

Kind of flattered, I said, "Well, yeah."

And he said, "Stay out of bars."

———————•→•———————

Jack Lemmon: "Tony is alone in doing something that I consider to be impossible—learning how to act on film and *in* film. He was a kid going to the drama workshop with Walter Matthau, studying with Piscator for a few months, and the next thing you know— bam!—he's off to Hollywood. Two seconds later, he's a star—as a *kid*. Those were the days when that could happen.

"Now I can promise you that when I did my first film, I was

thrown, and I had behind me about four hundred live television shows, four seasons of summer stock and a lead on Broadway. But I was so thrown by shooting out of sequence, jumping into the middle of a scene—three or four sentences and you're out of it. I couldn't do it. I just could not do it. I was totally thrown by the whole technique of film.

"A lot of actors never could handle it. You were not playing whole scenes. You got no rehearsal, or damn little, except during the shooting itself. Out of context and out of sequence. It's murder. There is no question in my mind that any performance on film is much more difficult to give compared to the performance that you could give on stage.

"Tony was always so damn good with good material. No actor can be good with bad material, but he was so bright, he could cover bad crap with his technique. He could have just been the beautiful young leading man, handsome and charming as hell, with a great personality, sensitive, all of those qualities he has, but he didn't. He wanted to be a good actor, and he's the only guy I know who learned his craft successfully—literally, learned how to act—on film. Nobody else comes to my mind who did this."

—JACK LEMMON TO B.P., April 22, 1993

I'm not sure when it started to happen. All I knew was that I started to like it. *Like* isn't the right word—more fascinated and awed by its magic. The "it" was making movies. There were so many elements to remember and then forget as soon as you remembered them. Mostly it was a matter of forgetting your own existence and allowing the situation, the physical locations, the strangers who were supposed to be your lovers or enemies, to become part of your existence. To be suspended, so to speak, in another world for five or six minutes. It took stamina more than anything else: strong legs, learn your lines, and don't let anyone or anything interfere with the moment at hand.

You found yourself surrounded by a hundred people: propmen, assistant directors, producers, writers, script girls, art and set directors, messengers, special-effects guys, clapper boys, extras, other actors, actresses, production managers, and their assistants—all of their collective energies poured into one small set in the corner of a sound stage surrounded by fifteen other sound stages in this huge studio complex.

Out near the front gate were the main offices, commissaries, dressing rooms, newsstands, gym, parking lots, huge prop and set departments, horses, wranglers, and a small river. There were planes, cars, boats, wagons, cannons, tenements, Arabian streets, Paris streets, London streets, midwestern streets—all ending by a waterfront overlooking a lake. There was half of a steamship. There was every imaginable kind of furniture and artifact. If they didn't have it, they rented it, and when you came on the set to shoot that scene in your lady's boudoir, man, you were in a real lady's chamber with hot and cold running water.

I was making entrances through doors, windows, cellars, roofs, and chimneys. I'd be in bed with a slave girl, riding a horse with a blonde, having champagne with a redhead, taking a brunette home to Mother. Some of them came to work stiff with fear or stiff with booze. Some prepared and knew every word, others didn't know their names. Big-titted, small-titted, men, women, children, dogs, cats, pigs, chickens, cows—these were my companions in those countless scenes with the cameras cranking.

They were all real and unreal at the same time. So was that physical world. Most of the time, to me, it all felt real—except that it all started nowhere and ended nowhere.

C·H·A·P·T·E·R S·I·X

JANET LEIGH

Let me tell you about the first time I saw Janet Leigh: I walked into a cocktail party at RKO, and there she was. Up to that point, I hadn't known too much about her. I don't remember seeing too many of her films. She'd just come from the set of *Jet Pilot*, a movie she was making with John Wayne for Howard Hughes, and Hughes was hot in pursuit. He was very interested in Janet. I looked over, and there was Howard talking with Janet, hovering in the corner. He was still out and about then. He hadn't yet become the Kleenex-over-the-phone recluse. I started to go over toward them, and he kind of stepped aside and walked away. I didn't know what that meant. I had only seen him on a couple of occasions before that, and we never spoke or met. I didn't really care what it meant, or what he thought. All I cared about was Janet Leigh.*

That blond hair was done up in two cinnamon-roll buns on each side of her head, like earphones, with a part in the center. Her face was exquisite—and those beautiful bosoms and tiny waist. It just devastated me to look at this woman. She had an incredible figure, and there was a sweetness about her that I found most appealing. She was wearing a silk blouse, and it was very hard not to be aroused by her—not just me but every guy there. I noticed how everybody responded to her, and I said, "I want her, I want her to be mine." And toward that aim I was dedicated.

*Janet Leigh was Jeanette Helen Morrison, a California music student, when she was discovered in 1947 by Norma Shearer and put under MGM contract. She played ingenues in such pictures as *The Romance of Rosy Ridge* (1947), *Words and Music* (1948), and *Little Women* (1949) until "re-discovered" by Howard Hughes and given better parts in RKO's *Holiday Affair* (1949) and *Two Tickets to Broadway* (1951).

Janet Leigh: "Oh, God, *Jet Pilot* nearly caused me a nervous break-down. When we were doing retakes at George Air Force Base, Victorville, on location, Tony tried to call me. We were shooting about five or six o'clock, and we saw this plane going around, and somebody made a crack, 'Oh, it's Hughes coming to see how we're doing up here.' And it *was* Hughes. He landed, and he insisted that Jules Furthman, the producer, and Josef von Sternberg, the director, and John Wayne and I go to dinner. I wouldn't have gone if it had been just me, but since they were all there, I didn't have much choice. I had said no to him a lot of times before. So we didn't get back from dinner until midnight or so, and Tony had called, and he was upset that I wasn't in. Normally, when I was shooting, I would have been in bed at nine-thirty or ten o'clock.

"Tony kept pretty close tabs on me in those days, and so did Hughes. But something in my deportment that night must have convinced Howard to give up. I never heard from him again."*

Our relationship was very hot, very physical in those early years. That was a major part of it—the actual touching and holding. We both needed each other physically, and we were a perfect match. In a world of imperfection, we were perfect at that time. Little did we or anybody know that would wane, that the ultimate end of perfection is imperfection. People won't accept that, and they drive each other crazy by thinking it's something that can be maintained forever.

I think another reason we were drawn to each other was because the novelty of that social scene was starting to wear off. At least it was for me. I couldn't take too many more of those sit-down dinner parties on the lawns, covered over with a cellophane contraceptive to keep out the cold or keep in the hot, and those gas heaters smelling of kerosene mixed with beef Stroganoff, Chanel No. 5, and menopause No. 3:

Jet Pilot was a curious Hughes film, updating his *Hell's Angels* interest in aviation with a Cold War theme. Some of the stunt flying was done by Chuck Yeager. It was completed in 1950 but not released for seven years.

"Hey, Tony!"

"Hey, baby, what's happening? Sorry, I got to go."

"So soon?"

"It's six already. I got to be at the studio in an hour; gotta go home and change my clothes, feed the dog."

"Can't you stay just another ten minutes?"

"Can't, baby. You know how mad your husband gets when I'm not on time . . ." Each day went like that. Muse and fuse. A lot of superficiality. I think Janet felt the same.

Was she the love of my life? That's very hard to say. I was very devoted to Janet and very much in love with her. I had never lived with a woman before. I didn't know what it meant to live with a woman. All I knew was that men made love to women. I didn't know that you also lived with them. I couldn't equate a love affair to anything in my mother and father's marriage because, especially in their last years, they could barely stand each other. I had no role models. Whatever I learned about how to behave with a woman was in the movies, the way men like Cary Grant did it—all very superficial.

I never read Janet's book—I was afraid to—until Barry Paris pressed a copy into my hands and made me.* She was very kind toward me in it, and I'll always be grateful to her for that. I remember that there was a lot of opposition to the marriage. MGM was leaning on Janet to drop me, but she said no, I'm not going to break up with him. Leonard Goldstein at Universal was strongly opposed. The studios tried to stop it; they were worried about the box-office impact. Jerry Lewis came to me and said, "Don't get married." There we were, all ready to do it, and we were being bombarded with these doubts. Janet heard about it and said, "All right, forget it." She was upset.

We were very confused. We needed some time to talk about it and be alone, so we got in the car and drove out of New York to visit my brother Julie's grave in Riverside, New Jersey. Every now and then, when I'm back East, I still do that—go to see the stone and pray. It's a very meaningful thing for me, and that day it was more than ever. It was so serene. It seemed to calm us both down. Somehow I got the feeling Julie approved.

The studios didn't want *any* potentially big players to get married; they felt it was a detriment to the career. There I was, hell bent on a career, and

---

* Janet Leigh, *There Really Was a Hollywood* (Garden City, N.Y.: Doubleday & Co., 1984).

TC and Janet Leigh: "It just devastated me to look at this woman."

there I was ready to get married. That was contradictory, to their way of thinking. But I felt that I was able to maintain a personal life. It was a profession that didn't *allow* any personal life—your personal and professional lives were one—but I was determined to have both. I even thought one might contribute to the other. A lot of performers didn't show you or let you into their lives. Marlon Brando, for instance, didn't give anything of his personal life. That was his choice, and I respected it. But once I surrendered to being a public figure, it seemed to me that everything was fair game. In retrospect, maybe I should have behaved differently. But you can't live your life like that. At that particular time, those were my needs, and I was not about to deny myself.

112

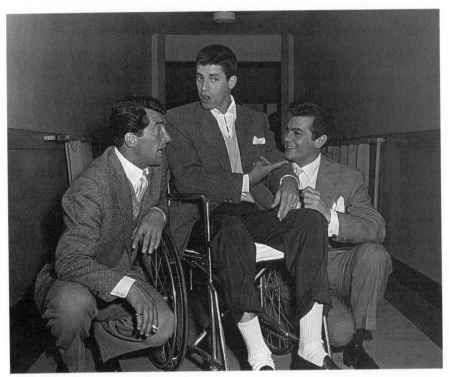

Dean Martin, Jerry Lewis (recovering from a fall), and TC cavorting at Universal (1952)

Neither was Janet Leigh. She was in Pittsburgh in April 1951, making a baseball film, *Angels in the Outfield*, with Paul Douglas, directed by Clarence Brown. It costarred the real Pittsburgh Pirates, whose home-run king was Ralph Kiner. At the season opener, Janet recalls, "I got my high heel stuck in the mud, and big Ralph Kiner just picked me up and carried me off the field. The papers made a lot of it and talked about a romance, which was silly. My heart belonged to Tony. But when he came to Pittsburgh to see me and saw the stories, he said, 'What have you been up to?' I said, 'It's just publicity—I can't help it that my heel got stuck!' It couldn't have been better for the picture. But he was very disturbed about it."

113

Despite all such personal, professional, and religious obstacles, they were married on June 4, 1951. Jerry and Patti Lewis—who arrived late—were the best man and matron of honor. After the wedding they drove through TC's old Bronx neighborhood, where he spotted a relative sitting on a stoop and yelled out, "We just got married! This is Mrs. Schwartz!" *Momeleh* and *Papeleh* Schwartz were as pleased as anyone.

Countless film celebrities attended the wedding party at Danny's Hideaway, the anarchy presided over (more or less) by Jerry Lewis and Dean Martin. The honeymoon would be a romantic one in Paris, but for the moment, the bride and groom's primary challenge was to make it back to their suite at the Waldorf Towers.

There Janet disposed of the gorgeous blonde sent up by Tony's pals as a gag, and at long last, they were alone. "When the hotel door closed and I looked at my husband," she recalled in her memoirs, "there were no barriers, no hesitations, no psychological compromises—only freedom, a flow of tender feelings, an unconditional surrender to unity."

—B.P.

It wasn't until I married Janet that I learned a bit. She was very helpful to me in social graces. I was from New York City, then three years in the navy, and to come into this kind of society—I didn't know which fork to use, and Janet would help me. I would pick one up, and she would nod her head yes or no. She was, in those early years, the most important person to me.

Once we did Edward R. Murrow's *Person to Person* show on live television. Ed—in CBS's New York studio—was supposed to "lead" us through our house on Coldwater Canyon in Beverly Hills and ask questions about it. They got everything set up, but there was a horrendous storm going on. Murrow did the introduction and managed to get in one question, and then—nothing. Silence. No audio. "What are we going to do?" Panic. So I just did it myself. I said, "This is my house, these are my electric lights, this is our bedroom . . ." I just narrated the whole show live—ad-libbing on national television. No big deal. I didn't find it that difficult, but everybody else was so pleased! They acted like it was a miracle. They didn't figure actors could put two words together or take one step without being directed. I felt that distinctly from them, and I think Janet did too.

Janet was a remarkable, very interesting actress. When I first met her, I didn't give her that much credit. I didn't think of her as an actress. To me she was a voluptuous, beautiful woman who had every right to be in the movies, but I wasn't able to relate to her acting talent one way or the other. Now, when I look back at the films she made, I see there were a lot of really wonderful per-formances. She was excellent in

Janet Leigh as a rising MGM star (1949)

Holiday Affair (1949) with Robert Mitchum, and in *Just This Once* (1952) with Peter Lawford—fabulous. As Bess opposite me in *Houdini*, I thought she held up her end beautifully.

When the *Houdini* project was first proposed to me, they didn't have a leading lady yet. Janet and I were just married then, and George Pal, the producer, said, "Let's do it with Tony and Janet, if we can get her." They thought it would be a good teaming, and it was. It was very successful. I was on loan-out to Paramount, and they had to get Janet from MGM. The studios got a lot of money for it, but we just got our regular salaries.

George Pal was always intrigued by the fantastic. Before *Houdini,* he made science fiction films like *Destination Moon* (1950) and *The War of the Worlds* (1953). He was the first to capitalize on the novelty of me and Janet as a husband-and-wife team.

Houdini (1874–1926) was really Ehrich Weiss from Appleton, Wisconsin, and I had to learn a lot about him. When his widow died, she willed three hundred of Harry's tricks to an illusionist named Dunninger, who was hired by Paramount to provide technical assistance. But George Boston was the one who taught me all the tricks. I worked with him every day for about

115

four months before the picture started on escapes and sleight of hand. I was a pretty quick study, and it stayed with me for life. I still practice it, and I've been inducted into the Magicians Society here and in Japan.

So George Boston was the magician, George Pal was the producer, and George Marshall was the director—three Georges. George Marshall was not the secretary of state. He was an ex-football player with a broken nose, and the most sensitive of all Georges. Charming and funny and considerate. I loved working with him.

———————•·•———————

Houdini (1953) was the first of five films Tony Curtis and Janet Leigh made together, the others being: *The Black Shield of Falworth* (1954), *The Vikings* (1958), *The Perfect Furlough* (1958), and *Who Was That Lady?* (1960). TC was twenty-eight; Janet Leigh, twenty-six. At its outset, Houdini is reduced to playing Bruto the Wild Man in Schultz's Dime Museum, running around half-naked to frighten the customers and, on the side, chase girls. (Old German character actor Sig Rumann played Schultz as apoplectically as in all his great Marx Brothers films.) Everything changes when our young hero gets a look at Bess. "I'm gonna show her some of my magic," he says, madly in love. The first of their many close-ups together reveals that the chemistry is real.

Houdini's career takes off with his romance. His death-defying escapes make him the toast of Europe and America. But the death of his beloved mother (Angela Clarke) plunges him into a two-year withdrawal in which he concentrates all his energies on trying to reach her through a variety of shyster mediums. His return to show business is highlighted by a brilliant underwater safe-cracking scene beneath the ice. TC is superb in it—and received severe burns due to ice exposure for his trouble.

Critics were disturbed about his lack of aging. The public was not. Curtis and Leigh were "the elite of the milkshake set," wrote James Robert Parish in *Hollywood's Great Love Teams*, and their honest, amiable personalities and tremendous good looks "made sweet box-office music." It was getting sweeter all the time. Initially, the wife was making more money than the husband—but

116

not for long. *Houdini* was his breakthrough picture on a wider scale, and Mrs. Curtis was magnanimous about it.

"In our work together, there was no question about billing, my husband came first," she said. "I would do the same thing today. I'm liberated. I've worked all my life, earned a good living, fortunately. But I felt—and this was just me, it didn't have to be any other woman—that I was his wife, and I wasn't going to emasculate him and take top billing just because I was in the business longer. I just didn't believe in that, and I don't today. Every woman or man has to make his own judgment on that. When I was single it was me, career. When I was married, it was husband, career. When I had children, it was husband, children, career. That's the way it had to be for me."

—B.P.

There was such incredible publicity about us, all those magazine layouts, about Janet and me as the fabulous, ideal First Couple of Hollywood. There was no bigger pair. Debbie Reynolds and Eddie Fisher could've been our maid and butler by comparison. No other husband-and-wife team came close to us until Richard Burton and Elizabeth Taylor, but that was ten years later. They did it through scandal. We did it through the movies and people's affection.

In those days, I was still mostly concerned that my hair looked okay, my suit was cut right, and that they would give me an eye light and wipe out the circles of the night before. But gradually I was figuring out a few other things about the movies.

One revelation still sticks in my mind. I was making *Forbidden* (1953) with Joanne Dru, and I needed a pocket handkerchief. There wasn't time to go get one, so the wardrobe man carefully folded up a Kleenex and arranged it just so in this beautifully tailored jacket I was wearing. From a distance you couldn't really tell the difference. But something was wrong the whole time I was shooting that scene. I was walking around like a wealthy dandy, barking orders on the phone, making passes at the secretaries, acting tough—but knowing that handkerchief in my pocket was a fucking Kleenex, I just couldn't be at ease. The words seemed clumsy coming out of my mouth. If the lapels on my suit were too big or if the shoulder pads were too much—things like that distracted me. I knew something was wrong. I wanted it right.

He came, he sawed, he conquered: TC and Janet Leigh in *Houdini* (1953)

Learning the ropes involved a hundred little things that you could learn only as they were happening. In one of those first films, I remember the actor I was playing opposite kept standing a little bit in front of me when the camera started to roll. He was looking for some little physical and psychological edge so as to be able to dominate the scene. He didn't want me to move at all because I was cute and maybe "fleshing out" my part a little more than it was supposed to be. So he came on with that old trick that actors have used ever since movies began: He'd move an inch over the line. That inch forced me a little to his left and forced the camera to pull around ever so slightly. All of a sudden, instead of an over-the-shoulder two-shot, he's now in a quarter-profile position. The cameraman digs but doesn't say anything. I move two inches to my right by shifting my weight to my right foot, and now *I'm* covering *him*.

It was situations like that that made me appreciate the art, or the artlessness, of movie acting. If I believed it, they believed it. If I had doubts about myself or the people I was working with, it was impossible to hide, and it always permeated the scene. Was there really anything more to it than just memorizing lines and listening carefully?

Yes and no. Learn your lines, and when you think you've learned them, learn them again. Don't let anyone trap or fool you. Always be early, never late, for a cue. Be ahead of everybody. Sense that other character's needs and desires, and try to orchestrate it so that your own line, your own response, is happening on the spot, spontaneous and real, responding to that moment and that character and not to some direction from a guy in a beret behind the camera.

It was cruel work sometimes. I saw young people and old people—even animals—crumble under the pressure, not able to remember from one line to the next, apologizing, having to read their lines from blackboards, sweating, throwing up, asking for five minutes to get themselves together. Part of it, for a lot of them, was that Method-acting crap. I went through some of that myself, and I could sympathize with them. In the beginning, I thought if you had to be angry in a scene, you *really* had to get angry, which was so exhausting. Gradually I realized that I had to be able to have all those emotions and thoughts and images at my fingertips.

I tried to keep Michael Gordon's lesson in my mind: "All you want is a tip." A director would say to me, "Now, what I want here is for you to be a little angry, but not angry enough to kill the joy of your love for her. I want your emotions to be turned inside out. I want you angry but still sensitive because you know Harry will be back for Miriam, and Miriam won't know how to respond to Nancy, and Nancy and Charlie won't be back from the yacht in time for Sally's birthday party for Edna. I'd like you to be a bit anxiety ridden, yet not allow that to disturb your perfect equilibrium of mind and soul. Got it?"

I'd look at him and say, "You want me to come in and smile, right?"

Right.

It took a while to gain confidence, but once I did, there was no place I felt as full and alive as on a set. To be all those people on a back lot in California—a doctor, a lawyer, a football player, a deaf man, a brave man, a coward, a thief—and get paid for it. I liked the money, the fame, the dames, the games. But that wasn't the best part. The best part, for those few minutes a day, was to forget your own reality (even though I enjoyed that too) and be someone else, someplace else.

Beachhead (1954) was a time and place and film with which TC deeply identified from his personal World War II experience in the Pacific. It was directed by Stuart Heisler (1894–1979), who had an eye for both visual action and suspense. The story concerned four marines sent on a hazardous mission to confirm radio reports from a French planter on a Japanese-held island. Mary Murphy, the love interest and sole woman in a tiny cast of seven, played the planter's daughter. (Murphy married actor Dale Robertson and later co-starred with TC again in 1963's *Forty Pounds of Trouble*.) She soon sprains her ankle and—in the time-honored tradition of war films—is largely a drain on the men: Curtis and Frank Lovejoy both have eyes for her, between skirmishes with "the Nips" and harrowing efforts to evade their booby traps.

"I'm not afraid," she says bravely.

"That solves everything," replies a very bitter and cynical TC.

The entire film, especially its action-packed climax, was filmed in tense, *cinema verité* style on location in Kauai, Hawaii. The extremely dark, moody color photography of Gordon Avil was properly recognized by the critics.

TC's performance, for a change, was also properly recognized. "Curtis turns in his best job yet," said *Variety*, "with an intelligent mixture of toughness and good humor." All in all, it is a gritty downer of a war picture and one of the best of that genre, with a disturbing sense of authenticity and truth.

—B.P.

Making *Beachhead* was a very intense experience for me because it hit close to home and my own reality. It gave me my first long exposure to Hawaii, which I fell in love with and where I bought some real estate, but I was relieved when the film was over.

Johnny Dark (1954) was a racing movie and a lark by comparison. It was directed by George Sherman, a tiny little man who used to reach up, pat me on the back, and say, "You're doing great, kid!" Of course, I loved that about him, and I have good memories of that film. When a scene went well, I'd forget about all the lights and turmoil around me, and all the cameramen and prop people and script girls would fade into nothing. Whether I got laid the night before or not, it didn't make any difference. I was able to drive all of those things out of my mind. I found myself just attacking the problem at hand, and when I finally said, "I love you," I believed it. That girl in front of me, Piper Laurie, believed it. The director believed it. I felt free.

I only had so much time to accomplish the scene—to walk across the room and explain why my car was a better design than my rival's. I had to stop at the bar, get the champagne from the fridge, get two glasses, open the bottle, all the while explaining the difference between my fuel-injection carbureted V-8 and my competitor's, always sensing that girl there. She was warm and desirable—she wanted me, I wanted her. The car was ready, but somehow I felt uneasy and wanted to check it out myself. Meanwhile, back at the garage, that prick of a rival was neatly eliminating one of the integral parts of my carbureted V-8, and that warm, desirable creature in that cozy penthouse down in Malibu overlooking the Pacific was trying to keep me distracted for just another hour or so. . . .

I loved the challenge of that kind of part. But I also tried to get into whatever parts they threw my way. *The Black Shield of Falworth* (1954) was another swashbuckler, and I was back again with Rudy Maté as the director. It was another crazy story about knights in armor and damsels in distress, but it was the first and last one I ever did with Janet. It was also Universal's first film in CinemaScope, which the studios were then introducing to try to offset television. It gave you a nicer, wider picture. I had worked before with Rudy a lot, but Janet never had, and I tried to alert her in advance to one of his little idiosyncrasies.

Janet Leigh: "Rudy Maté was a sweet, gentle man with a slight affliction that was rather funny. He had a tick with his head. Tony told me about it. He said that after doing a take on *The Prince Who Was a Thief,* he'd look over, and Rudy would be sitting there shaking his head back and forth in a negative way. Tony thought, *Oh, God, it must have been awful,* but then Rudy would come up and say, 'That was very good, my boy, very good.' It took Tony a while to realize that it was an affliction, not disapproval. So when we did *Black Shield,* I looked over and, sure enough, there was Rudy shaking his head. I thought, *Thank God Tony warned me,* because that would throw you. Every actor is insecure. And every director has a different way—but none quite like Rudy's."

As Robert Parish notes, MGM had its *Knights of the Round Table* (1953), Warner Bros. its *King Richard and the Crusaders* (1954), and 20th Century–Fox its *Prince Valiant* (1954; with Janet Leigh). Universal's *Black Shield* had a stellar cast, including Herbert Marshall as the Earl of Mackworth and Ian Keith as

TC, Mary Murphy, and Frank Lovejoy looking for reinforcements in the World War II film *Beachhead* (1954)

King Henry IV, though it was more concerned with the Cinema-Scope wide-screen process than with the screenplay or characterizations. Even so, it had fine swashbuckling combat sequences, and it did exceptionally well in the action-trade market where it was aimed.

—B.P.

So This Is Paris (1954) was my one and only musical. It was Universal's attempt to compete with RKO and MGM in that area; kind of a cross between *An American in Paris* and *On the Town*, about a couple of sailors on leave in Paris. The difference was that MGM would spend millions on something like that, whereas Universal made *So This Is Paris* in exactly twenty-two days at a cost of about $250. They were definitely in economy mode. Those pictures were thrown together in no time at all. How could I do three movies in a year if they weren't? Dick Quine was the director, and Charles Hoffman wrote the screenplay—modest guys who were hired to come in

Piper Laurie and TC on the racetrack in *Johnny Dark* (1954)

and do the job quick. I got good notices, but I never told Gene Kelly because I was afraid he might be jealous. One day I asked Gene what he thought of my dancing, and he replied, "Keep fencing."

Nobody ever asked me to be a song-and-dance man again.

I was more comfortable in *Six Bridges to Cross* (1955) which was based on the famous Brinks robbery of 1950—the so-called "perfect crime." It was directed by Joe Pevney and shot in Boston, where it happened, and it was the first movie Sal Mineo ever appeared in, playing me as a boy. I had to do a publicity tour to promote it, and there was a lot of craziness.

———•-•———

Gene Singer: "Tony said, 'I'm going to Boston, and I want you to meet me there.' At that time, the adoration for Tony Curtis in this country was equaled only by that for Sinatra. Girls went absolutely ape over him. He had to get off at South Station because they were ripping his clothes off, tearing off his buttons—any piece of him they could get their hands on. That was in the afternoon, and he was shaken up.

"When he got to the hotel in Boston, he stayed in his suite all day. I didn't see him until evening, before the premiere. He said, 'I want you to be with me tonight.' He was afraid something was going to happen, and so was I. Imagine thousands of girls screaming at you and ripping off their brassieres!

The moody hero taking a cigarette break in his dressing room during the making of *The Black Shield of Falworth* (1954)

"But he had to make an appearance, and that's what he did. We went to the theater by a circuitous route in the limo, and once he got there it went all right. But by that time the girls had doubled in number outside, and the security people said, 'Why don't you have your friend wear your coat and hat? We'll say Tony's in that car and get them away from the door so you can get in another car and escape.'

"It was frightening. Those screaming girls looked in the car and realized after five seconds that it wasn't Tony Curtis, that blue-eyed devil—it was Gene Singer. But by that time, Tony got away."

—GENE SINGER TO B.P., October 13, 1992

In 1955 I did my last swashbuckler, *The Purple Mask*, in which I had to do a lot of fencing—just like Gene Kelly told me to do. I had my own personal fencing instructor, and we practiced between every take and planned every move carefully. During one session I was supposed to parry, but I didn't parry quite enough and took the blade right in my cheek. *Zap!* I felt the tip go straight in. He pulled it out, and we kept on fencing, but I said to myself, "I think something's wrong."

TC with his Hungarian fencing instructor Joseph Vince, on the set

The assistant director eventually came over and said, "We're ready for you, Tony." I said, "I've got this hole in my cheek." He said, "Okay, wait a minute." In those days they didn't hold up production for anything. He just got a nurse to put a flesh-colored Band-Aid on the hole, and we went right on working. When we finished shooting for the day—and not before—they took me to the hospital, and I got a few stitches. That's the way they did things then at Universal and, as far as I know, at all the other studios too.

The Purple Mask had to do with Napoleon and the Royalists who were opposed to him, of which I was the main man. I had a mask like Zorro and kept saving people from the guillotine. It was an action film, no more or less than it was intended to be, and we all—Colleen Miller, Gene Barry, Dan O'Herlihy, and I—did the best we could. But I was disturbed by Angela Lansbury, who had a small part in that film. She wrote a book in which she said, "I needed the money so badly that I played a seamstress in a Tony Curtis film." I thought that was unkind and unnecessary, and fuck her if she can't take a joke. I found her to be most disagreeable and arrogant.

I have much better memories of *The Rawhide Years* (1956), the last one I made with Rudy Maté, and the only Western in which I was the star. My leading lady was Colleen Miller again, a lovely woman I still enjoy seeing up at the Hefner mansion. Universal hyped the fact that she'd been a member of the Tony Curtis fan club in San Francisco before she got into films herself. But the person I remember most, and learned more from than anybody in the movies, was a stunt man in that film named Davey Sharpe.

Davey started out in the silents and by the late thirties was the most important stunt man of his time. I had met him when I started out. He was about forty-four then, but he doubled me in those early cowboy pictures. He taught me how to ride a horse and how to enter a scene on top of one. He was extraordinary—a man I loved very much. So now we were both on the back lot at Universal, doing *The Rawhide Years,* and I had a very difficult, complicated shot of climbing out of a window, jumping onto a horse, and galloping off. It was about a twelve-foot drop from the window, and of course Davey was going to do the stunt.

During the rehearsals, Davey always smoked a cigar so they couldn't film him without his knowing about it—a common trick. He'd never take that cigar out of his mouth until just before the take. I loved to watch him work—the way he judged distances. He was very mathematical. He made sure everything was right so he wouldn't be hurt. On this particular shot he looked it over carefully, and when the director said "Action!" Davey came out the window, balanced himself precariously on the ledge of the balcony, and then leaped over a wagon toward the horse. But something went wrong, and the horse wasn't there when he landed. He hit the wagon, bounced off, rolled onto the ground and up against a building, and just lay there stunned. Everybody ran up to him, and the assistant director, Tommy Shore, said,

126

"Dave, are you all right?" Davey just looked up at him and said, "It would have killed an ordinary man."

Dave Sharpe gave me another piece of advice I never forgot: "Don't walk if you can run. Don't run if you can fly. Never stand still, always move a little. After all, you're in a moving picture." The stunt men I knew were fine men, and I liked to be in their company. Some were ornery and mean, but I always respected them. Once I did one of my own stunts, jumping from a second-story window, but forgot to put on my kneepads. I hit the ground and ended up in the hospital for a week and a half.

By that time, my cowboy career was pretty much over anyway. I'd met John Wayne in 1953 when I was doing *Houdini* at Paramount, and he said, "Hey, kid, come over here." We walked along together on the lot. "I've been watching you. You're doing great." I said, "Thank you, Mr. Wayne." He said, "Maybe we'll do a Western together." I said, "That would be great. I really would like that." And then he walked away.

I never did work with him.

As far as I was concerned, I was on my way out of Universal. I felt stuck there. So was Rock Hudson. He and Piper Laurie did *Has Anybody Seen My Gal?* (1952), and not only didn't anybody see the gal, nobody saw the picture. Rock's dilemma was that he did everything they told him at Universal. Henry Willson, his agent, made him unavailable for other movies and organized his life in such a way that he was locked into that seven- or fourteen-year contract, and they wouldn't let him go. He was constantly being used because he was under contract, but they never gave him a really substantial movie. He did *Giant* on the outside as a loan-out. Maybe he could have asserted himself more, I don't really know. All I knew was that I didn't want that to happen to me.

Universal's movies were changing. The people there were changing. Those early pictures were ingenuous, charming, funny, but then the pictures at Universal started to fall away. I had a seven-year contract with them, but after the fourth or fifth year, Lew Wasserman reorganized it so I could do outside films.

Trapeze (1956), for United Artists, wasn't my first outside movie, but it was the most important of my career so far. Carol Reed was very introspective, and I knew the minute I met him that I was in good hands as far as the directing was concerned—very knowledgeable, incisive. Burt Lancaster started out as a circus acrobat in his youth, and he'd wanted to do a circus picture ever since. So this was it. The original book (*The Killing Frost*) was a really dark story about a French circus, but a lot of the darkness was eliminated to make it more palatable for the movies.

At Burt's request I did a great deal of training with Eddie Ward of Ringling Brothers so they could keep the doubling to a minimum. Some of the aerial stunts were so dangerous, even the *doubles* had doubles. But I did a lot of the ground tumbling, and some of the flying too. Burt and I did everything we could to make it easier in the cutting. I did a good chunk of the early bar work in the film, and that was really Burt and me walking on our hands. Robert Krasker, the photographer, was brilliant. As if there weren't enough problems, he was working with a whole new color system on that film.

This was Burt's company—Hecht-Lancaster Productions—and at first I didn't know what to expect. But with Burt it was a free and open experience. We got along great and became even closer friends. I'd only been in movies about six years, but he was well established. To star in a movie with Burt Lancaster was quite a coup for me then, thanks to Lew Wasserman, who arranged it.

We'd start shooting at noon and work till 8:00 with no lunch break. Sometimes we'd start at 5:00 P.M. and work till 2:00 or 3:00 in the morning. In one of the scenes I was waiting outside a bar for Burt to finish drinking and come out. Carol Reed insisted the street always be wet down so it would reflect the light and give a nightlike look.

I was sitting there on the sidewalk about thirty-five feet from Burt, waiting for the shot to begin, and I saw him looking at me. We looked at each other, just kind of gazing. Then Burt took a cushion off one of the chairs and flung it toward me like you'd skip a pebble across water. That pillow hit the ground and bounced three or four times; I lifted up my ass, and that thing just slid under me perfectly and stopped. I'll never forget that. It was such a perfect gesture of friendship. That was during an early part of the shooting, and from then on the film took on another level of consciousness for me. That's the way Burt and I related.

Gina Lollobrigida was a major player in Italy, but only in Italy—maybe France too. She, Anna Magnani, and Sophia Loren were the major players out of that Italian market. So when Gina joined us in *Trapeze*, that was a major coup, to bring her into an American production. It was guaranteed European and Italian box office. She was a charming woman, never any trouble, always on time. Carol Reed had a crush on her, and I think Gina encouraged it. If the director or the cameraman had a crush on you, you knew you were going to be all right in the movie. She flirted with all of us, which was consistent with her character in the film. But she had a lovely husband and family, and when the picture was over, and Janet and I went to Rome, Gina gave us a beautiful ancient stone carving, the head of a ram, which I still have and cherish.

Trapeze (1956), in CinemaScope and garish color, was filmed entirely at the Cirque d'Hiver and Billancourt studio in Paris. It opens with a Johann Strauss waltz—more than a decade before *2001: A Space Odyssey*—as Lancaster makes a graceful but ill-fated attempt at "the triple."

Enter TC as Tino Orsini, sexy and muscular in his leather jacket. Crippled Burt is now just a rigger, but TC lures him back into the ring. Lollobrigida, the hot-blooded Italian with an agenda of her own, shows up and vamps both TC and Lancaster but good, insinuating herself into their act. The act will be improved, says the manager. "By a *dame*?" asks Lancaster.

Burt Lancaster, Gina Lollobrigida, and TC as the high-wire ménage à trois in *Trapeze* (1956)

129

She comes between them in more ways than one. An upside-down kiss between Lancaster and Lollobrigida on the trapeze is matched photographically only by the fight for her affections between Lancaster and Curtis in midshow. Yet despite or because of it, TC does the triple—without a net!—in the breathlessly exciting trapeze sequence that ends the film.

Trapeze was a major film smash of 1956, eventually grossing $7.5 million in North America alone. At the Berlin Film Festival that year, Lancaster was named best actor. TC, said *The Hollywood Reporter*, "has had to overcome the fact that he is a very handsome young man. He has done it so that his appearance is now secondary to a talent and vitality that mark him as one of the most important young stars."

—B.P.

While I was shooting *Trapeze* in Paris, Janet was in London getting ready to go to Africa that summer to work on a British movie called *Safari* (1956) for Columbia with Victor Mature. I went over to visit her, and helped her out with a benefit appearance she got roped into doing.* The next day we went to see Marlene Dietrich's closing night at the Cafe de Paris in London. Noel Coward introduced her. I was awestruck, in a way, but the truth is, I didn't quite know what to make of her.

A few days later, back in Paris, I met Dietrich at a social gathering. Janet wasn't with me. Marlene was propped up against a fireplace, resting her elbow on it and holding a very delicate champagne glass in her hand, flirting with me, and I was flirting with her. Marlene and Tony. I remember saying I was kind of lonely, and she said, "How can a good-looking man like you be lonely?" I said, "Well, you know, my wife's not here." And she said, "Don't let a little thing like that stop you."

We never went any further than that. She was a little drunk or maybe just out of it. She looked quite old to me, and as delicate as her champagne

*Janet Leigh recalls that TC rescued her that night by putting on her makeup at the last moment: "I had never been on the stage. I had studied with drama coaches, but I never learned to put on stage makeup because I always had makeup men. In movies, you don't do it yourself. I didn't know how. For that show in London, I came looking for my makeup man, and he wasn't there. So Tony did it. He did a pretty good job of it too."

130

glass. I was spellbound by her, but I was mostly caught up by the incredible reception the French people were giving Burt, Gina, and me in Paris. One day during *Trapeze* production there was a parade, and they put the three of us on one of the floats. It was astounding. Photographers from all over the world descended, and two hundred thousand people turned out to see us (Janet was there too) and all the elephants and circus animals. I couldn't believe that figure, but the police and the newspapers confirmed it.

In Hollywood, every time I won an award or was singled out or announced for a new film in the trade papers, I could feel the tension in the commissary. So what if I was a star in movie houses across the country and in Europe? In Hollywood I was an upstart, nouveau riche, morally unacceptable, uneducated, ill-mannered, probably a fag. They treated me like shit in Hollywood. The race was so intense there, you had to constantly fight the forces of envy and people's efforts to demean you so that they could have a little better shot at it themselves. Everybody was looking for that sweet smell of success. Come to think of it, that might make the title of a good movie. . . .

So I finished *Trapeze*, and Janet went to Africa to make *Safari*. She told me Victor Mature had the best line on the set there. He was nervous about having to get into the water with all these fucking alligators, and some assistant director said, "Don't worry, Mr. Mature. When we fire the gun, the alligators will go upstream." Victor nodded a little dubiously and said, "What if one of them is hard of hearing?"

BREAKING OUT

 To break the mold and develop from teen idol, it was a matter of the parts you got. If Universal had let me play some young man out of New York City—striving for something—and put me in movies like *Sweet Smell of Success, The Defiant Ones, Some Like It Hot* in the beginning, the studio bigshots would have seen that in me a lot earlier. But they didn't. Marlon, because of his beginnings in the theater, was able to get *The Men* and *Streetcar Named Desire*. They wouldn't dare give him *Son of Ali Baba*. But since I didn't have his kind of credentials or credibility, they put me in *The Prince Who Was a Thief* and then were stunned when I was able to play those other parts.

Branching out is hard in any profession, but it's hardest in the movies. Blake Edwards was trying to do the same thing at that time. He had been doing scripts for Dick Quine, and then he finally got a chance to direct a picture (*Bring Your Smile Along*, 1955), which was okay, nothing special, and then *Mister Cory* (1957) came along. I was a gambler from Chicago who hooks up with Charles Bickford and ends up running a casino. His name was Biloxi. I loved that name. This was just Blake's second picture, but it was a good part and gave me a chance to do something a little different.* The next one was another Joe Pevney movie called *The Midnight Story*

---

* *The Hollywood Reporter* commented: "Curtis can carry this kind of role perfectly. He is one of the few young stars of major value who has that contained recklessness, insouciance and bubbling good humor that regrettably has been lost in the current substitution of soiled T-shirts for the Byronic Collar." The fashion comment was pertinent: Universal was trumpeting TC's original design of a new suit he wore as Mister Cory: It had a short coat, narrow lapels, rounded shoulders, and split sleeve cuffs that could be unbuttoned and turned back. The trousers were high-waisted and tapered to an arrow leg line.

(1957), which was really better. I was an Italian motorcycle cop tracking down the killer of the priest who raised him, and I got to work with Gilbert Roland in it.* But there was never a film like *The Sweet Smell of Success*.

———————•—•———————

By his own admission, TC hounded Burt Lancaster for the part. Much impressed by TC personally and professionally during *Trapeze*, Lancaster now took a risk and cast him sharply against type for Hecht-Hill-Lancaster Productions' *Sweet Smell of Success* (1957). The tough, often shocking screenplay about journalistic corruption was written by the first-class team of Clifford Odets and Ernest Lehman from Lehman's novella, *Tell Me About It Tomorrow*. As J. J. Hunsecker of *The Globe*, New York's most powerful and unscrupulous columnist, Lancaster had one of the best roles of his career. Blackmail is his finest art. Thwarted by one intended victim, he says with chilling calm, "You're dead, son; get yourself buried." J.J. has incestuous designs on his own sister and a furious need to destroy her boyfriend, Marty Milner. "What's this boy got that Susie likes?" J.J. snarls. "Integrity— acute, like indigestion," answers Sidney Falco, one of his many fawning minions.

TC is Sidney, a conniving press agent willing to do anything to curry J.J.'s favor, including pimp his own girl (Barbara Nichols) and plant a pack of marijuana cigs in Milner's pocket. In short, he is despicable. "Sidney lives in moral twilight," muses J.J. His cruel irony alternates with rhapsodies on his own power: "I love this dirty town."

So does the camera of James Wong Howe, who captures the gritty nighttime feel of fifties Manhattan in every black-and-white frame. Elmer Bernstein's mood music and a jazz score by the Chico Hamilton Quintet further heighten the fast pace and the atmosphere.

---

*Said a British magazine, *Today's Cinema*, of that sleeper, which was shot on location in San Francisco's North Beach Italian neighborhood: "With each successive film Tony Curtis proves he must no longer be regarded as a mere pretty boy but as a serious actor. He puts in here a performance of considerable dramatic depth."

Its director was the underrated Alexander Mackendrick, a Scotsman whose Ealing Studios films in Britain included *The Ladykillers* (1955). Later, in Hollywood, he shot TC's *Don't Make Waves* (1967) with Sharon Tate, and eventually became dean of the film department at the California Institute of the Arts. He was an astute observer of film actors, and his take on Lancaster and TC is interesting:

"Match me, Sidney!" orders Hunsecker in *The Sweet Smell of Success* (1957).

"The stars had this neurosis which goes right to the edge. You have somehow to use this to get performances from these deep-sea monsters. There was this enormous difference between Burt Lancaster and Tony Curtis. Tony had a fantastic vanity, but no ego. He could act Burt off the screen, but [he lacks Lancaster's] granite quality of ego."

Sweet Smell of Success—dark and cynical, with its downbeat ending—was made the year before the British Angry Young Man school's "definitive" *Look Back in Anger*. In England, it was solidly hailed: "Curtis has never done anything better," said the *London Daily Herald*. "Curtis is astonishingly persuasive," wrote the *Sunday Express*.

It was a different story in America, where *Sweet Smell* got a poor box-office reception and mediocre reviews, largely because it hit too close to home among those with the power to boost or kill movies. Walter Winchell was said to have been enraged by it, and for good reason: As *Citizen Kane* was a thinly disguised tale of William Randolph Hearst, J. J. Hunsecker bore a strong resemblance to Winchell.

At Oscar time, the potboiler sensation *Peyton Place* took eight nominations (five for acting), while Lancaster, Curtis, and *Sweet Smell* were resoundingly ignored. In the best supporting actor category that year, no one approached TC's brilliantly unsympathetic performance—certainly not Russ Tamblyn and Arthur Kennedy (nominated for *Peyton Place*) or Red Buttons (the winner for *Sayonara*).

The consolation is film history. Two of two

TC as press agent Sidney Falco ingratiating himself with J. J. Hunsecker (Burt Lancaster), the all-powerful columnist, in *The Sweet Smell of Success* (1957)

dozen homages come from the films of Barry Levinson: In *Diner* (1982), a bizarre minor character keeps popping up and obsessively quoting TC's dialogue from the film, while in *Rain Man* (1988), Tom Cruise and his girlfriend curl up in their suite watching *Sweet Smell of Success* on TV.

Four decades after it was made, it is unanimously hailed as a classic.

—B.P.

For me Sidney Falco was crucial. That picture really put a lot of people in my pocket, and I owed it all to Burt. He and I were in New York for the opening and ended up at "21" one night with Rod Steiger and Harold Hecht. Inside the industry there was a lot of stir about that film, even among the oldtimers. While we were waiting to be seated, George Jessel came in and said, "Helluva movie, Tony." But life goes on, and so did George. He said, "You know, I just came back from Israel, and we have big problems there—lotta trouble in Israel." On and on. My friend Gene Singer was there, and he said innocently, "Gee, if there's so much trouble, why do you go there?" And Georgie lit into him. "What kind of a Jew are you? We're fighting for our country!" On and on. People turned around, staring. I always sympathized with Israel, and I gave money, but I never got involved emotionally the way a lot of those guys did, especially Jessel.

My main connection to George—again, this shows where my head was at—wasn't Israel. It was the fact that for a while I was taking out one of his girlfriends. He had a lot of them, but this was one of the "special" ones, he thought. I didn't *know* she was one of his girlfriends until after I started dating her. I don't remember her name, but he was keeping her in pretty royal style, and I was terribly embarrassed when I found out I was fucking his girlfriend. I did the honorable thing, though. Once I found out he was paying her bills, I didn't see her anymore. But I didn't know whether he would accept that as a proper explanation. For years, I thought, "Should I tell him?" Fortunately the subject never came up. It made me feel a little too much like Sidney Falco.

I did three pictures with Kirk Douglas, who is a wonderful man and friend: *The Vikings* (1958), *Spartacus* (1960), and *The List of Adrian Messenger* (1963). Janet and I were both in *The Vikings*, and since our daughter Kelly was just a baby, we took her along and deposited her in England while we went on location. It was shot in England, France, Germany, and mostly Norway, outside of Bergen, in a village on the Hardangerfjorden, the main location for six weeks that summer. You had to take planes, trains, cars, boats, and ferries to get there. Jerry Bresler, the producer, had all sorts of problems. Once, he rented a horse, but when the guy found out it was for Kirk, he doubled the price, and Jerry wouldn't pay it. So the guy cut off the whole unit's water supply. I guess he controlled both the horse *and* water market. We needed wolves for the picture, but they turned out to be a little too ferocious, so Jerry got a bunch of Alsatians and painted them black.

Kirk's company, Bryna Productions, made the film, and I coproduced with Curtleigh, the company Janet and I formed in 1956. Kirk and Jerry Bresler went to tremendous lengths for authenticity. We went to Denmark before the picture started and spent a lot of time in museums checking out props and costumes for the film. Every dish in that movie was absolutely

136

authentic. The men who played the Vikings were all Scandinavians, and they had to train all summer.

Kirk was very desirous that everybody got a fair deal, and everybody did. I felt the same kind of free, open, honest experience with Kirk on *The Vikings* as I did on *Trapeze* with Burt. Kirk wouldn't give in later when those Viking boat rowers threatened to go on strike for more money. But he gave everybody a bonus if they'd grow beards before we started shooting. So we all showed up with beards. The odd thing we learned about beards was that they were a different color from your hair. A redheaded guy can get a black beard. A black-haired guy can get a red beard. One was curly, one was straight. That was amusing.

But Kirk was really harassed during the whole production because he was one of the producers, and almost the director. Dick Fleischer really directed it, but he was distracted a lot by all the production problems. Did you ever notice that more actors become directors than directors become

Bearded TC with daughter Kelly on a location break in England during filming of *The Vikings* (1958)

actors? There's a reason for that: Of the two jobs, obviously directing is easier. Otherwise, actors wouldn't do it. Anyway, in Kirk's case, he was actively producing the movie and playing a main role in it at the same time, and he had his hands full.

The weather is notorious in Norway, even in the summertime. Out of

137

365 days, about 360 are rainy or overcast, and then you have five or six days of uninterrupted sunlight. We had to get a lot of work done in those five dry days. The weather was horrible when we started shooting, and it pretty much stayed that way. In one of the early scenes, I take out Kirk's eye with a hawk, and for the rest of the movie he had to wear a kind of egg-shaped contact lens implant to cover his whole eye. This thing was huge and very difficult for Kirk to deal with all the time. In those days, the technology couldn't make it any better or more delicately than that. Between every shot, Kirk had to take that thing out and then stick it back in, and it was painful and frustrating for him. He would just get it in, and we'd be doing a scene, and then all of a sudden the sun would disappear. We'd have to stop shooting. He'd say, "Can we try it in the shade?" They'd say, "No, we have to have sunlight," so we'd take a break and they'd take the eye out again. This routine went on and on, rain every day. Three quarters of the day it would rain, and then it would stop for just a few minutes, and we'd run out and try to shoot.

They put up a kind of tent for us to take refuge under when it rained. We would sit under this lean-to and then run out and do a scene and then run back undercover. In the middle of production, Kirk and I were huddled under that canopy in that miserable weather, waiting for the sun to come out. Finally, just when we thought we were ready to do the shot, it started to pour again. We're sitting there, and he has this awful thing over his eye, and when they came over to take it out, Kirk said, "Just leave me alone." The makeup guy went away. Kirk and I kept on sitting under that little lean-to, shivering and feeling miserable, thirty-five days behind schedule, hundreds of people standing around, money going down the drain. Big silence. Then Kirk Douglas looks at me with that bad eye and says, "Tony, you want to buy a company cheap?"

I said, "No, thank you, Kirk, I've got one of my own."

------ •·• ------

The Vikings (1958) was based on Edison Marshall's best-selling 1951 novel—the type that used to be known as a "bodice ripper." It opens in the ninth century with a Viking raid against England. King Ragnar (Ernest Borgnine) slays the English king and rapes his queen. The resulting child, Eric, becomes a Viking slave and grows up to be TC, in competition with Ragnar's son Einar (Douglas) for Morgana of Northumbria (Janet Leigh). "I want her to fight me the first time I take her—and the last," says Kirk, once he has her in captivity. Tony's gentler wooing is much more to her liking.

So are his scanty costumes, designed to show off as much of TC's attractive lower anatomy

TC delivering the death blow to half-brother Kirk Douglas in *The Vikings* (1958)

as the censors would allow. Jack Cardiff's location photography was nothing short of gorgeous, and Mario Nascimbene's music a perfect match. Fleischer's direction, recalled Leigh, "was very visual but also very passionate in the intimate scenes. He directed quietly. If we were moving in the right direction toward what the scene needed in pace and emotion, he would let us do it the way we tended to, naturally, in rehearsal. But also out of his quietness came those monumental action scenes, which took a tremendous amount of directing."

The battle to the death for Morgana was filmed in Fort La Lotte, a medieval castle with a real moat, drawbridge, towers, and slots for pouring boiling oil on attackers, overlooking the Gulf of St. Malo. TC and Kirk Douglas were both "remarkable athletes," says Leigh, "but the stunts they undertook made me sick with worry."

Indeed, the film was extremely violent for its day, and Douglas's torn-out eye was just the first of many dismemberments. Later, TC's hand is sliced off, Borgnine is forced to jump into a pit of howling wolves, and many Vikings are squashed beneath the stone wheels of the battering rams. Mrs. Curtis's fears were not unfounded: In one battle scene, a stray arrow hit her husband in the eye—a serious injury requiring hospitalization. But TC himself is sanguine about it:

"All of those action movies involved a certain number of injuries. I was banged up and hit around a lot, but you took that in your stride. I didn't think *The Vikings* was particularly bloody or more violent than the rest. It just looked like a good action movie to me."

It looked that way to Kirk Douglas too. As producer, he was to receive no salary but 60 percent of the profits. The film cost $3.5 million and took in exactly twice that amount at the box office. It was the number-five top-grossing picture of 1958, and Douglas earned a little more than $2 million for all his troubles in making it.

—B.P.

Our daughter Kelly and Kirk's son Peter made their movie debuts in *The Vikings* as babies in one of the scenes. But first Janet and I had to get her back from the governess we'd left her with in England. This was a woman named Ethel—the Nanny from Hell. She was a nightmare. She had spoiled the baby terribly, and she was a tyrant, and when we fired her, she put up a huge stink and threatened lawsuits and demanded a lot of money and drove us crazy for a long time. On top of that, while Janet and I were shooting the final interiors and retakes in Munich, my mother decided that was the perfect time to send my brother over to visit. So I had poor Bobby to deal with too. I couldn't have done it if Janet hadn't been as kind and helpful with him as she was. But it was a terrific strain, and we were glad to go home.

What I came home to was *The Defiant Ones* (1958), a racial story in which Sidney Poitier and I were escaped convicts on the lam in the South. I hated him and he hated me, but we could never get away from each other because we were chained together. Some reporter asks, "How come they chained a white man to a black?" The sheriff says, "The warden's got a sense of humor." I liked the story so much that I helped raise the $1 million budget through Curtleigh.

Sidney Poitier and TC bound together—and bound for tragedy—in Stanley Kramer's *The Defiant Ones* (1958)

At first they said I was too good-looking for the part; I didn't look enough like the asshole "nigger-hater" I was supposed to play. So I wore a false nose and made myself look uglier. I felt pretty strongly about wanting to do that movie.

At the beginning of the movie, Sidney is driving everybody crazy singing in the prison van. But then there's an accident, and he and I are the only ones that escape. We go through all sorts of trials and tribulations—shooting the rapids and then getting stuck in a horrendous clay pit. It was the hardest sequence in the film, and the one people talked about the most. There were no doubles. That was me and Sidney. I had a double named Bobby Hoy, an excellent stunt man who looked like me and did some of the water scenes, but most of it was done by me. It was a physically exhausting picture.

Stanley Kramer produced and directed it and, because of the racial climate of the time, he went out of his way to be more agreeable to Sidney. I noticed that in his direction and his behavior. I think he originally wanted Marlon, and when he couldn't get him, United Artists said, "We'll do it with Tony." So I don't know how much Stanley really wanted me. I only know he never treated me with the same reverence that he did Sidney. I wasn't mad about it. That's just the way it was. Sidney was a helluva talent, no matter what color he was, and this was a time when Hollywood was just starting to realize maybe it could do something positive for civil rights. In 1992, when I was asked to speak at the American Film Institute's ceremony honoring Sidney with a lifetime-achievement award, I said that first they offered my part to Marlon Brando, but he wanted to play the black guy. Then they offered it to Kirk Douglas, but he wanted to play *both* parts. Finally they offered it to me, and I said okay, as long as I could do it in drag.

Over the years, I've noticed that a lot of people still talk about *The Defiant Ones*, but I wonder how many of them recognize the guy in the movie who keeps playing the radio while everybody yells at him, "Shut it off, goddammit!" This guy, to me, was the most fascinating. He was Carl Switzer, who played Alfalfa, the one with the freckles and the cowlick in all those *Our Gang* comedies. He was so wonderful. As a kid, I loved him in those pictures, and there I was—and there *he* was—working in this same movie. He played poker all the time, and a few months later, he ended up getting shot in a game.* That's how much he loved his poker.

We were all down on our luck at times. Only rarely did an actor end up with any meaningful dough, and only if he had a manager that didn't cheat him and knew how to invest for him. If an actor waited for his residuals to make him rich—it never happened. It could only come from elsewhere—investments, real estate, wherever. Today, it's a little easier, because the money is so overwhelming. But even now, it's easy to lose it all. So how much money did "Alfalfa" make, even in his heyday? If he got a thousand dollars a week, that was a fortune in the thirties, but he wasn't getting a thousand dollars a week. The money he made was minimal, and the adults were all swindling him.

One day on *The Defiant Ones* set, Carl told me a great story about the time he and Spanky McFarland were doing a scene with a live bear. He said,

*Carl "Alfalfa" Switzer (1926–1959) was one of the most beloved child stars of the *Our Gang* films from 1935 through 1942. He later became a hunting and fishing guide in northern California and then a bartender. He was shot in a dispute over a fifty-dollar debt. The killing was ruled "justifiable homicide."

Carl Switzer as Our Gang's "Alfalfa" (1937) and in his last film role in *The Defiant Ones* (1958)

"Tony, I was frightened to death of this fucking bear. He was on a chain with a muzzle, but now and then the trainer would take it off, and the bear would growl and show its teeth, and we'd be scared shitless. The director says, 'I want you boys to come out of a bush, and in between you is this bear. You don't know it's there. I want the bear to lick one boy's face, then turn and lick the other boy.' But we wouldn't go near the thing.

"So the trainer says, 'Let me show you there's nothing to worry about.' He puts a little honey on his face, takes the muzzle off the bear, and says, 'Look, no problem! Just turn your head a little and the bear will—' And with that, the bear took a huge bite out of his face and jaw, blood everywhere!"

That was Carl Switzer's story, which I loved. I never saw him again.

———◆———

The Defiant Ones was not French film noir but American *blanc et noir*. "Everybody winds up alone," Curtis tells Poitier, "not just you—everybody." It is a traditional "buddy film" in some ways, but with a powerful social message. The near-lynch scene is a

143

Sidney Poitier, TC, and Sammy Davis, Jr., at the time of *Porgy and Bess*. Davis's caption for this photo: "I was captured by cannibals."

shock, and harrowingly effective. So, most of all, is the wrenching ending in which the biracial heroes (or antiheroes) almost make it onto their train to freedom.

The New York Film Critics voted it the best film of 1958, while the Motion Picture Academy nominated it but gave the Oscar to *Gigi. The Defiant Ones* did win Oscars for Sam Leavitt's superb

Oscar nominations for both stars: Al Hirshfeld caricature of TC and Poitier in *The Defiant Ones* (1958)

photography and for the lyrical screenplay of Nathan E. Douglas* and Harold Jacob Smith. TC and Poitier were both nominated for best actor, which split the vote and gave the Oscar to David Niven for *Separate Tables*.

Sidney Poitier has powerful memories of the experience:

"I didn't know Tony before *The Defiant Ones*. That picture brought us together. He was a consummate professional. There was a dash of the mischievous prankster, but he was always on time, always knew his lines, he knew what his character was about, and everybody liked him. When you're with Tony Curtis, you're with somebody very alive. He was—and is—one of the most 'up' people I have ever known.

"On *The Defiant Ones*, in terms of myself, Tony performed the most generous act I ever received from an actor in my life. My

---

*"Nathan E. Douglas" was a pseudonym for the blacklisted actor Nedrick Young, who took the Fifth Amendment when questioned by the House Un-American Activities Committee in 1953 and then turned to screenwriting.

contract called for me to be listed among the supporting actors. Tony had top billing alone, but he went to Stanley Kramer and said, 'I want you to put Sidney's name up there with mine.' And that's exactly what happened. That's how I got top billing for the first time in my life. I think that speaks a lot of him.

"It's an amazing film for 1957. It disturbed a lot of people—and *informed* them. We came along at the perfect time. For the likes of Tony Curtis and Sidney Poitier, the times couldn't have been better—as actors, as artists, as young adults. It was an emotional time with civil rights and the beginning of the Vietnam War, all kinds of explosive events and circumstances and conditions. Our lives encompassed those moments. We might have had a small, minuscule effect on some of them. There was a connectedness between our business and those events. It was a marvelous thing, and so is having the film record of it."

—SIDNEY POITIER TO B.P., June 3, 1993

Frank Sinatra and I became friends when I first came to California. I met him at a party at the home of Charlie Vidor, the director, right after Janet and I started going together. I was in a movie he made at Universal called *Meet Danny Wilson* (1952): Jeff Chandler and I played ourselves, as spectators in the club where Frank was singing. A couple years later, that so-called "Rat Pack" was my group, but I didn't do pictures with them. Frank and I were major players, but most of the rest of them were not—no disrespect to Peter Lawford or Sammy Davis or Joey Bishop or Angie Dickinson. Lew Wasserman wouldn't allow me to be in pictures like *Robin and the Seven Hoods* because my career was going in a different direction.

Socially I was involved with them way before, but *Kings Go Forth* (1958) was the first and only "real" film I made with Frank. It was for United Artists, right after *The Defiant Ones* and right before Douglas Sirk's remake of *Imitation of Life* (1959). All those films had racial themes, which had to be handled very delicately in those days.

Frank was the star and the narrator of *Kings Go Forth*, which was about the mop-up operations in France at the end of World War II—the so-called "champagne campaign" around the Riviera. He was Sam, the tough

146

Frank Sinatra and Tony seeking relief while filming *Kings Go Forth* (1958)

sergeant, and I was one of the replacements in his unit—the rich kid with "something to prove." Natalie Wood was the local girl. She and Frank fall in love, she tells him her father was an American Negro, he overcomes his prejudice. But then I move in, and she falls in love with me, and we sleep together. I pretend I want to marry her, but I'm just jerking her

147

around. In the big scene, Frank makes me confess to Natalie and Leora Dana (her mother):

TC: I'm not gonna marry you, Monique.
DANA: You never planned to, did you? You scum!
TC: I don't like that word coming from you.
DANA: Get out of my house.
TC: Mrs. Blair, on several occasions I've been engaged to marry, and on several occasions I've been *not* engaged to marry, if you follow me. A lot of these girls I wouldn't take to a country club, but with the exception of your daughter, Mrs. Blair, all of them were white. . . . Sam, look, you understand—it was like a new kick for me.

Sinatra punches me out.

It was the most difficult scene I ever had to play, admitting I was just fooling around and dumping her because she's half-black. Natalie, of course, didn't look remotely Negro. But in those days a black girl could not have played that part. You could never have hired Dorothy Dandridge. That sliver of racism could only barely surface. So Natalie jumps in the river, and Frank and I pledge to kill each other, but we have to kill some Nazis first. I get shot, and Frank goes back to Natalie, without an arm. In the fifties that was enough to balance everything out. It was a nice, ambiguous ending.

Delmer Daves was an interesting director on that film. He was an amateur geologist, and he'd come up to me and say, "Look at this beautiful stone," and hand me some rock with a certain strata in it.* Movies like *Kings Go Forth* were made for very little money. If the cast budget was $600,000, that was a lot, and the percentage of cast money in the total financing was usually 40 percent to 50 percent, so that picture couldn't have cost more than maybe $1.5 million. It wasn't extremely successful.† The racial subtlety of the story was beyond a lot of people. Leora Dana says at one point,

---

*Delmer Daves (1904–1977) was an actor, writer (*Petrified Forest*), and director for Warners, Fox, United Artists et al.—a meticulous craftsman with a penchant for crane shots and an understanding of characters in conflict with their environments. His first hit was Cary Grant's *Destination Tokyo* (1943), but he was at his hottest in 1958–1959, during which he directed *Kings Go Forth*, *The Badlanders*, *The Hanging Tree*, and *A Summer Place*.

† But the men's performances were. Typical of the praise was *The Hollywood Reporter*'s: "Sinatra is superb [and] Curtis is equally fine as the reckless show-off who arouses pity by his very shallowness. By sheer insouciance, Curtis makes this intriguing and repulsive individual completely believable."

"I was married to a black man," but if you weren't listening for a second, you could easily miss it.

I did three pictures with Natalie Wood, and I thought we complemented each other well in all of them.* Personally, on and off the set, we were very good friends. She was engaging and sweet, with an impudent kind of personality. Her younger sister Lana was also an actress. When I first saw Lana, I thought she was the most beautiful woman I'd ever seen—voluptuous, long legs—I was ready to take her out any time I could. Natalie had the beauty, but she didn't have the figure her sister had. On the other hand, Lana's career never quite made it. Natalie started very young and slowly finessed her way into a major career. Her sister was never given that kind of a push. She and Natalie didn't get along as well as they should have. There was rivalry there. I think Lana felt Natalie could have done more for her. But why should she have? She had her own problems, in and out of the movies. With Natalie, they were trying to hype the Jimmy Dean relationship and then the Warren Beatty relationship. Always something. I think her head was spinning.

Natalie and R. J. Wagner got married about the same time Janet and I did, and the four of us used to hang out together. R.J. was a funny and charming guy, and a great golfer. He came from a very well-to-do family and was very well-educated, while I was the kid gangster out of New York. We were so different that we hit it off really well, and we're still friends. On that first picture there was a lot of chemistry between her and me, but I never made any move in Natalie's direction. I respected her and R.J. I kept her at arm's length. After she had separated from R.J., there were times when we ran into each other, and something was on the verge of happening. But I'm getting into a delicate area here: the whole matter of what were called, crudely, the "fucking privileges." There were strong feelings between me and Natalie, but never at the expense of R. J. Wagner or Janet Leigh. Later, R.J. and Natalie rented my house in London at 49 Chester Square. After that we didn't see each other for a while, and then Natalie died so unnecessarily.

Natalie was constantly searching, pursuing something inside of her. She was never quite content. There was always a distraction in her life. She was a gifted actress, but she had certain demons that drove her. She never achieved the greatness she wanted. She was never that major player she

* The other two were *Sex and the Single Girl* (1964) and *The Great Race* (1965).

wanted to be. In those days, among the women, it was really only Elizabeth Taylor and Marilyn Monroe. With all due respect to Janet, I don't know of any other major women players then. Jeanne Crain? No way. Go down the list. Bette Davis and Susan Hayward were another generation. You could argue that Doris Day and Audrey Hepburn were in that "major" category, but I'm not sure. Natalie was successful, but at the same time she always seemed to be struggling. I know she struggled in *Kings Go Forth,* trying to play half French and half black and not really getting that odd combination to work.

They held the premiere of *Kings Go Forth* in Monte Carlo on June 14, 1958, under the auspices of Princess Grace and Prince Rainier, as a benefit for the U.N. refugee fund. I was there, and I remember that the film itself was shunted aside in favor of the social experience. Grace Kelly and I had socialized a lot in Los Angeles, and when I was in Europe I would run across her now and then. We always had a good relationship. Once in Monte Carlo she asked me if Dominic's was still the restaurant of choice in Hollywood. I said yes. Dominic's was a little chop house on Beverly Boulevard. Another time she said, "Do you still go dancing?" I said yes, and she asked me what places were still around from the old days, and I said, "Well, Mocambo, for one." She looked up and away and just said, "I remember Mocambo . . ." with a wistful tone in her voice.

The Perfect Furlough (1958) was TC's third film with Janet Leigh and second under the direction of Blake Edwards. Lieutenant Colonel Leigh is a military psychologist called in to help solve a serious morale crisis at the Army's top-secret experimental station in the Arctic. The 104 bachelors stationed there are restless. "We sent them a bunch of do-it-yourself kits, but the men don't seem to be interested in doing it themselves," complains one officer. Leigh's prescription is to devise the Perfect Furlough for one of the men—picked by lottery—and let the others experience it vicariously.

Dissolve to TC in his frozen Quonset, bearded, disheveled and demoralized, throwing darts (with amazing real-life accuracy) to pass the time. Informed of the furlough lottery, he scams to win it. Cut to the clean-shaven and dashing Tony arriving in Paris,

150

where his Don Juan reputation has preceded him: "Obviously an overactive libido," says Leigh, frowning over the report. "His file reads like a stag film." It is her duty to chaperone and stop him from going too far with dream date Linda Cristal, the "Argentine bombshell." Lusty soldier and starlet begin their frolics in an airplane berth (such things existed in 1958). Janet breaks it up. Once on land, two beefy MPs are stationed outside his hotel-room door, but he slides down a sheet-rope to Cristal's room. In the film's most risqué sight gag, Leigh catches him in the act, and his champagne bottle explodes—prematurely.

TC slips away. "He's loose in Paris?" someone asks. "Everyone's loose in Paris," is the response.

More skirmishes follow until Leigh replaces Linda as TC's romantic target. Soon enough he is massaging her back and she is setting aside her concerns about military-code infractions in order to relax into the clinch. "Face it, Lieutenant Colonel, this guy bugs you," says the Eve Arden-esque Elaine Stritch. Leigh replies archly that a bug is something you find crawling in your bed. "I rest my case," says Stritch.

A good time, and good timing, are had by Curtis and Leigh, who lend restraint and credibility to their love scenes. But just when Janet is hooked, Cristal reveals she is pregnant, and everyone assumes TC is the father. The temperature rises. He shifts into macho mode with Leigh.

"Take your hands off me!" she orders, when he grabs her and tries to explain.

"Shut up," he says.

"You're talking to an officer."

"Shut up, *sir*."

He abducts her by force, takes her out to the French countryside, pushes her into a wine vat—in short, loosens her up. Stop trying to save the world from drowning in a sea of sex, he tells her, and jump in with the rest of the swimmers. Cristal's secret husband in Argentina is the daddy, not Tony. Back at his cozy hotel room, she's got to get out of those wet clothes, of course. But what to wear for dinner? Taking a cue from Scarlett O'Hara, Leigh handily fashions a stunning dinner dress out of a bed sheet and curtain cord—with a little behind-the-scenes help from costume designer Bill Thomas. She is now gorgeous, cool, and self-confident, just in time for the denouement.

Edwards's heavy-handed direction gets worse before it gets better (simply by *ending*). Supporting players Elaine Stritch and Keenan Wynn are reliably amusing, and twenty-two-year-old Troy Donahue, just a year or so out of Columbia University, shows up briefly. But it is Curtis and Leigh who rescue

Mr. and Mrs. Tony Curtis in a publicity pose for *The Perfect Furlough* (1958)

the film, working naturally and credibly together to make the most of the material. It's the fifties, after all—with some exceptions, a vast wasteland of scripts. This one was written by Stanley Shapiro, who won an Oscar the following year for *Pillow Talk*, and who wrote *Operation Petticoat* and *That Touch of Mink* for Cary Grant soon after. The Curtises took what he gave them and turned it into a good service comedy, despite the severe limitations of that genre.

The perfectly complementary team of *The Perfect Furlough* was also, at this point, enjoying what everyone considered the Perfect Marriage. No such thing exists, of course—then or now—but, if not perfect, theirs was fun, vibrant, and full of activity. Janet recalls life with Tony then as "unpredictable and spur-of-the-moment: 'Let's do this' or 'Guess who's coming for dinner?' What used to drive me crazy was his penchant for cars. The IRS nearly investigated us one year because they thought we were in the used-car business, so many transferred through our possession. Tony was just crazy about cars, and I never knew when he was going to bring a new one home."

152

The Curtises in those days also starred in some films that never reached the theaters: the private home movies of Jerry and Patti Lewis. *Sunset Boulevard* and *Watch on the Rhine* had been fabulous hits; the Lewis parodies of them were called *Fairfax Avenue* and *Watch on the Lime*, starring Tony and Janet, among others. "It was very serious work," Leigh recalls, "except that we were hysterical all the time. But we had a real director—Jerry—and he had all the equipment, the lights, the script, and the professional cast. Danny Arnold was the writer. It was first-rate. We even had a premiere with a red carpet leading out from Jerry's house to his screening room in the back.

"Tony was great in those because he always had a great sense of humor. We used to play 'Guggenheim,' that game where you'd get a five-letter word (say, 'tiara') and five categories (say, 'movies,' 'countries,' 'ways of death'), and then you'd get ten minutes to fill in words starting with each of those letters. You handed your paper in and got a certain amount of points for your answers, depending on how many other people believed you. One time there was a word with a *U* in it—I think it was *tulip*—and the category was ways of death. Everybody was stumped. Nobody could think of a method of murder that started with *U*. But Tony wouldn't give up. He pondered over it for a long time and then, very calmly and with a completely straight face, he wrote, 'Up the ass with a bullet.' "

—Janet Leigh to B.P., October 14, 1992.

153

C·H·A·P·T·E·R E·I·G·H·T

SOME LIKE IT HOT

In *Some Like It Hot*, I was really doing three characters under the cover of one. There was Joe, the musician; vain, shallow, only interested in going from job to job. There was that woman Josephine: aloof, arrogant, well educated, frightened of men. There was that rich, indolent, bored millionaire who happens to talk like Cary Grant for some reason. Each of them had a little seed from my own life, or lives.

United Artists originally wanted Bob Hope and Danny Kaye to play the guys, and Mitzi Gaynor for Sugar. Then they wanted Frank Sinatra. He read the story and was interested at first but changed his mind.

I think Lew Wasserman had a great deal to do with getting me in that picture. He knew that the idea of Tony Curtis and Jack Lemmon, in drag, with Marilyn Monroe singing and Billy Wilder directing—this one was going to go down in the history books.

We were making it at the Goldwyn Studios off Formosa and Melrose, and the men's stuff was going to be easy. It was the ladies' stuff that had me worried. Billy brought in a female impersonator to work with Jack and me and teach us things like how to hold our hands. If we held them up, our muscles showed. If we held them palm down, the muscles disappeared. When we walked in heels, we threw our weight forward and our bottoms under. We had our legs and chests shaved, eyebrows plucked, extensive makeup tests with lipstick and eyelashes and a variety of wigs with different cuts and colors. Our hips were padded underneath the dresses. We had a voice coach to help us pitch our voices higher.

To find the appropriate bra was no easy matter. I'm a 36D myself. The woman I was to be, I decided, was a little bit of Grace Kelly for the debutante

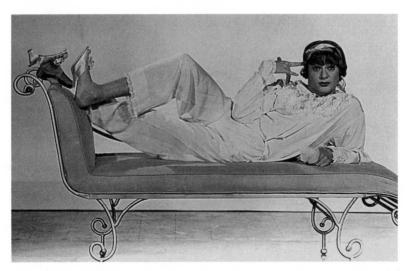

TC at his most seductive, reclining as Josephine for the publicity of *Some Like It Hot* (1959)

look, ZaSu Pitts for comedy style, and, of course, my darling mother for heart.* After four or five days of makeup and hair and wardrobe tests, I told Jack, "Listen, I'm sorry, but you don't make a good-looking woman." He was ugly as a woman. I was a little more attractive, but that's genetics. Anyway, we were sitting in my dressing room, and I said to Jack, "We may look good on the set, but how do we look in real life?"

"I don't know."

"Well, why don't we test it? Let's go to the ladies room."

"I don't think I want to do that."

"Come on, let's just try it out."

So we marched down past the commissary, into the ladies room, and went right to the mirrors. There were a couple of women standing around. I immediately took out my lipstick and started putting it on, watching the women coming in and out. The girls would come out of the stalls, come up behind us, fix their makeup, wash their hands—not one of them gave

---

* Jack Lemmon underwent a similar mental sex-change operation, and with similar results. "My mother came on the set," he recalls, "and they took a portrait of us together. I had the wig on, and we did the Lemmon-family grin, and when I saw it—my God, we looked like an older and younger sister! I'd been modeling the makeup and the hair unconsciously after my mother."

us a second look. When we got out of the ladies room, Jack said, "We made it." I said, "No, we're just so ugly, they don't even see us."

So we went back to the makeup men, Emil Levine and Harry Ray, and said, "Guys, you gotta make us a little better-looking. Figure something out." They gave us a little more eye shadow and a little more mascara, and we put on three-inch heels instead of the two-inch ones we were wearing. I had my busts enlarged. Jack had his waist pulled in. Back to the ladies room we went. And as soon as we walked in there, a girl said, "Hi, Tony."

I said, "Let's go, Jack." That pretty much settled which makeup was better.

Some Like It Hot was peak Curtis, peak Lemmon, peak Monroe, and certainly peak Wilder. Nineteen fifty-eight was the director's watershed year. The four Mirisch brothers had left Allied Artists to form their own independent production company. Wilder's deal with them gave him complete freedom of subject, screenplay, casting, direction, final cut, and a 25-percent share of net profits on each film.

Some Like It Hot grew out of a 1932 German musical film called *Fanfaren der Liebe* ("Fanfares of Love"), written by Robert Thoeren, in which two unemployed musicians don various disguises to scam their way into jobs. They blacken their faces to play with Negro bands, wear rings in their ears to work as gypsies, dress up as girls to play in a women's combo, and so on. The current version was set in 1929 Chicago and did away with all disguises except the female one. The brilliant script was cowritten by Wilder and I. A. L. Diamond.*

In 1958 Marilyn Monroe was in a state of depression following a miscarriage. By one account, her husband, playwright

---

* Diamond was born Itek Dommnici in 1920 in Romania. (The *A* and the *L* never stood for anything.) At nine, he came to America and grew up in Brooklyn as plain old "Izzy." He went to Hollywood directly out of Columbia University and wrote routine film scripts until linking up with Wilder—and immortality—beginning with *Love in the Afternoon* (1957), just a year before *Some Like It Hot*. Malcolm X and black militancy were then on the rise, which prompted Wilder to observe that "if Izzy Diamond ever becomes a Black Muslim, he will have to change his name to I. A. L. X."

156

Arthur Miller, felt it would raise her spirits to make another Billy Wilder comedy after the success of *The Seven Year Itch* three years earlier. By another account, she took the part because Miller needed money to pay his legal fees stemming from the House Un-American Activities Committee witch-hunt. In any case, when they all met to finalize the deal, Miller put one arm around Wilder, the other around Diamond, and began, in a pedantic tone: "The difference between comedy and tragedy is . . ." Everybody rolled their eyes. Marilyn looked nervous—and remained nervous throughout the whole production. TC says that after each scene, she called out "Coffee!" and was brought a thermos containing straight vermouth.

Wilder hated color. He had made *The Seven Year Itch* in color only because Monroe's contract demanded it. He felt the Curtis-Lemmon drag makeup would be too obvious and vulgar—its effect ruined—in full color. *Some Like It Hot* would be shot in glorious black and white. The film opens with TC (who got second billing after Monroe) playing sax in a speakeasy band, with Jack Lemmon on bass. They lose their jobs, accidentally witness the Saint Valentine's Day Massacre, and hightail it out of town a step ahead of George Raft as gangster Spats Colombo, on a train to Florida, disguised as Josephine and Daphne for their new jobs in an all-girl band. Monroe is Sugar Kane, the singer and ukelele player—formerly Sugar Kowalchik.

Lemmon's character is a frenetic nervous wreck. TC is a more restrained and believable "girl." The script contains a fabulous array of lecherous male stereotypes and ditzy females to match. A hideous midget bellboy repeatedly hits on TC ("I like 'em big and tough!"). An ironic muted trumpet plays—*wah-wah*—every time Monroe's derriere appears. On her first entrance she gets two blasts of locomotive steam on her bum as she boards the train. She neither sings nor dances very well in "Runnin' Wild," her first song, or for that matter in "I'm Through with Love," but it doesn't matter in the least. She is riveting. What is it about her—and, for that matter, about Tony Curtis? It is not just beauty, but something about them as human beings—a vulnerability of some kind.

Once ensconced at the "Seminole-Ritz" Hotel in Miami (actually the Hotel Coronado del Mar in San Diego), Lemmon is hotly pursued by Joe E. Brown. TC pursues Marilyn, but it's difficult to do so in drag. That prompts his yachting outfit and vocal impersonation of Cary Grant. First he scares away a little boy on the beach and expropriates his shell collection—a fine example of Billy Wilder's nasty sense of humor. TC's Grant imitation is legendary, as is his dialogue with Monroe:

"You play the market?" he asks her.

"No, the ukelele."

Curtis–Cary as the phony Shell heir gets the title line: "I guess some like it hot, but I prefer classical music myself." When Lemmon–Daphne intrudes on his wooing of Monroe, TC threatens him through clenched teeth: "I heard a very sad story about a girl from Bryn Mawr. She squealed on her roommate, and they found her strangled with her own brassiere!"

Monroe and her dresses are incredibly sexy—breasts outlined completely and nude looking, most notably in the "topless" gown she wears during "I Wanna Be Loved By You." In the end, TC frantically peddles his bicycle to get to the beach and meet Marilyn before she finds out who he really is. At the last second, in a typical Wilder touch, he remembers to remove his earrings.

Wilder and Diamond had a strict rule never to divulge who wrote what in their joint scripts. But in this case Wilder made an exception: Joe E. Brown's famous curtain line, "Nobody's perfect!", was written by Diamond.

Some Like It Hot came in $500,000 over budget, at a total cost of $2.8 million, which was unusually expensive for a comedy in 1958. But it was number three at the box office in 1959, earning $7 million that year (and another $8 million by 1964); Tony Curtis never had a more important 5 percent piece of the action. The film made history, as did TC's reply to a reporter who asked what it was like making love to Marilyn Monroe: "It was like kissing Hitler," he said.

—B.P.

Billy Wilder: "I never met anyone as utterly mean as Marilyn Monroe. Nor as utterly fabulous on the screen, and that includes

TC as the ersatz Shell Oil heir with Marilyn Monroe as Sugar, in a see-through dress, during *Some Like It Hot* (1959)

Garbo. I was at first thinking about Sinatra for one of the parts. I knew Mr. Tony Curtis back when he was making *Houdini* at Paramount. For *Some Like It Hot* I wanted a straight leading man and a comedian. I did not know who was going to be in it until seeing Jack Lemmon in *Operation Mad Ball* [1957]. Then I felt that he and Tony would make a great pair. I was sure Tony was right for it, because he was quite handsome, and when he tells Monroe that he is one of the Shell Oil family, she has to be able to believe it. It was a farce, right? Tony is so open and animated. But when we were making tests of the guys in costume, he put on the makeup and the wig and then suddenly froze. He was too frightened or embarrassed, with the high heels and all. Gradually he felt more secure.

"At one point, I brought in a female impersonator named Barbette to work with him and Jack. I remembered Barbette from my younger days in Europe—a wonderful performer, very well known as a ladies impersonator. He had a few afternoons with the guys and taught them how to walk, what to do with their hands, and a few basic things. It couldn't be *too* good; it had to be kind of awkward, for the audience to be in on the joke, to really get the laughs out of it. If it's too perfect, it's just not so funny.

"Tony's famous quote, 'It was like kissing Hitler'—he did not quite mean it. Tony and Jack suffered because she was never on time. In a scene where she had one line and they had all the rest of the dialogue, we'd have to do it eighty times because she forgot her one line. She paid absolutely no attention to anybody. She never thought, *We're doing eighty takes, and those guys are standing there. They're cramping, they're not going to get any better—in fact, it may kind of curdle on us.* That's what he meant when he said it was like kissing Hitler.

"Tony's enormous contribution came when I said, 'After you have stolen the yachtsman's clothes and you begin your relation with Marilyn, you have to speak differently—not the English of a Brooklyn musician. What can you do?' He said, 'I can do Cary Grant.' I said, 'Do it.' And he did. And it was a huge, wonderful plus for the picture. I did not know he could do such a perfect imitation. I discussed it with Cary Grant afterward and he was roaring with laughter. He loved it. So that was not in the script. I just wanted him to talk Bostonian or some other kind of 'rich' accent different from the one he had as a musician.

"That scene at dawn, after spending the night with Monroe on the boat, when he comes through the window and Lemmon is lying on the bed working the maracas and telling him he's engaged—this is a scene of about two minutes, but it is the biggest sustained laugh I ever had in any one of my pictures. I must say, very cleverly, I gave Lemmon the maracas so we could get the

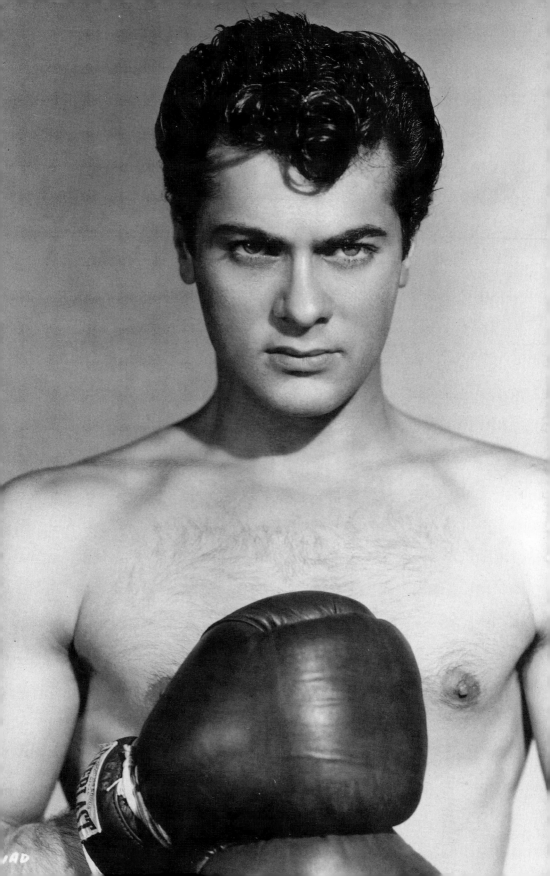

laugh but have it quiet again when the next straight line comes. In the theater you could just wait until the laugh is over, but in film you have to guess. After the preview I knew how much to prolong that interplay with the maracas according to how much time was needed to cover the laugh.

"Another thing about timing: When you first see them as girls, you see their legs, which is already funny: slightly bowlegged Mr. Lemmon and hairy Mr. Curtis. Then I went up with the camera as they were walking down to the train in the station. It got such an enormous laugh in the preview that I had to put in every take I shot as they went by the same three cars—I only had three cars. I used every single inch of film to make it longer. They go by the same cars five times, but people don't know it. That's when film-making gets to be fun.

"Also, a very ingenious idea of screenwriting, if I say so my-self: On the telephone to the agent, he pretends to be a girl because they've got to get out of town fast. But I did not go into any crap of borrowing the dresses and wigs from a girlfriend—nothing. Just 'Cut!' and the two guys are walking down to the train dressed like women. It's the immediacy of it, you know. The hell with how they got the dresses. Just the end result."

—BILLY WILDER TO B.P., October 16, 1992

Jack Lemmon: "Tony had his hands full with Marilyn. She was ill at the time, but we didn't know that until later. All we knew then was that she was driving everybody nuts. You might do forty takes with Marilyn, or you might do one, and Billy's gonna print the one that's best for her. I figured that out fairly early and made up my mind, if I let this get to me, it's going to hurt my perfor-mance. But it was easier for me, especially in the second half, be-cause I'm off with a rose in my mouth doing tangos with Joe E. Brown, while Tony has those long scenes with Marilyn.

"She got worse than ever during that stretch. She just sat in the damn dressing room and wouldn't come out. Billy was dri-ven to distraction by it and said, 'I will never ever work with her again as long as I live.' He got into bitter disputes with Arthur

Miller. Telegrams were flying back and forth. Billy was tremendously upset by her behavior.*

"I don't think it was 'temperamental.' It was just *selfish*. It was totally about *her*. She would stop take after take after take. You'd be doing a long scene like Tony's on the yacht, and she kept stopping the take when *she* didn't like it—not waiting for Billy. You're into twenty, thirty takes, and if you're Tony, you're going to slit her throat, because if you 'go by it,' you lose it after a while.

Jack Lemmon in his Daphne costume with TC's mother, Helen Schwartz, on the *Some Like It Hot* set

"In one scene, she knocks at the door, Tony and I throw our wigs on real quick, she comes in and says, 'Where is that bourbon?' She sees it lying in an open drawer. 'Oh, there it is.' And she picks it up. That's it. Eight words. But she could not get them out. She kept stopping and stopping. Billy was going bananas. I have never seen a director come up with so many different ways to tell her how to play it after each of these takes. She'd say, 'Sorry,' and walk out the door, shaking her hands to relax her fingers.

---

*Another Wilder remark on the subject was: "I knew we were in midflight, and there was a nut on the plane." Wilder's public criticism of Monroe sparked the famous telegram war in which Miller blamed Wilder for a second miscarriage Marilyn suffered just twelve hours after the final shooting day. The back-and-forth vollies included this one from Wilder:

"Had you, dear Arthur, been not her husband but her writer and director, and been subjected to all the indignities I was, you would have thrown her out on her can, thermos bottle and all, to avoid a nervous breakdown. I did the braver thing. I had a nervous breakdown."

Wilder later apologized, and Marilyn was encouraged to do the same. She phoned Wilder after a recording session for the *Some Like It Hot* soundtrack album, but Wilder's wife, Audrey, said he was out. "Well, when you see him, will you give him a message from me?" she asked. "Please tell him to go fuck himself." Pause. "And my warmest personal regards to you, Audrey."

We've got one hundred fifty thousand feet of film of her shaking her fingers. Tony and I are just standing there, and our legs are getting tired because of the goddamned high heels, so we made a bet. I said, 'What do you think it's gonna go to?' He says, 'Fifty.' I say, 'Ten bucks she does it in forty.' I forget who won the ten bucks, but we got up to about take forty-eight. After take forty-two, Billy is getting dazed, and when she stopped again, he said, 'Marilyn, possibly—' He got that far, and she said, 'Don't talk to me now. I'll forget how I want to play it.' I have never seen a director stopped so cold—Billy Wilder, the fastest mind on earth. He was absolutely stunned, and he just shook his head and walked back. When she got those eight words out, you can bet your ass it was printed. So if you've got Tony's part, you're unlucky compared with Lemmon.

"And oh, God, that Barbette! She came over—or *he* came over—and worked with us for a few days, and then he quit because he couldn't stand me. We came in one day, and he wasn't there. Billy was laughing his ass off. He said, 'Barbette came to me and said, "Tony is wonderful and he'll be perfect. Lemmon is totally impossible. He refuses to do what I tell him. I wash my hands of it." ' He made them book him on the next transatlantic.

"I felt the two of us should be different, but Barbette wanted us to walk the same. He said, 'Always cross one foot in front of the other.' It's interesting. When you walk forward, if you cross one foot over the other, you walk like a woman. No man on earth ever did it. It makes you swivel your hips a little, and it's totally feminine. That's fine, except I didn't want to do it. You didn't want them both doing the same schtick, and Tony was much more successful at the imitation. I was clumsy, I was an asshole, the shoes were killing me, my ankles were turning. But Tony could carry it off with a great aloofness; he just put his head up in the air and pouted his lips. His Josephine was fearless about it, but my Daphne was scared shitless.

"The result, in my opinion, was the greatest film comedy ever. I couldn't care less who played my part. It was the best comedy script I ever read. When I first read it, I was lying down on a couch, and I literally *fell off that couch*. It was the only time that happened to me. Billy was absolutely at the height of his powers. Next

we jumped right into *The Apartment*, and he won three Academy
Awards. Right after that, *Irma la Douce*. Billy was really flying."
—JACK LEMMON TO B.P., April 22, 1993

There's been a lot of bullshit written about that Hitler remark of mine.
It was just a throwaway line. Somebody asked me what it was like making
love to Marilyn, and I said, "What do you want me to say? It was like kissing

TC with Marilyn Monroe before *Some Like It Hot* production began

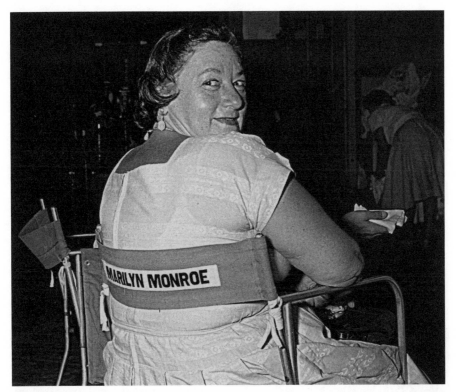

Seeing is believing: Helen Schwartz coyly usurps the Sex Queen's throne on the set of *Some Like It Hot.*

Hitler."* We would do thirty, thirty-five takes. I'd say, "Billy, how many fuckin' takes are we gonna do?" Billy would say, "When Marilyn gets it right, that's the take I'm going to use." The odd thing was, it could take her forty or fifty takes to get out one line, but sometimes she did a whole long scene—like the one in the train berth with Jack and all the girls piled inside—on the first take. You never knew.

---

* Monroe's own response to the Hitler remark has recently surfaced. In *Marilyn Monroe: The Last Interview* (PBS, July 20, 1992), Richard Meryman of *Life* magazine, just six weeks before her death, asked her about TC's Hitler comment. Her reaction was angry and not wholly coherent: "That's his problem. . . . It's not *him*, it's somebody else. . . . Out with *him*—get somebody else!" After *Some Like It Hot*, Monroe made one more film, *The Misfits* (1961). Her final attempt was *Something's Got to Give* (1962) for Fox, during which she was absent twenty-one of thirty-three shooting days. She was fired and died a few days later on August 5, 1962.

I didn't have much to do with Marilyn during *Some Like It Hot*, although we had something to do with each other in the early days. My friend Howard Duff had a house on the beach in Malibu and he told me to use it anytime I wanted. So one Friday afternoon, in '49 or '50, I asked Marilyn if she wanted to spend the day there, and she said yes. I picked her up, we stopped for some groceries, and drove down. That night I decided to build a fire, which I had no idea how to do. I burned my hand and then the steaks. In pulling the cork out of the bottle, I spilled red wine all over my white pants and her white blouse, which we immediately took off and rinsed out. I put too much vinegar in the salad, and the potatoes were only half baked. Other than that, I was the perfect chef.

After dinner, we sat on the beach under stars and talked about what we wanted to accomplish with our lives. She was as sweet and caring then as any twenty-two- or twenty-three-year-old girl I knew. We spent the night there and dreamed of the future with joy and optimism. Things happen to you when you get older. But that's another story.

Anyway, on *Some Like It Hot*, everything was going well up until around the middle of the movie when she just lost all control—too much alcohol or pills or too much I-don't-know-what. Emotionally, she was devastated.

A lot of people ask me what Janet thought about my making such a hot movie with Marilyn, but Janet wasn't concerned about it. She was pregnant with Jamie when I was doing *Some Like It Hot*.* Of all my leading ladies, Marilyn was the least threat to anybody. In my Universal contracts, I thought one of those small-print clauses said I had to have affairs with all of my leading ladies. I was sure that was part of the contract, and with two or three exceptions, I did. One of those few leading ladies I didn't have an affair with was Jack Lemmon. It just didn't seem right to me. I had some aversion to his charms. Maybe I just had too much respect for him. At any rate, he was just not appealing to me. Neither was Marilyn at that point.

She was truly incapable of memorizing the simplest lines. Paula Strasberg† would huddle with her before and after every scene. She was on the set all day through the whole movie, about five feet two inches, always

---

*TC's private publication, "Anthony's Almanac," contained a letters-to-the-editor column in which someone asked: If you were to do a picture on location with Liz Taylor, what would your wife say? TC's answer for Janet: "Tony, are you getting a percentage of the net or the gross?"

†Wife of Lee and mother of Susan, Paula Strasberg was then Monroe's acting coach and almost constant companion.

166

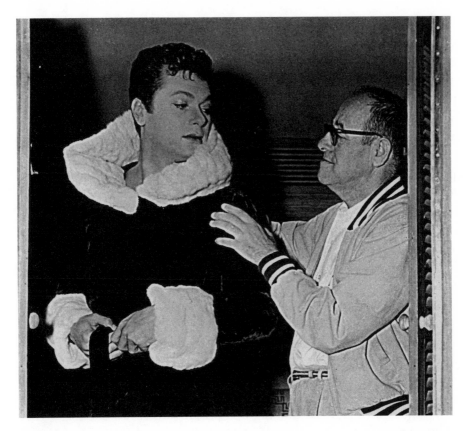

TC being drag-fitted by Orry-Kelly: "You know," he told Marilyn, "Tony's ass is better-looking than yours."

dressed in black. Billy hated it, but he had no choice. If you wanted Marilyn, you got Paula. She was getting fifteen hundred dollars a week. You had to go through Paula for everything, so Marilyn could never fully connect with anybody she was acting with. Paula followed her around with a big black umbrella, holding it up in the air over this blond monster, all the time whispering in her ear, "Relax, relax . . ." And there was Jack before each shot, saying, "Magic time! Magic time!" Between "Magic time!" and "Relax!" I was going apeshit. Mine was, "Keep your pecker up." Each of us had our own little mantra to get ready for a scene.

The first time Marilyn showed up on the set, we were shooting the train sequence on the MGM back lot. Paula was there, hovering behind Marilyn and making a pain in the ass of herself, letting everybody know that she motivated and manipulated Marilyn. They were doing the shot of Marilyn walking down at the train station. At the end of the rehearsal, she would look not at Billy but at Paula, who was sitting on the side with the umbrella and trying to act like she wasn't around. Privately she was saying, "I am King Shit here."

This was the first day of shooting, and we did it in one take. "Cut!" Marilyn looked over at Paula. Billy stood up, looked at Paula, and said, "How was that for you, Paula?" That was the end of Paula Strasberg on *Some Like It Hot*. She hung around, but from then on she was nothing but an umbrella carrier. Billy knew the score. He never said anything else—just that once on the set in front of everyone, and it stopped her cold.

I was always on time. So was Jack. That made things worse, because we were always having to stand around—in drag—waiting for Marilyn. We had to wear these horrible steel jockstraps, and one big problem, you can imagine, was what to do when you had to pee. I rigged up this funnel-and-hose thing. It was uncomfortable, but it did the trick, and I always wore it when I was in costume. I always had that little pipe to relief. I worked it out myself. I never mentioned it to anybody, but the logistics of it were amazing. I should have patented it. It ranged around my thigh and abdomen and down the inside of one leg, then hid behind the silk stocking that I was wearing, so that I could unroll it, take care of business, and roll it up again without ever standing up or sitting down. People said, "That Tony—how does he do it? Strapped all day long in those women's clothes, never whimpers, never has to go to the bathroom!" Jack didn't have this device. Once he sort of caught me and said, "What the fuck are you doing?" I said, "Never mind; I'm inventing something." I never shared it with him because he was too conservative. He would never have gone for it.

I liked working with Jack a lot but I never felt secure on *Some Like It Hot*. It had nothing to do with Jack. It was that almost all my scenes were aimed in Marilyn's or Jack's direction. I was the straight man for both of them. I was disappointed. Billy was very pleasant and nice to me, and always has been. But I had a way of attaching myself to people, thinking of them as older brothers and fathers. I felt like a stepson with Billy Wilder. I never felt he really cared that much for me. Maybe it was paranoia, but that was my feeling.

So I have some rough memories of making that picture, but some funny ones too. Orry-Kelly, who was the costume designer and a very gay guy in all senses of the word, told me that one day when he was fitting Marilyn he said, "You know, Tony's ass is better-looking than yours." And Marilyn said, "Oh, yeah? Well, he doesn't have tits like these!" Then she yanked open her blouse to prove it.

But, you know, the whole thing wasn't just Marilyn Monroe. That movie involved all sorts of inside movie-history jokes and people and connections, including Edward G. Robinson. When Billy first told me I was going to be in it, he said, "It's you, Marilyn, Sinatra, and Edward G. Robinson and George Raft as the gangsters." Then he called back and said, "I'm putting in Jack instead of Frank, but Edward G. is still in." What he didn't know was that Robinson and Raft had come to blows on a Warners picture, *Manpower*, back in 1941. There was a photograph of them fistfighting in *Life* magazine. They hated each other, and Robinson vowed he'd never work with Raft again.

In the meantime, Billy had hired his son, Edward G. Robinson, Junior, to play the guy who stands there flipping a coin when George Raft comes into the hotel for the gangster convention, which was called The Friends of Italian Opera—you could never get away with that now. Raft grabs the coin and says, "Where'd you learn a cheap trick like that?" That was an in-joke referring to the exact same thing Raft did in *Scarface* with Paul Muni. Edward G. junior didn't know how to flip a coin. He would throw it up flat into the air and try to catch it. It took him a while to learn how to do it right. So when Edward G. senior dropped out at the last minute, Billy was livid because the only reason he'd hired junior was as a favor to senior, who was supposed to play Little Bonaparte, the head gangster. Billy had to recast it with Nehemiah Persoff.

Nicky Persoff was just fine, but I was disappointed because I wanted to work with Edward G. Robinson. He spoke impeccable Yiddish, by the way. He liked the fact that I was so handsome and came out of New York. He had an extraordinary art collection until he got divorced and had to split it with his wife. In an unhappy marriage you'll give up anything to get out. That same year, when he was doing *A Hole in the Head* with Frank Sinatra, I went to visit him and Frank on the set, and during a break Edward G. told me about his early life in New York and how he got into movies. Fascinating man. He'd lean over and grab my cheek and go, "*Shöne punim!*" ("Beautiful face!")

Toward the end of *Some Like It Hot*, during the gangster convention, there's a scene where a guy bursts out of a cake and guns down George Raft. Billy was having a horrible time with Marilyn, who was making everybody's life miserable. I got the bright idea of hiring a stripper with big tits to jump out of that cake. Everybody was singing "For He's a Jolly Good Fellow" and then, instead of the guy with the machine gun, this girl leaps out and goes over and gives Billy a big kiss.

I just wanted to make a little gesture, because Billy was so much under the gun, no pun intended. At the beginning of production, David O. Selznick had told him, "You want machine guns and dead bodies and gags in the same picture? Forget about it, Billy. You'll never make it work."

The December 1958 sneak preview of *Some Like It Hot* at the Bay Theatre in Pacific Palisades, California, seemed to prove Selznick right: It was a disaster during which only one person in the audience of eight hundred was heard to laugh. When the lights came up, Wilder rushed down the aisle to shake the hand of his one fan, who turned out to be Steve Allen. Also present was Wilder's old friend Joseph Mankiewicz, producer of the new Tennessee Williams picture *Suddenly Last Summer*, which had also been previewed that night—much more receptively—right before *Some Like It Hot*. Mankiewicz put his arm around Wilder and said, "It's all right, Billy; it happens to all of us." Wilder, who hated sympathy, replied, "I was thinking, Joe, that in *Suddenly Last Summer* you violated one of the basic rules of the movie business: not to offend big pressure groups. This picture will offend the vegetarians."

Things were different in New York, where *Some Like It Hot* was sneaked at the Loews Lexington on Fiftieth Street. When Joe E. Brown said "Nobody's perfect!" the balcony nearly collapsed from the reverberations of laughter. Upon leaving Loews Lexington, Marilyn Monroe had to be pushed through the avalanche of fans into a limo in order to get out alive. The man standing on the street and banging on the roof of her car was Montgomery Clift, who was supposed to leave with her but couldn't get in.

The reception was similar everywhere else, including at the film's first screening in Russia at the peak of the Cold War in 1964. TC personally carried the film there under his arm. An interpreter simultaneously translated the dialogue, and at the end, when he

Helen and Manuel Schwartz with lovely daughter TC on the *Some Like It Hot* set

said, *"Nikto nye bezuprechniy!"* ("Nobody's perfect!"), the Muscovites exploded.

Jack Lemmon was nominated for an Academy Award as best actor. TC and Joe E. Brown were overlooked, even for best supporting actor nominations, though many thought their performances the highlights. Billy Wilder lost out both for best director and for best screenplay. The only one of the film's six nominations to win was Orry-Kelly's for costumes—for which TC could take at least a partial measure of credit. Otherwise, this was *Ben Hur*'s year to sweep just about everything.

—B.P.

You would think that "womanizing" might have rubbed off on me. But it didn't. As soon as the picture was over, I went back to being Tony Curtis, the man. As for the Oscars, I always believed the old saying that the only thing you can rely on the Academy for is free movies at the end of the year.

A long time afterward, when my son Nicholas saw *Some Like It Hot*, he said, "Dad, you were great. What I loved was that weird New York–English accent you did. Where did you get that?"

He didn't know from Cary Grant, which was fine. It had to work on both levels. But it was important to me that Cary liked it, because I always loved Cary. I had watched him all my life. His *Destination Tokyo* made me volunteer for submarine service. He had such class! I met him at the Academy Awards one time and told him I really admired the way he dressed. He said, "Really? Take a look." He pulled up his trousers, and he had on white socks with his tuxedo. He had class, but also a great sense of humor.

Later, when I was working on a Hollywood novel called *Starstruck,* I called him and said "Cary, I've written a book, and I want you to hear a little bit of it." He said okay, so I read the part where this aspiring young actress looks out her window and sees Cary Grant coming around the corner: "He had light gray slacks with cuffs, blue double-breasted jacket, brass naval buttons, black and white shoes, an open white shirt, and ascot. He must have had a haircut the day before. The back of his neck was sharp and clean. Corky was at the window screaming, 'Jesus Christ, it's Cary Grant!' "

He interrupted and said, "No, Tony—say, 'Cary Grant, it's Jesus Christ!' "

I was doing so well those days that Universal asked me what kind of movie I wanted to make next, and I said, "a service comedy about submarines." They said, "Fine, we'll get Jeff Chandler or Robert Taylor to play the captain." I said, "No, I want Cary Grant." They got back to me later and said, "Robert Taylor wants to play that part very much, and he'll give you five percent of his ten percent of the gross." I said, "No, I want Cary Grant."

That's what I wanted, and that's what I got. Suddenly I was making *Operation Petticoat* with Cary Grant. It was a fabulous experience. What a period of time. Everything just rolled and became a reality. I said I wouldn't take second billing to anybody except Cary Grant, because I didn't have to. Cary ended up getting half a million, and I only got sixty or sixty-five grand for that movie, but I didn't care. I wanted that relationship with him.

Operation Petticoat (1959) was the third of four TC films directed by Blake Edwards. It contained TC's ultimate billing fantasy—

"Cary Grant and Tony Curtis"—fulfilled at age thirty-four. Grant played Admiral Matt Sherman, commander of the war sub *Sea Tiger*, which was about to be junked. Audiences would obligingly ignore his accent: What Cary wants, Cary gets in suspension of disbelief.

TC is Lieutenant Nick Holden, the new supply officer—a lovable, scheming scavenger. "In confusion, there is profit," he says. His character is a kind of 1959 Michael J. Fox.

TC saluting as the devilish Lieutenant Nick Holden in *Operation Petticoat* (1959)

Grant grills Curtis about his credentials as a "recreation officer." TC says he came from a New York neighborhood known as Noah's Ark: "Wherever you went, you made sure you traveled in pairs." His philosophy about money is succinct: "Steal it or marry it." He is at his most roguish, and the genuine feeling between the two stars is striking. Leonard Maltin called them "a dynamic duo."

Overall, it is a warm, innocent war comedy-drama—very Eisenhower era. TC as a naughty but all-American boy is male-bonding with Grant, who, in turn, is trying to deal with his own libido and his crew's. Blake Edwards's fast-paced direction contained more than a few patriotic tugs at the heartstrings. It was a kind of latter-day *The Best Years of Our Lives*—perhaps the last successful example of a genre that would soon be out of vogue.

With a running time of two hours and four minutes, *Operation Petticoat* was a virtual epic for Universal. The Oscar-nominated script by Stanley Shapiro and Maurice Michlin lost out to *Pillow Talk*, but it was number three at the box office, grossing

173

$9.5 million, with a $6.8 million profit, and one of *three* Tony Curtis films in the top twenty that year. Generational footnote: *Operation Petticoat*'s 1977 television remake costarred Jamie Lee Curtis as one of the army nurses.

—B.P.

When Cary and I were making *Operation Petticoat* in Key West, Florida, he had a limo and driver in his contract. All the rest of us were picked up in a big van and taken to and from the location every day. One morning Cary came over to me and said, "Tony, come with me." All the other people were very jealous as we drove off, but it was great fun for me.

We went back to the West Coast after that, and one day after we finished shooting in San Diego, Cary said, "Tony, do you want to drive up [to

TC with beloved role model and mentor Cary Grant in the mid-fifties in Hollywood

Los Angeles] with me?" I said that would be great. He had this Rolls-Royce and a driver, and there I was, driving up Route 405 with Cary Grant. He told me he loved those parts of the freeway that were piled up on top of each other. You looked down and saw five different layers. He was so alert and attentive to his environment.

I stayed close to Cary always and really admired him. There was a lot to admire. His phone number never changed. He gave it to everybody. Now and then I'd go up to his house and have breakfast with him. We'd sit on his terrace, and I'd tell him the trials and tribulations of being an actor (as if he didn't know), what was going on in my life, this or that party, and he'd sit there and say, "Tony, Tony, Tony!" He loved it. I was one of the guys on the street for him. I was one of the voices for him, one of the eyes.

Acting was an ongoing subject of conversation between us. One thing he said was really important for me: "Tony, you must forget that you're in a movie." I didn't understand that until another day when he was talking about how to judge a bottle of white wine. He said, "When it's chilled, it should taste like a perfectly cool glass of water—so artful, it's artless." When he said that to me, all of a sudden I understood what he meant about acting. So artful, it looks artless. He said, "Tony, just relate to the person you're working with, just be *with* them. Even if they can't play the part properly and you don't believe a word of the dialogue, you must *use* that. Use everything you hear and be ready to adjust like a good acrobat." He'd been an acrobat when he was young—he'd worked in a circus—and acting to him was like balancing on a wire, constantly adjusting the weight, one side to the other, never secure in the middle. It was always those delicate little adjustments, he said, and that's the way an actor had to be too. That was Cary Grant's gift to me, and I always loved him for it.

Who Was That Lady? (1960), directed by George Sidney, was the final joint appearance of Tony Curtis and Janet Leigh. It was based on the 1958 Norman Krasna play *Who Was That Lady I Saw You With?*—which made for a title song Dean Martin could run with. He sings it during the credits as the camera takes us on a tour of Columbia University, ending up in the science building. There, a tight-skirted coed is planting a passionate kiss on TC, her chemistry professor, but they are caught in the act by his

TC and Janet Leigh in *Who Was That Lady?* (1960)

pathologically jealous wife, Janet Leigh. On the grounds of that one kiss, she announces she's filing for a divorce.

TC enlists his pal Dino to help concoct an excuse for why he was kissing the girl. The alibi: He and TC are undercover FBI agents assigned to ferret out Communist spies. The kiss was strictly in the line of duty. Leigh is dubious, but their fake FBI cards and real guns finally convince her, and she dissolves into remorse. "Ann, you're not to think of me as a hero," says TC. "But if anything happens, I want to be buried in Arlington Cemetery."

Cut to their clothes on the floor and the happy husband and wife playing footsie in bed. Minutes later he is showing her his secret jiujitsu holds, jumping on top of her for a make-out session on the couch. They are surely the horniest couple alive, and this is about as far as a major Hollywood studio can go in 1960: Rampant sex and bed scenes are allowed, so long as you're married.

Plot complication comes in the form of the Coogle sisters, Gloria (Barbara Nichols) and Flo (Joi Lansing), the first of many

176

whose "loyalty" Martin plans to check out. At their table in a Chinese restaurant he explains to TC: "I met these girls when they were trying out for Ted Mack's Amateur Hour. He said they didn't look like amateurs." Martin's character—pre–alcohol awareness—plays to his real-life image. As soon as the waiter delivers the first round of drinks, he orders the second round. "The trouble with drinking—you break it up, it's a shock to your nervous system. Steady drinking is the safest."

The plot and the slapstick thicken when Leigh and the real FBI converge on the restaurant for a shootout. *Real* Russian agents show up (Simon Oakland and Larry Storch) and kidnap Martin, Curtis, and Leigh. TC is given sodium Pentothal to make him spill his U.S. defense "secrets":

STORCH: Let's play a little game, shall we? Do you like doctors? . . .

TC: Dr. Eberstadt . . . He's building the bridge . . .

STORCH: A bridge? Where is this bridge? *Where will it be??*

TC: [*long pause, slowly opens mouth and inserts finger*] In my upper right molar . . .

STORCH: [*politely to Oakland*] May I? Now I am goink to induce fear. [*grabs TC*] Mr. Wilson, do you love your wife? [*threatens to kill her, TC breaks down.*] He's a difficult subject. Sentimental . . .

The timing is hilarious, as are Storch's delivery and TC in support. Again, his job is largely that of straight man, generously helping Storch steal the psychological-warfare scene. It is Krasna's best dialogue and the funniest sequence in the film. The patriotic denouement further parodies the espionage game and turns the film—almost unwittingly—into a highly topical political farce. *Who Was That Lady?* and its Cold War agenda came a year before Billy Wilder's East-West comedy *One, Two, Three.*

Janet Leigh is her usual restrained, soft-spoken self. Her cardboard character has little relation to what any real woman would do or say, but she pretends not to notice. TC at one point pokes fun at his own native dialect: "They're genuine cultured pearls, as against uncultured *poils*, which they ain't." Dino—just three years after the Martin and Lewis breakup—proves strong on his own. (At his FBI interrogation, to the annoyance of the G-men,

177

he taps the microphone and says, "Testing! Testing!" as if beginning a nightclub act.) Jack Benny has a funny cameo. Groucho Marx visited the set one day and later made a trailer for the film, which also features a fine jazz score by André Previn.

Who Was That Lady? is a revealing sliver of the life and times. It ended up a respectable number nineteen on the year's list of top box-office hits, taking in $3 million. No one can watch it today and dismiss Curtis and Leigh as anything other than the smoothest screen team of the decade.

—B.P.

------◆------

It was Cary's influence and my own interest in circus skills that made me do a little one-hour television film called *The Young Juggler,* which nobody but me remembers. It was the story of St. Barnaby, the patron saint of variety acts, and it gave me a chance to do something I couldn't have done in the movies. We made it for $200,000, but it had an expensive look: color, with big Universal sets. I knew where all the good sets there were, and I made sure we got them. We planned to add footage and release it later as a film, but that never materialized.*

Around then, I quit going to the shrinks, who had cost me $30,000 over the previous four years. Instead, I took up photography and did more painting and decided I'd learn how to play the flute, for some reason. I also had to learn how to play the saxophone for *The Rat Race* (1960), which was Garson Kanin's story about a jazz musician trying to make it in a sleazy club run by Don Rickles. I liked working with Robert Mulligan,† who was just starting to direct, and with Debbie Reynolds. When we wrapped the film, she gave me a fine set of art supplies, and I gave her one of my paintings. Mulligan's pictures always had a lot of atmosphere. He tried to deal with real people and situations.

The Young Juggler, coproduced by Curtleigh, aired March 29, 1960, on NBC-TV.

†Mulligan was a TV director until 1957 when his first feature film, *Fear Strikes Out,* was much acclaimed. His later intimate dramas, mostly produced by Alan J. Pakula, include TC's *The Great Imposter* (1961), *To Kill a Mockingbird* (1962), *Love with the Proper Stranger* (1963), *Baby the Rain Must Fall* (1965), *Up the Down Staircase* (1967), and *The Summer of '42* (1971).

There was another movie around that same time that was based on a real situation—*my* real situation—even though I didn't have anything to do with the film. I always thought it was amusing that Billy Wilder, Jack Lemmon, and a few million people in the theaters were the beneficiaries of my private life and never knew it. The reason it came about was because there were a lot of beautiful girls who were extras and bit players that I wanted to fuck, and I did—either in the back seat of my car or in my dressing room or somewhere else. Like I said, I somehow felt my contract said I could get laid anytime I wanted. All I needed was a girl who would agree and a place to do it.

Most of the time the problem wasn't the girl, it was the place. I couldn't do it at home and, unlike the Beatles, I couldn't do it in the road. The car and the dressing room were too restricting. But my pal Nicky Blair—the actor and later restaurateur—had a little place off Laurel Canyon. One night I was on my way to pick up a date near there, driving up in the hills in the rain. I didn't quite know where we were going to go. I saw Nicky sitting in his little MG on the side of the road, so I stopped and said, "Nick, what are you doing?" He said, "My car is stuck. I'm waiting for the auto club to come." I thought for a second and said, "Listen, I'm sorry about your car, but since you're stuck here for a while, do you think—" He interrupted and said, "Go ahead, use the place."

So from then on, I'd pick up a girl and then call Nicky and say, "I've got to use the place." He'd sigh and say okay, and I'd drive up there in my Rolls and hide it under an awning, as if nobody knew. How could you miss the fucking thing? My license was "TC1," and that car was known all over the city.

The idea that it might make a film treatment came from Sidney Skolsky the columnist, a tiny little hawk-nosed gentleman. He ran across Nicky sitting in his car one day and said, "Why don't you go home?" Nicky says, "I can't go home—Tony's up there with a girl." Sidney says, "But it's your apartment, isn't it?" Nicky says, "Yeah, but Tony's my pal, and he's been getting me some jobs . . ."

So Skolsky wrote it up as a treatment and sold it, and it became *The Apartment*. When Billy Wilder was preparing the project, he said, "Tony, you're too good-looking for the Nicky Blair part." Jack Lemmon ended up with it.

C·H·A·P·T·E·R N·I·N·E

NEW FRONTIERS

Spartacus (1960) was an epic and a milestone for everybody involved: $12 million budget, shot in Super-Technirama, three hours long, a hundred different sets, and eight thousand extras. Spartacus freed ninety thousand slaves and led the two-year revolt in which they defeated nine armies sent by the Roman Senate. It was Dalton Trumbo's first Hollywood screenplay under his own name, since being blacklisted during the McCarthy era.

Anthony Mann was supposed to direct it, but Kirk Douglas replaced him with Stanley Kubrick. Some people thought Kubrick was an odd choice because he had a kind of cynical approach. I thought he was brilliant. He understood human frailty, very much like Billy Wilder—only Billy saw everything humorously. Kubrick's films are not funny. *Dr. Strangelove* and *Lolita* had a great deal of humor, but always with that bizarre, black view underneath.

Most of the actors and the crew in *Spartacus* thought of Kubrick as an upstart. It was Kirk's production company and it was Kirk's idea to hire him, but Kirk became ambivalent about him after a while. He had to keep defending him to the studio, and, consequently, he started to put pressure on Stanley, and they got somewhat antagonistic toward each other. The pressure had to do with the shooting schedule. They wanted him to shoot quicker, and they wanted him to make cuts and not to cover as much as he did in every scene. They wanted the standard over-the-shoulder shots and two-shots; nothing complicated. Stanley was asking for shots where the camera moved creatively, Kubrick-style, and the studio didn't want him to do that.

Universal was so heavy-handed about everything, including production values. It wouldn't give him room to move, and so Kubrick became obstreperous. He always wanted that scope, and he had to really maneuver to get *Spartacus* made. He was a genius with the camera, but as far as I was concerned, Stanley's greatest effectiveness was in his one-on-one relationships with actors. He was so good with actors in general—and with me in particular—so appreciative. He was a very fine person. My favorite director, in fact.

Spartacus started out rather modestly. I was only supposed to do a short time on it. It would eat up one of my Universal commitments, and that was the pleasure of it as an outside project. The next thing I knew, it was a nine-month production, and it eventually stretched into a year. This picture went on and on, with the slaves and the Romans and the armies and the gladiators and the battles. One day Jean Simmons and I were sitting on the back lot, up in the hills somewhere, waiting to do a shot. Kubrick was down below with fifteen hundred men charging up the mountain. I'd been on the movie five months by that time, when I was supposed to be on it only twelve days. I turned to her and said, "Who do you have to fuck to get off this picture?"

Finally we started doing night shootings. This was the sequence where the slave army has been captured, and they're all being crucified, and Kirk and I—Spartacus and Antoninus—are waiting for our turns the next morning. The Laurence Olivier character is coming down to officiate. We are the last two to be crucified, and we have this heavy, philosophical discussion about it.

"I don't want you to die this way."

"Well, that's the way it's going to be." No one knows he's Spartacus yet.

So we're sitting at the foot of this big hill by a wagon. Off in the background, just out of camera range, is the freeway. This is going to disillusion a lot of people who think it was shot at the gates of Rome, but it wasn't. It was on Barham Boulevard and the 101 Freeway, with a straight view maybe fifteen hundred feet or more all the way to the top of that hill. We shot that scene from nine at night to five or six in the morning. Night shooting, believe me, is the pits in the picture business. Everybody was exhausted.

As far as the eye could see, from that wagon where Kirk and I were sitting to the horizon on top of that hill, stood a long row of crosses with bodies on them, diminishing as they got higher up—all of Spartacus's friends who were being crucified. Kubrick insisted on having live people on most of them, with a few mannequins here and there because he wanted people to see them writhe and moan while Kirk and I were sitting at the foot of that steep hill, doing our scene. "What is it all about, Spartacus?" "Well, Antoninus, life is not a bowl of cherries." Moans and groans from above. "Then what is life?" "Ah! Well may you ask . . ." More moans and groans. Kubrick wanted the moans and groans and writhing bodies on film during this dialogue so it wouldn't look static in the back.

As we rehearsed it, Kubrick didn't pay much attention to them. He just kept giving orders to Marshall Green, the first assistant director, a huge man whose father was a film director I had worked with [Alfred E. Green, director of *Sierra*]. "Do this, Marshall, do that!" Marshall's real job was to make sure Kubrick got his night's work done. Kubrick hadn't picked Marshall to work with. He was just the A.D. assigned by the studio, which meant he didn't care about Kubrick, only about Kubrick getting his work done. Everybody knew it. That's the way it worked. Universal was watching Kubrick like some mad creature from outer space, and Marshall was their point man.

We rehearsed and rehearsed until Kubrick got the men writhing and groaning pretty much the way he wanted. Finally he said, "Let's start shooting."

"Spartacus, what is the meaning of life?"

Moans and groans.

"Life is not a bowl of cherries, Antoninus."

Kubrick says, "Cut." He looks up and says, "On the cherries line, the man on the third cross on the left is supposed to move. You didn't move." The guy says, "I'm sorry."

This went on and on. Forty minutes of starting and stopping and starting and stopping. Almost right, but not quite. Finally he says, "Let's do it," and we started the take again.

"Spartacus, what is the meaning of life?"

Moaning and groaning from up on the hill.

"Life is not a bowl of—"

Kubrick says, "Cut! Son of a bitch . . ." Some mild obscenity—nothing overwhelming. Stanley never lost his temper. I'm sitting only four feet from Kubrick. We all thought it was a perfect take. Kubrick says to Marshall Green, "Come here." Marshall, this huge man with huge feet, schlepps over. It's the middle of the night, he's dead tired, he's been eating lousy, he's been standing around and smoking for eight hours.

"Marshall, the guy up there on the twentieth cross on the left is supposed to struggle, but he didn't move at all. I want you to go up there and

182

TC and Kirk Douglas awaiting crucifixion in *Spartacus* (1960)

tell him that on the 'cherries' cue and the handkerchief signal from you, he's got to move. I can't use the megaphone to tell him during the shot because it'll screw up the dialogue."

Marshall looks at him with daggers. If looks could kill, Kubrick is dead. So Marshall turns around and starts walking up this incredible incline—like a StairMaster, it's so steep—to the highest point of the hill. It took him three minutes to trudge all the way up to a cross right near the end. There must have been 35 crosses on either side, and this was just about the farthest one. Marshall schlepped all the way up and stood at the foot of that crucifix and looked up. The moonlight silhouetted him looking up at this cross. It looked as if the light of God was shining on him. I was watching him, and I distinctly remember thinking, *God, that eerie light—that's the way it must have been when Jesus was on the cross.*

Marshall stood there for about thirty seconds, looking up at this guy on the cross and walking around it. The way he was changing position, it looked like he was saying, "What's the matter with you? You fucked up the last take. Why didn't you move?" And the guy must have been saying,

183

"Listen, I've been strapped up here for an hour now. It's getting uncomfortable." And Marshall is saying something like, "Well, I'll talk to Stanley, but please—in the next shot, *move*!" The guy says, "Okay, okay." That's the dialogue I imagined.

Marshall turns around and walks slowly back down that hill, never looking right or left, just down at his feet. It takes him another three minutes, but it seems like an hour. He doesn't look at anybody or anything along the way. He just lumbers straight up to Kubrick and says, "It's a fucking dummy."

Stanley took that information with the same grace with which he took everything else. No display of surprise or regret. Just some calm reply like, "Oh. Then put on wires and wiggle it."

Even though it took forever, I loved watching the way Kubrick worked and dealt with these guys—Russell Metty, the cinematographer, for example. Metty was an ace cameraman under contract to Universal. He was a boisterous, red-faced man who had been around for years. He always had a coffee cup loaded with Jack Daniel's. You'd walk by and get a powerful whiff of that. He was gregarious and friendly, and as things turned out, he got a fucking Oscar for the photography on *Spartacus*. He was twenty years older than I was and like an older brother to me. "Come here, kid," he'd say, and let me look through the camera. He was one of my mentors, and I liked him very much. But he hated Stanley Kubrick. To Russ Metty, Kubrick was just a kid, barely shaving. "This guy is going to direct this movie? He's going to tell me where to put the camera? They've got to be kidding." That was the attitude. There was always some animosity between them—nothing too overt, but always a little needling.

We were on stage twelve at Universal doing the scene where Kirk makes a deal with Herbert Lom, the merchant, to get the ships for Spartacus's people to escape. We rehearsed it three or four times, and then the stand-ins went in so Metty could do his lighting. When that was finished, Marshall Green said, "We're ready," and in came Kirk, me, and Herbert. Kubrick was sitting on the side, and Metty was in his big high chair with his coffee cup, watching. Kubrick never said anything, and I wasn't quite sure what his attitude was. With Kubrick it was hard to tell because his mind was always popping all over the place. Finally he got up, looked over the shot, and went over to Russ Metty and said, "I can't see the actors' faces."

Telling a cameraman you can't see the actors' faces is like telling the Boston Strangler there are no necks around or like telling a bartender there's no alcohol or like telling a motorcycle cop there's no gasoline or like telling Robin Hood there are no arrows for his quiver. It's just unheard of. Russ Metty, who was red-faced to begin with, got purple. He never said a word, but he was fuming in that high chair with his name on the back. Big silence. Everybody held their breath.

By chance, next to his high chair, there was a little light no larger than the circumference of, say, a beer bottle—a little thin-necked spotlight with shutters on it, about five feet tall, on a tripod. Russ Metty just lifted up his foot and gave it a big kick, and it skewered its way onto the set and into the scene. That was Russ's way of saying "Fuck you!" to Kubrick. That light just went rolling in and came to a halt there. When it stopped, Metty looked at Kubrick and said, "Now is there enough light?" Kubrick just looked at it, looked back at Russ, and said, "Now there's too much light."

Almost everybody treated Kubrick that way. They had no idea who they were dealing with. Later on they'd lionize and canonize him at Universal and everywhere else, but not in those days. *Spartacus* cost $12 million and was the most expensive film Universal ever made. It ended up grossing $14 or $15 million, but they were scared shitless at the time. Stanley was a few years younger than me, about thirty-two. We were all still babies. We looked like babies. The major players in that movie all looked like we were in our twenties. Even Larry Olivier and Peter Ustinov and all the stunt men looked young, although they were in their forties and early fifties. Kirk was forty-three and didn't want a lot of young men in the movie. The ages were scaled up so that nobody would look too much younger than he was.

That happens a lot in movies. When Alan Ladd was making pictures, anybody who was five feet nine inches or taller would tower over him. So everybody had to be five feet six inches or under. It's the same today when they put together a picture with people like Al Pacino or Dustin Hoffman or Joe Pesci. Everybody is scaled down to their size. The agents and the casting directors won't tell you that, but Tony will. If the star is five feet six inches, nobody's going to go much over that.

That's part and parcel of the business. You couldn't count the number of movies where people were eliminated because of religion or background or heritage. On a John Huston or John Ford movie, they were almost all Irish. If you work for Francis Ford Coppola, it doesn't hurt to be Italian. A lot of pictures were all-Jewish, and if your name was Schwartz, you were in; if not, forget about it. That's the name of the game.

Kirk never had any ethnic qualifications like that, but he had other problems on *Spartacus*. One of them was that famous bath scene where Olivier comes on to me—he's Crassus, trying to seduce Antoninus, the slave. They only filmed it in a medium shot, which made me suspicious at the time. Why no close-ups? I remember that a guy named Otto, Kirk's stand-in, said he thought it was disgusting to have two men in that tub together. That was the only nervousness I noticed during the shooting, but they must have known it would never end up in the movie, which is why they shot it without even a voice track. When it was rereleased a year or so ago, they had to get Anthony Hopkins to do Olivier's voice, and I did mine.

There was a lot of publicity about that "new" scene between me and Olivier being put back in *Spartacus*. That, plus the famous drag act in *Some Like It Hot,* convinced a lot of people I was a homosexual. One woman interviewed some guy who said he was my secret lover for ten years. He *wishes.* If you're in the movie profession, people can't wait to print that a man and a man or a woman and a woman are in love. They're pretty sure that will demean and humiliate you. When I was a handsome young boy just starting out, the first rumor people heard was that I was a fairy or a queer or a fag—that was automatic. That was how those columnists could "equalize" you if they wanted to. They got their information from certain girls—usually ugly girls—who would call me "faggot" because they didn't think they had a chance with me (and they didn't), or from guys in the business who were jealous. That was a good way of getting even. So they labeled you with those names, and the hatred behind it was just the same as people who called you "kike." I never felt the need to deny anything or defend myself then, and I certainly don't now. I've had close relationships with homosexual men all my adult life.

Did Larry Olivier make passes at me during *Spartacus*? Never. Once when we were filming, he said, "Tony, where do you get arms like that?" I said, "Come with me." We went behind the dressing rooms, and I said, "Get down on your face." He got down. I said, "You were worried, right? Let's do push-ups." So we did push-ups, and from then on we did them every day before we went to work. I'd say, "Come on, Larry," and we'd do our push-ups. He got into it, and one day he said, "I owe you one."

He paid me back by giving me little insights into acting. Once he told me, "You know, Tony, clothes make the actor. Dress the part, look at yourself, and you *are* the part. Put the clothes on, and you'll slowly begin to see

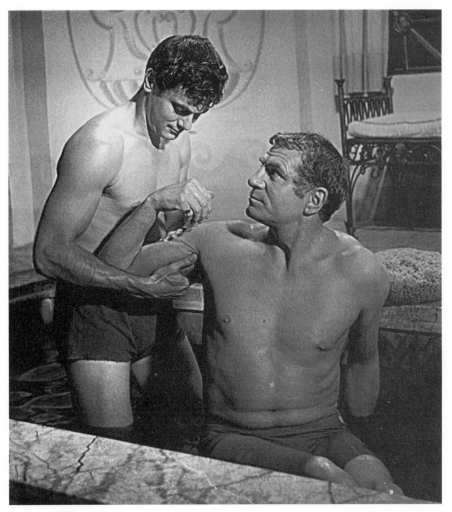

TC and Laurence Olivier in the infamous bathtub scene, censored and later restored, of *Spartacus* (1960)

an image of what you want to be." Olivier wasn't into the Method school at all. None of us were, because it was so destructive. It drove you crazy because it was all just jerking off in Macy's window, all in the brain. I don't care what anybody says, it really harmed people like Marilyn and James Dean. It drove the actor out of himself so that he didn't exist anymore. If you watch Dean in *Giant* . . . what a clumsy performance. He's so out of it, playing with a rope, that self-conscious, idiosyncratic thing. I said it before, but I have to say it again: They took the idiosyncrasies and genius of one man, Marlon Brando, and tried to make a school of acting out of it. Other people tried to mimic him and do that introspective thing, but it was Marlon's own personal brand of madness, and it couldn't be duplicated.

To tell you the truth, I never really thought of the movies as an art form. I thought of it as a means of entertaining people, of letting them forget whatever it is they want to forget for a few hours in a dark theater. It's not as complicated as a lot of actors like to make it out to be. For me it always came back to Michael Gordon's line, "All you want is a tip." Once I was watching Dan Duryea when I was making *The Rawhide Years* with him at Universal. He came in the door and started the dialogue, and the director yelled "Cut!" and went up to him and said, "Dan, the intent of what you are about to do is important. She's been unfaithful, and you don't want her to know that you know, but by the same token, you don't want her to get away with it because if she knows that you know, then she might really hurt you. . . ." On and on. When he was finally finished, Dan said, "You want me to come in sooner?" The director looked dumbfounded and then just said, "Yes." That little moment really gave me an insight into movie acting. You come in sooner or later—nothing much more complicated than that. Your technique should do the rest.

A few years after *Spartacus*, Larry Olivier wrote an article for *Life* magazine saying a lot of these same things, only much more eloquently. I wrote him a letter telling him it was the best thing I'd ever read about acting and reminiscing about our days on *Spartacus*. He wrote back and thanked me, and I've always cherished that reply.* To me it's worth more than all of Stanislavski's and Strasberg's lectures put together.

———————————•◆•———————————

Robert Mulligan, having recently directed *The Rat Race*, now wanted to show off TC's versatility as Ferdinand Demara, Jr., a real-life "human chameleon," in *The Great Imposter* (1960). In an early flashback, Karl Malden as Father Devlin tells him, "Face facts—settle for less." But TC cannot. He poses as a monk candidate for abbot Raymond Massey and soon after, when jailed, becomes editor of the prison newspaper. Ex-con Frank Gorshin

* Olivier's piece appeared in the May 14, 1964, *Life*. His letter to TC is dated May 22, 1964.

188

later tries to blackmail him, and he schemes his way onto a Korean warship, posing as a dentist for a hilarious tooth-pulling scene with Captain Edmond O'Brien. Things get more serious when TC has to perform delicate surgery during a storm.

Is it a drama or a comedy? Mulligan's direction makes it hard to tell. "I remember that whole picture as being an absolute kick," he said later. "It was such fun . . . because the character was so crazy and yet so real. This guy had actually lived all those lives. I was

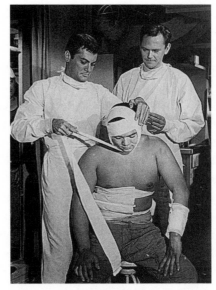

TC as "human chameleon" Ferdinand Demara masquerading as a doctor, while Richard Sargent looks on, in *The Great Imposter* (1960)

intrigued by [his saying] the reason he was successful was that most people don't know who they are. Whoever he presented himself as—a doctor, a lawyer, a teacher, a priest, anything he wanted to be—if he did it with authority, people accepted it."

Saturday Review and others accepted TC's achievement in the role: "Through hard work, [Curtis] has made himself an actor. Demara's many facets afford him a rare opportunity to demonstrate what movie acting is all about."

—B.P.

* * *

"The New Frontier" was what Jack Kennedy called his administration, and it turned out to be a pretty good description of the early sixties and of my career. For a while, Janet and I were very involved in politics—not always of our own choosing—in and out of the industry. Ronald Reagan was the president of the Screen Actors Guild, and I was on the negotiating committee for a strike scheduled for March 1960. It was eventually called off before it got started, but everybody was scared to death about it at the time.

Ron came over to our house on Summit Drive and gave a big speech while Janet and I and everybody else sat there. He was very affable and friendly, very much the same way he was later as President. But in those days he was a very dedicated and devoted labor man.

Then came his General Electric relationship. He became their spokesperson, and that turned him around. When he saw the value of it and the way they treated him, it became an expedient. It took care of his bills. He had to make a living like everyone else. Janet and I did a commercial for GE once, and they gave us a whole new kitchen. What was wrong with that? It was payment for the commercial. Nancy was always sweet with me, and she still is. That has never changed. We're not friends, but they always remember me and are very nice when they see me, and vice versa. I never voted for him, though. I only voted for the Kennedys and for the Democrats.

I'm completely apolitical now, but at that time I was political because of my relationship with the Kennedys. Peter Lawford's wife, Pat, who was Jack Kennedy's sister, asked Janet and me if we would host a luncheon for JFK during the campaign, and of course we said yes. Pat Lawford was always a good friend. She was very supportive of Janet and me. I still see her in New York. Wherever I have an opening, there's sweet Pat with her daughter or son. We keep in touch. In 1960 Janet was more into the campaigning than I was, but I got involved too.

I liked Jack and Jackie a lot. Even before the campaign, when Janet and I were living on San Ysidro Drive, Jackie and Pat Lawford would come by our house while Jack was usually spending time with Peter. That's when we first met. To be honest, they were no more important to me than a lot of other people—the meaning comes later on, you know. It's only later that people say, "You really made a movie with Marilyn?" "You really knew President Kennedy?" At the time, Marilyn is an ordinary woman. Jack Kennedy is an ordinary man. Tony Curtis is ordinary. Everybody is ordinary. You find yourselves in the same room together, and you either hit it off or you don't.

After the election, of course, things changed. During the inauguration in Washington, at this big reception, I looked up and saw the President coming across that crowded room, waving at me. "Come here," he said. I went over to him, and he put his arm around me and said, "Tony, my father and I ran *The Great Imposter* down in Palm Beach last week, and when you pulled that guy's tooth out, we just collapsed. I had to tell you that."

That was the President of the United States to Bernard Schwartz of the Bronx.

TC with Gary Cooper and poet Carl Sandburg at a Los Angeles reading in the late fifties

But an even more amazing moment happened a few days before that. About a week before the inauguration, I flew down to Palm Beach with Joe Kennedy, who for some reason loved me very much. I really got to know him much better than I got to know Jack. We had a great relationship. Why old Joe Kennedy liked me so much, I don't know, but he did. He just got a kick out of my movies, and he liked me to come down and play golf with him. That's all I knew. So I'm down there with him, and we're sitting in his little study in that compound down there, having a drink, and the phone rings. He picks it up.

"Yes, son? How are you? Fine. Tony's here with me." He turns to me and says, "Jack says hello." Then he goes back to the receiver. "Why, yes, of course I'd like to hear it."

Joe sat there listening and gestured for me to come over and sit down next to him, and then he held the phone out a little so I could hear. What do I hear? The President-elect of the United States reading his inaugural

191

speech to his father—and me—over the phone. "Ask not what your country can do for you; ask what you can do for your country." That's the truth. I heard it before anybody else in the country except his own dad. But to be honest, when I heard "Ask not what your country can do for you," I didn't realize the importance of it. All I knew was that the President of the United States was reading this to his father and I was privy to it. Then Joe took the phone back.

"Yes, son," he said, "yes, I like it very much. It's excellent. Thank you." And then he hung up. Joe never made any other comment. Nothing. What a thing that was—to read your father your inauguration speech. To think that a son would do that for his father. That's what the Kennedys were about. That's the way I remember them—not how they fucked or didn't fuck Marilyn Monroe. If you know that story about them, all the rest is shit.

I never really saw that much of Jack, but as I said, Joe and I played golf a lot at the Tamarisk Course in Palm Springs. He loved Janet very much—both her personality and her big tits. One day he said, "Tony, how can I make a pass at your wife when I like you as much as I like her?" Old Ambassador Joe Kennedy and Tony Curtis, fifty years between us—what strange friends. But there we were, buddy-buddy, laughing and scratching. I was in good shape, and once when I hit into a sand trap, we drove over and I jumped out of the golf cart into the sand trap in exactly the position I was going to shoot from. I just leaped out right to where the ball was, hit it out, and then leaped back into the cart, leaving just two footprints in the middle of the sand. I said, "Come on, Joe, let's get out of here. Let the next guy figure it out."

Joe told that story to everybody. A couple years later I was in Paris making a movie when Sargent Shriver was ambassador to France. Rose Kennedy was there, and she said, "Tony, show Sarge what you did with the ambassador when you played golf." The old man had told her this story. "Just do it!" she demanded. We were standing in the back of the ambassador's house in Paris, which had steps down onto a lawn. So, with great dexterity, if I do say so, I leaped off the back steps and landed on the grass, then reversed it and leaped back.

I loved every one of the Kennedys—Papa, Jack, Bobby—I had good relationships with them all, and I still do. Maria Shriver came to Las Vegas with Arnold Schwarzenegger a few months ago to see my art exhibit. I remember when she was a little baby. That's how far back the Schwartzes and the Kennedys go. Whenever I was in Washington I'd go to Bobby's compound and fool around with all those kids in the backyard, throwing footballs and hanging out.

That house in Palm Beach has an incredible history. And Rose still lives in it—can you imagine?—at 103. I used to be afraid to fly, but Ambassador Joe got me to fly from New York to Palm Beach after all the excitement of that "Happy Birthday" Marilyn sang to Jack in 1962 at Madison Square Garden. Janet and I were both there. I've read that she was supposed to be doing a big come-on to Jack at that event—but don't believe it. I heard on TV that the Kennedys gave her poison suppositories. Give me a fucking break.

After *Some Like It Hot* in 1959, Marilyn Monroe was finished—she was slovenly and unappealing. Kennedy was elected in 1960. She was going downhill fast, and she busted up with Arthur Miller just about a year later. Who would want to have an affair with her then? If she had an affair with the Kennedys, it had to be in 1955 or maybe 1956. After that she was unmanageable, unpleasant, dirty—no one wants to acknowledge that. People have a time warp. They imagine the Marilyn that the Kennedys were supposedly jumping on was the Marilyn of the early fifties. But she wasn't.

Let me tell you: The Kennedys didn't murder Marilyn. The Mafia didn't murder Marilyn. *Marilyn* killed Marilyn. Why would a man like Jack or Bob Kennedy go out with a half-drunken, out-of-control woman, particularly when she was married to Joe DiMaggio and Arthur Miller? There were no Kennedys around her in 1957. By 1959, when *Some Like It Hot* was finished, I predicted she'd never make another movie. It was truly my feeling that she would commit suicide. And I only missed it by a film and a half. So when did she start fucking around with the Kennedys? When did they shovel her into an airplane to Washington or to the beach? She was such a great cocksucker? Forget it. Nobody's that good. It's too farfetched.

Joe Kennedy's affair with Gloria Swanson? It happened, I guess. What is the big deal? It's the same as with Marilyn and Jack. All those overanxious, unhappy writers keep hitting us over the head with this old news. Joe Kennedy fucked Gloria Swanson sixty years ago? That ejaculation is still important sixty years later? To *him* it was, but why should it be important to other people? There's no sense of perspective, let alone propriety, in our concept of intercourse. That may sound funny coming from me, but that's the way I feel.

I could understand why a guy like Frank Sinatra got turned off by the world pounding on him all the time, and why he pulled into himself in a lot of ways. But he and I got to know each other better in those days. He would call me up and I'd hear that unmistakable voice on the other end of the line say, "Bernie."

"Francis?"

"We're going to Las Vegas."

"We are? When?"

"Tonight. You're driving."

He'd show up in his car and I'd get in the driver's seat.

I marveled at him. I still do. Actually, Frank always was a loner. I respected him for that. He didn't advertise in the trades, and he didn't give a fuck who was president of the Screen Actors Guild or whether David Selznick invited him to his latest screening. He always had something else to do. There was no club that was too big or too small for Frank Sinatra, if he wanted to do it and if you paid his price. If you didn't know how or where to find him, then you didn't want him badly enough.

Forget about all the movies and all the recordings for a minute. People always want to hear and see him in person even more. Name any city in the United States—they'll do anything to get him, and no matter where he goes, Sinatra works the place like no man in show business before or since. His band is never arranged in the conventional rows of musicians sitting behind the star. Frank has them all around him, like daisies in a field. A cluster here, a group to his right, maybe a single girl cellist over there. Through his whole act, he strolls around as though he's some Italian poet making up the verses as he goes along. He does this for thirty minutes, then walks off for a fifteen-minute intermission.

Precisely when the fifteen minutes are up, he comes back onstage with his Jack Daniel's in a glass for the real magic of the evening. The second act lasts anywhere from forty minutes to *two hours* and forty minutes, depending on how he feels and the chemistry that night. This is the consummate artist. This is Picasso in front of a canvas—deft, clean, and melodious. Frank is the only singer in the world who can do four hours onstage and still have a hundred songs left in his repertoire. If a song moves him, it moves you. Frank transmits the emotion of it like no other singer. He strikes you inside your chest, not in your brain. Nothing comes between him and his audience.

Onstage and offstage, he wanted to be obligated to no man or woman. Frank knew a lot of people, but none of them knew him. No one got too close to him. They loved him, but he wasn't too sure about them. Frank is one of the most fortunate men in his profession because he has it on his terms. And I am one of the most fortunate to know him and be his friend— not "intimate" friend, just friend. That's good enough for me.

I was fortunate to know a lot of incredible people. Ernie Kovacs comes to mind. He was also a good friend of mine in that period. He was one of the heaviest drinkers I ever knew. That car crash in 1962 was because he was drinking. A compulsive man. Had cocaine been around, he'd have been into that too. We spoke Hungarian with each other. He was the most gregarious man I ever met; wonderful personality. Always a big cigar, always a big gambler. He had a house up in Beverly Hills with a garage in the front, and we played poker in that garage sometimes three nights a week with guys like Dean Martin. Ernie would lose $20,000 at a crack and owe everybody, but everybody would eventually get paid. I loved him. We had a great time together—such a gifted, funny man, with such flair. The booze did him in.

Those were the civil rights days, as well as the "Rat Pack" days. With Sammy Davis, you got both. For me, the civil rights issue was like Israel and the 1960 election and other political areas: I was never on the front lines. I just tried to live it in my life and do what I could when a chance like *The Defiant Ones* or *The Outsider* came along.*

Harry Belafonte and I went to that same New York Dramatic Workshop together in the forties when we were kids. We always stayed very good friends, and of course later on I introduced him to Janet. She loved him, and we went to see him a lot in New York at the Village Vanguard, where he used to sing. We were only married a little while when Harry came out to California to make *Bright Road,* and one day he and I decided to visit Janet on the set of *Walking My Baby Back Home* (1953). There was a set photographer on hand and he said, "Let's get a picture." Janet got in between and put one arm around Harry and the other around me. It wound up in *Ebony*, and she got a lot of hate mail for having the audacity to touch a black man. She was furious about it.

---

* *The Outsider* (1961), directed by Delbert Mann, was the true story of Ira Hamilton Hayes, the Pima Indian who was one of six U.S. Marines to raise the flag on Iwo Jima during World War II. Racism and alcohol addiction subsequently brought him to a tragic end. For the role, TC darkened his skin, covered his curls with a straight wig, and refashioned his nose and chin with putty. His serious, sensitive portrayal of Hayes was consciousness-raising and widely praised.

Janet's energy level was very high and she was fearless, ready to take on anything in those days. I watched her develop more and more as an actress. Her performance in *Psycho* (1960) was incredible—she walks away with that movie. She was the only one that brought a kind of brittle vulnerability to it. Everybody else was bigger than life. But there she is, trying to hide that money, fucking a guy in a motel room—so gritty, and at a time when nobody wanted to deal with that or show that; least of all Universal, least of all Alfred Hitchcock. She was right on the edge of being raunchy. A remarkable actress.

When Janet was making *Psycho,* I'd go on the set and watch them work. Hitchcock had everything planned down to the smallest detail, and he came to the set each day absolutely prepared. Every shot in the movie was laid out on a storyboard. He would set up the stage and the cameras and show the cameraman the drawings, and they would match the shots exactly. That shower scene, for example, was pure geometry—this intricate combination of angles and body parts that rose up somehow in his brain. Then he just plugged the actors into the mathematical equation. Some actors didn't like it because it wasn't "personal" enough for them. They didn't think they had enough room to be creative. His singleness of purpose and concentration were too demanding for them. But we all know now how effective that method was.

In private, Hitchcock was most gracious, and his wife, Alma, was a charming woman. Janet and I met them long before *Psycho* through the good graces of Lew and Edie Wasserman. One night the Hitchcocks had us, the Wassermans, and three or four other couples over for dinner, and we had the most wonderful time. After dinner we were sitting in his drawing room, smoking those Monte Cristo Havana cigars that he loved so much. He once gave me six boxes of them because I smoked cigars in those days. So we were all sitting there, and it got quiet for a moment. Then he said, "I have an opening for a film. May I share it with you?" He had that wonderful, slow, deliberate way of speaking. Of course everybody said, "Please do," and so he started in:

"A small plane—a little twin-engine aircraft—is flying somewhere on a clear day. In the aircraft is a man who is just zipping up his jumpsuit. We don't see his face. He's wearing goggles and a helmet. He puts a parachute on his back and straps himself into it. The pilot looks over his shoulder and gestures to him to get ready.

"With that, the man in the jumpsuit opens the hatch of the airplane. The wind rushes in and for the first time we see, through this man's eyes, outside the aircraft. The altitude is about fifteen thousand feet—not so high, but high enough. We see hills and mountains in the distance down below. This chap with the jumpsuit and the parachute steps up to the open door, stands there for a moment with his hands holding the hinges, and looks over his shoulder at the pilot. The pilot nods, holds up his hand, and counts down with his fingers: five, four, three, two, one! The man in the jumpsuit leaps out of the plane like a frog, arms and legs outstretched.

"Eerie quiet. We're now outside the aircraft, which we hear getting farther and farther away. All of a sudden we hear the rush of the wind past his body. Cut to the goggles and helmet, nothing more. Quiet. Then he reaches down and pulls the ripcord. The parachute billows out and, after a minute, he settles down neatly on an empty road.

"He gathers up his parachute, folds it, puts it under a rock and looks for something. There, just fifty yards from him, sits a motorcycle under a tree. A beautiful bike, black. He walks up to it, carefully takes a key out of his jumpsuit pocket, inserts it in the ignition of the Harley-Davidson, starts it, revs up. He's still wearing his gloves and goggles, and off he goes—through some countryside and down the country dirt roads.

"Next he's on cement—not a big highway, a two-lane. Next thing you know he's coming into a little village with houses going by, the suburbs. Pretty soon we're in the heart of a throbbing city: lights, action, cops, people on the streets. The man on the motorcycle just keeps going. Finally he turns left, turns right, pulls into an alley behind a building, and stops. He puts the bike in park, takes the key out, and gets off. He walks up to a steel door in the back of the building. You can hear the noise of the city in the background. He knocks three times, takes out a different key, opens the door.

"He steps into a rather dark hallway that we can't see very clearly. He shuts the door. We go with him as he walks into a kind of locker area. It seems like a kitchen of some sort. We're not quite sure. He goes up to a locker, takes off his helmet and glasses, and now for the first time we see the actor who has the lead. He zips out of the jumpsuit. Underneath he's impeccably dressed in a tuxedo, black bow tie, fingers manicured, patent-leather shoes shined—everything about him impeccable.

"He walks through the kitchen, goes up to a stairway, takes a beautiful white linen napkin, drapes it over his left forearm, opens a door, and steps inside the most elegant restaurant. Until now, we have never heard his voice. He looks, walks up to a certain table, and says, 'May I help you?' "

Hitchcock stopped there. We all sat and waited. Everyone's eyes were big. You could feel the anticipation in the room. Silence. Finally, somebody said, "Yes? Then what?" He looked back with that long, blank expression on his face and said, "That's as far as I've gotten."

He never solicited anybody else's idea of how to finish it. He probably had more in his head, or maybe he didn't. That was his little joke—to get everybody so excited about it and then leave them hanging. He never said he was going to tell us a movie. He said he was going to tell us an *opening*. He was the most wonderful, fascinating man.

Janet Leigh: "When I first knew Tony, he was funny and earnest and loving and caring. He was also suspicious and didn't trust easily. I think his family misfortunes left a mark that became more pronounced as time went on, maybe because they were pushed down inside him earlier in life.

"At the same time, he was eager to please. When he went to MCA, they gave him a little pin that said, 'Don't listen to me, whatever I say. Call my agent.' People would come up and tell him, 'I've got a great script for you,' or a director would say, 'You'll really love this,' and he'd always say, 'Sure.' He was grateful they wanted him. I knew that feeling too: 'Wow, they really want me for a picture!'

"As success came, he handled it well in the beginning. But there came a time when he didn't want to know about responsibilities or problems. He felt, 'If I earn a million dollars, I can spend a million dollars.' There were other problems we had, typical family ones. We had two children, and when you're running a house, you have to have a certain order. You have a schedule, and it was like I became not a mother figure to him but a discipline figure. You can't be so spur-of-the-moment when you have children. Dinner would have to be at seven-thirty or eight, or whenever he or I would get home, and he didn't like the constraints.

"Later, after we were separated, somebody visited his apartment and Tony said, 'I don't have to eat, I don't have to wash my clothes—I don't *have* to do anything.' It was a kind of rebellion, I think. Tony's parents were wonderful, but they were almost helpless in many ways. They depended on him for everything, and it was a huge burden for a young man. His younger brother, Bobby, had terrible problems. A lot of things in his life can be explained by his feeling a responsibility, in different ways, for his two tragic brothers. I think all those things were a part of why he wanted out of the marriage. It just got to him.

"People asked me why I didn't blast Tony in my book, and I said, 'Why would I blast him? We were married ten and a half years. I loved him very much. We had two beautiful children.' The fact that we divorced was just two people going in different directions. We've all done things we're not proud of, but the disintegration of a relationship does not mean that one or the other person is bad. At one point, I have to say that I was very disappointed in Tony, but I feel that the man who was disappointing me was not really Tony—it was the problem with his dependencies. I have to believe that was the reason he acted the way he did. If you understand what's really behind it, you can't be bitter, even though it hurts a lot at the time."

—JANET LEIGH TO B.P., October 14, 1992

Kelly Curtis: "My parents met each other while they were both in the process of inventing themselves. It was Bernie Schwartz meeting Jeanette Morrison, and then Tony Curtis meeting Janet Leigh. But I think throughout the whole marriage there were still many encounters with their old selves, or worse, with their *mismatched* selves. As long as Janet was dealing with Tony, or Bernie was dealing with Jeanette, things were okay. But when Janet ran into Bernie, or Tony ran into Jeanette—trouble. Their wires got crossed. That's how I think of it, from what I remember or found out later on. They were four such diverse personalities. They could've been their own bridge table."

—KELLY CURTIS TO B.P., March 20, 1993

I wasn't trained for marriage and children. I didn't get that training as a kid in New York. My parents were always bickering, still living in Hungary in their minds. I would run out of that Hungarian environment and into those harsh streets to get away mentally as well as physically. I had no knowledge of women until I got in the navy, and even that was chaotic.

The frustrations I felt, being married to Janet, were not all her fault by any means, but it seemed like it at the time. I resented the way she would insist we go to a party or a film premiere when I'd been working all day on a film and was exhausted at night. I had very little personal life as it was, and partygoing just made my time with Janet for lovemaking or living so much less. Our personal life was becoming nonexistent, and I thought that justified sexual relationships with other women, even prostitutes. Those encounters relieved me physically but demeaned me and provoked more feelings of shame.

Sometimes I felt she was jealous of the success I was achieving, because she had been successful and established in films when I was still starting out. She seemed to become more irritable, and we both began to drink more than before, which affected our behavior. That drove me to more feelings of guilt and anger, especially when she wouldn't support me in a business decision or side with me when I needed to turn down a picture. She and my agents wanted me to take every job that came along. I acquiesced because it seemed like she withheld her pleasant ways from me if I didn't. These things were going around in my head, and I wanted out.

Janet was always close to the children. In 1962 when we broke up, Kelly was five and Jamie was three, and they stayed with her. There was a long time after that when I didn't get along with my daughters, because I didn't see them. Not that Janet was stopping me. I was suffering a lot. I couldn't be bothered with anybody. But those girls turned out wonderfully, and Janet deserves most of the credit for that. They're crazy about her. She married a stockbroker named Bob Brandt, who's a fine man, and they've stayed married for thirty years. She always went out of her way to be good to people, loyal to friends, and devoted to those girls. She's a very fine and very gentle and very sensitive woman, and I admire her.

200

C·H·A·P·T·E·R T·E·N

YENTAS AND AGENTS
BUT NO THERAPY BARS

 Right before we decided to break up, in the fall of 1961, Janet's father committed suicide in California. She was terribly upset, as anybody would be. Afterward, I thought it might help take her mind off things if I brought her, Kelly, and Jamie with me to Argentina, where I was making *Taras Bulba.* It turned out not to be such a good idea. Janet got food poisoning, I got a throat infection, and Jamie got hurt in a fall. So they went home early.

My costar in that movie was a German actress, Christine Kaufmann.* I started seeing Christine during *Taras Bulba,* but she had nothing to do with the bust-up of my marriage. It coincided, and there was a lot of heat that Christine caused it, but that wasn't true. My relationship with Janet had become untenable long before that.

It sounds ironic, but I think you have to "divorce" yourself from a marriage to have it work. You've got to pull yourself out of it, or back from it, somehow. In a marriage, people want everything: the fucking privileges, the food privileges, the comfort privileges. You want all of those privileges. Men and women both. But after the first week, you just cannot fulfill all

---

*Christine Kaufmann, then seventeen years old, was born in Lengdorf, Austria, in 1945. She went to school in Munich and made her movie debut as a child star in 1952. Among her many films before *Taras Bulba* were *Der schweigende Engel* (1954), the remake of *Mädchen in Uniform* (1958), *The Last Days of Pompeii* (1959), and Kirk Douglas's *Town Without Pity* (1961).

201

those expectations. There are just too many of them, and we're all so full of such peculiar idiosyncrasies.

Instead of a booze bar every six blocks, imagine if there was a "therapy bar," a recovery environment. You're going down the street, all stressed out, and you look over—"Oh, there's one of those therapy bars." You go in and see ten strangers sitting there, and you start talking with them.

"This woman, she's such a pain in the ass, I don't know what to do. I'm supposed to be home now for dinner, but I don't want to. I want to go visit this other girl. What should I do?" One guy says, "Well, you're not going to solve it tonight. What would make you happy?" I just want to see this girl tonight. "Then do it, but try to resolve it the next time." The guy next to him says, "Nah, you shouldn't do that. I think you should go home to your wife and talk about it." I make up my mind, say thanks a lot, hop in my car, and drive off—never see those people again. If something like that existed for people when they needed it, then marriages might work. But it doesn't.

We always like it a little fatter or thinner, a little hairier or less hairy, stronger or weaker. We like it soft, we like it hard. Things are always changing, and we should have the privilege of changing too, but we don't. Society's laws won't allow it. All of a sudden I don't want someone anymore, even though I used to desperately. Your combination of feelings changes. If you're not married, you say, thank God I didn't invest any more time and energy. But in marriage, your investment is huge, and so is the agony of getting out.

———————————

Taras Bulba (1962) was directed by J. Lee Thompson, fresh from the success of his *The Guns of Navarone* the year before. The script, based on the novel by Nikolai Gogol, was cowritten by Waldo Salt, his first screenplay since being blacklisted. The film began as a Burt Lancaster project but devolved to TC, who got first billing over Yul Brynner. It was shot in Salta, Argentina, a Spanish colonial town in the Andean foothills, where ten thousand gauchos were hired to play the Cossack, Polish, and Turkish armies. An elite group of forty was trained by TC in the proper use of swords, for close-ups.

In sixteenth-century Ukraine, the Cossacks join the Polish army to defeat the Turks in a stunning opening battle sequence.

TC as Yul Brynner's son Andrei in *Taras Bulba* (1962)

But the treacherous Poles quickly turn on—and massacre—their allies. Yul Brynner, as Taras, vows that his baby son Andrei (the future TC) will not live with a Polish collar. There is scorched earth galore as the Cossacks scatter across the steppes.

Twenty years later Andrei "rides like a Cossack and fights like a Cossack—we'll teach him to *drink* like a Cossack," says Yul as TC makes his first entrance to the strains of a Ukrainian drinking song. Father and son engage in the first of their periodic macho tests of strength throughout the film. Then it's off to Kiev, where TC is to learn Polish ways and be whipped by sadistic Polish monks.

There he falls in love with Polish princess Christine Kaufmann, who has an unearthly, almost Oriental beauty. TC's own beauty is a match for hers. His deep-blue eyes devour her as he conjugates the Latin verb *amare* ("to love"), and the music swells.

Their love scenes—one upside-down kiss, in particular—are quite convincing.

TC has many sword fights and more S&M beefcake beatings in store for "dishonoring" Kaufmann and killing her brother. The plot now borrows from *Romeo and Juliet:* Kaufmann is banished, and TC is determined to have her, regardless of the Cossack family wrath he incurs. Vaulting in and out of the saddle, he demonstrates again that no one of this film era moves better or with greater agility. *The London Daily Mail* noted that "what Tony Curtis does would have left even Fairbanks Sr. breathless."

Brynner now has a song—*The King and Him,* perhaps—followed by more whips, girls, and an orgy. These Cossacks are a barbaric but lovable bunch. They have an inborn, irresistible urge to do trampoline tricks, to splash each other while bathing in the river, and to wrestle and hug. Winsome, watery-eyed Christine Kaufmann and her mother, the film's two perfunctory women, must meanwhile represent all Femininity on an allotment of just three or four lines of dialogue.

Taras assembles his mounted men and becomes the new hetman. In grim Cossack fashion they all march over the old one on their way to the finale: a siege, a plague, and a climactic battle with incredibly gripping shots of men and horses falling over a cliff.* Kaufmann is to be burned at the stake but is rescued by TC at the last minute. "I'm a man before I'm a Cossack," he tells his father—for which Taras Bulba shoots his own son dead.

—B.P.

———————•◦•———————

Making *Taras Bulba* was an unforgettable experience, and Yul Brynner, a charming and funny man, was to me the most fascinating of those players. He had a fabulous pomposity about him. An aloofness. A sense of grandeur about himself and everything he did. That was the nature of the man, and that was the way he behaved, both on and off the set. It was never, "Hey, let's go out and play ball." I liked working with him very much. I'll

*"Bring out the dead!" is the grisly call throughout the plague scene, during which enemy guards taunt the Cossacks. It is grim and effective—and the source of a later wickedly funny parody in *Monty Python and the Holy Grail* (1975).

never forget that moment when, as my father, he shoots me. I was amazed when I saw the rushes—the way Thompson did it. I'd never seen that on the screen before. Usually in a scene like that, the man would be covered with blood, but all you saw in *Taras Bulba* was one tiny, clean hole in the breastplate.

There were other amazing scenes too, especially with the animals. There's the fat guy who lifts up the horse on his back and then accuses me of cowardice, so we have to have a duel—walking over a plank and jumping across that chasm with the snakes and the bear pit below, almost falling in. And in all those battle scenes, you can bet your ass there was no ASPCA on hand to observe the treatment of the horses.

Did you ever hear of the "Flying W"? It was a leather strap they put on the forelegs of a horse. It had a loop through which they rigged a rope or wire around the front legs and then down the horse's middle in a W shape. One end of it was fastened to the ground or a concrete pike, and the other end was let out. The horse came galloping in, and when it reached the end of the slack, that Flying W would yank its legs backward to make it stumble and fall. Many horses' necks were broken that way. Next time you watch an old Western, look and see if the horses fall face forward. If they do, it's because of the Flying W, which was finally outlawed.

There was no ASPCA for the actors either. Those guys were just catapulting off those horses at incredible speeds into rocks, trees, buildings—whatever. It was a dangerous profession for man and beast alike.

And it was dangerous financially as well as physically. I learned some bitter lessons during that production with United Artists in Argentina. They gave me a per-diem living expense of about $1,000 a week, and rented a house for me at $500 a week, which was automatically taken out of the per diem. I was there for about eight weeks, so that came to about $4,000—a lot of money then. The film company got the Argentine army to work in the picture. They put two thousand men in costume, and all they had to give them was a box lunch. On the books, it was $5 a man for box lunches—$10,000 total for the lunch expense, billed to the company. But in reality the lunches only cost about 32 cents. And that house I was renting for $500 a week really only cost $50 a week.

So where did all that fucking money go?

Creative accountants can do anything with figures, and they did it in such a way that you couldn't find anything wrong unless you were personally involved in the financial details, which I was. Lew Wasserman arranged for me to be a part-owner, and I took that seriously. I watched what was happening. They'd say, "We're going to have a hundred horses," but only twelve old nags would show up, and the company would still be charged for a hundred. That was part of the game. Now and then a courier would fly from Buenos Aires to Switzerland to make a deposit in some un-numbered account. *Jawohl, mein Herr!* Jawohl, your *own* hair.

Taras Bulba started out with a $3 million budget and ended up costing $9 million and grossing maybe $10 million. At the $3 million budget, I would have made a lot of money. But at $9 million, I didn't make anything. It was one of the first movies I had a piece of—and I felt ripped off. In the middle of production, I went to New York and told the honchos in that company, "I'm not going back to work unless you pay me the money you stole from me. That $500 a week you took for the $50 house rental; where's the other $450?" They carried on like I was holding them up at gunpoint. But they were stealing from me, and I didn't think that was fair. And I got every dime of that money before I reported back to that set.

When I got back to Hollywood at the end of 1961, Janet and I separated and I moved out. The divorce came through about six months later. She got custody of Kelly and Jamie, and remarried the next day. About six months after that, on February 8, 1963, Christine and I got married at the Riviera Hotel in Las Vegas. Kirk Douglas was best man and his wife, Anne, was matron of honor. We moved to a two-bedroom house in Coldwater Canyon, and Christine announced that she was giving up her acting career.

I didn't see Jamie or Kelly for a long time. That was when I started to despise those fan magazines. They kept printing headlines like "TONY, COME HOME, YOUR DAUGHTERS MISS YOU—WHY DID YOU ABANDON THEM?" There was so much pressure and anger and envy then, and still today. Once you're successful in the movie business, everybody's gunning for you. I can't tell you how many people would love to bump off Arnold Schwarzenegger. What Arnold generates, thirty-seven other people could live on, so other actors, agents, and directors are automatically his enemies. Nobody's your friend. They make you think they are, but in the grand scheme of things it's a war. And the press is a big part of it.

Sob sisters like Rona Barrett and Radie Harris and Joyce Haber, when she was writing her column, are cancers on the rectum of the industry. After I married Christine and we were living in a big mansion, Barrett announced,

"Tony Curtis and his teenaged bride are having troubles." All those Hedda Hopper types loved that idea. It was hot stuff for them. Barrett also tried to get me kicked off *The Boston Strangler*. While we were rehearsing that picture in Boston, I was doing a stunt and I leaped up and grabbed hold of an overhead board that wasn't attached properly. I broke the bridge of my nose, and we had to take three days off shooting. Rona Barrett said they wanted to fire me from the picture because I wasn't doing a good job.

She kept picking on my marriage with Christine Kaufmann, and one day she wrote that we were breaking up. In fact, we weren't. So I sent her a signed telegram that said, "DEAR YENTA: YOU'D BETTER CHECK YOUR FACTS BEFORE YOU PRINT ANYTHING."

They had to scrape her off the wall. Nobody talked to her like that. For a yenta to be called a yenta was very difficult to take. She told my press agent, Warren Cowan, "I'm going to ruin him in this town." Warren told me about it. What Rona didn't know was that you're not allowed to make a threat like that—there's a law against threatening a person's livelihood. I told Warren, "You tell her I don't want to see my fucking name in that column again. I could sue her for that, and I'll call you in for the deposition, Warren." So a deal was struck that she wouldn't mention my name again and we wouldn't sue her, and that was that.

Rona Barrett had a license plate that said "Miss Rona." It should have said "Miss Take" or "Miss Fortune" or "Miss Carriage." I thought about her recently when I read Julia Phillips's book *You'll Never Eat Lunch in This Town Again*. I thought, if Rona had written it about me, she would have called it *You'll Never Eat Pussy in This Town Again*.

There was only one reason why the industry put up with hacks like that: If the studios had had to pay for all their publicity, it would've cost them another $100 million apiece. It made better sense to get connected with a few newspaper and TV men or women and sweeten their kitties with free liquor and vacations, among other things. Those people were leeches, sucking off the film industry. Some of them diddled themselves into thinking that anyone actually cared whether they liked or didn't like a movie.

I remember once seeing Louella Parsons at her house in Beverly Hills, doing the Twist in a sparkling blue minidress. During the holidays her home was a cornucopia of gifts tumbling out through the windows and doors—boxes and boxes from the studio heads, who'd send her Steuben glass, David Orgell silver, clothes, plane tickets, anything and everything. People bribed her with gifts because of the free publicity. The studios didn't have to pay for it, and they didn't give a fuck what she said as long as she printed the name of the movie and when it would be released. If Louella or Hedda liked somebody, he got in the column. If you were in that column a lot, you became a pusher for items.

"Louella, dear, there's a friend of mine, Ann-Margret—she's just starting out. Could you say something nice about her? And by the way, we're going to Acapulco for Christmas. Would you like to come along?"

"Oh, really? What should I write about her?"

That's the way the game was played, and it's still the way it's played. Do you think Rex Reed or Gene Shalit knows anything about movies? They are nothing but rumormongers and tools of the distributors. There should be term limits for reviewers: six months, rotating. Reed writes these awful books about Hollywood. They kiss him, feed him, wine and dine him, and he's the worst enemy the picture business ever had. David Susskind once made some crack about me being "a no-talent with no taste" and marrying Christine Kaufmann so I could "examine the postwar Germany." I came out of the Beverly Hills Hotel a year or two later and there was David Susskind. He said, "Tony, let's forget about what happened." I said, "I ain't forgetting," and walked away from him. He was just an unsuccessful theatrical producer, and his frustration about that was overwhelming. I don't have any respect for those people. They're vindictive, envious, shallow, self-serving, and mean-spirited. Other than that, they're wonderful and I love them.

------ •◦• ------

Paramount production executive Tommy Culla: "The first time I saw Tony and Christine Kaufmann was in New York at the Sherry-Netherland Hotel. They had just wrapped *Taras Bulba*. Christine was wearing a beautiful full-length caftan. This woman was unconsciably pretty, and Tony came out wearing a tailored towel with a button—with that physique of his, and he was tanned. He and Christine were besotted with one another. A year or so later I had occasion to take them to *Fiddler on the Roof,* which Tony loved, and at the end of the show, when those two went up the aisle, no one was looking at the stage. All eyes were on Tony and Christine.

"Tony is a very fastidious man, and he kept his cars that way too. We were coming out of the Beverly Hills Hotel one morning, under that beautiful rotunda, and the fella pulled his car up. Tony walked over and tipped him and then looked at the top of the car. It had what you'd call a little *schmidjik* in Yiddish—a spot. Tony opened his glove compartment and took out a little spritz. He had his driving gloves on, as always. He spritzed the roof and took off that spot. The carhop was paralyzed. Tony didn't make a three-act play out of it. He just did it, because he didn't want to drive around the rest of the day with that spot on his car. To me, for some odd reason, that always represented Tony Curtis at his elegant best."

—TOMMY CULLA to B.P., February 14, 1993

After *Taras Bulba,* Christine went back to Germany for a while and I made *Forty Pounds of Trouble* (1963) here. When that picture was over, I went over to be with her in Munich, where she was working on a movie. Her father had been a *Luftwaffe* pilot, and her mother a French nurse. Christine told me that after the liberation, her mother's head was shaved because she was accused of collaborating with the Germans.

I bought a green four-door Jaguar in London and drove it from London to Munich. I was staying at the Bayerischer Hof, a beautiful old hotel. My plan was to ship the car back to America after visiting Christine. They were shooting at night. I would visit her on the set. We'd sit in the Jaguar, the heater would warm it up, she'd go over, do a little work, and then come back. Some of the other cast members would come over too and use the car like a warmed-up dressing room.

I did this for two or three nights and arrived back at the hotel about five-thirty or six, just when the sun was coming up. I'd sleep a few hours at the hotel, then go sightseeing and meet Christine for an early dinner before she went to work. That was what the routine was like.

One morning I got back to the hotel after spending the night on location with her and the German film crew. Everybody seemed friendly enough, right? When I got to the hotel, I gave the car keys to the doorman, and he said, "May I show you something?" He took me around to the back of the Jaguar. Someone had stuffed rags into the exhaust pipe and taped it up with black masking tape that night on the set. When I was waiting for Christine, I would get tired and fall asleep sometimes. Someone was going to carbon-monoxide me.

TC and Christine Kaufmann in *Wild and Wonderful* (1964)

I immediately flashed to what those countless Jews went through in Germany. The force of it was overwhelming. There I was in Munich, an hour's drive from Dachau. It was as if that evil was still lurking there, twenty years later. Christine Kaufmann was their pick of the season. She was going to become the biggest German movie star of the day; they never counted on Christine not fulfilling her destiny. But that was the symbolism: Their rising Aryan star with an American Jew. Why else would anybody want to bump me off?

I never brought that car to America. To me it had been violated, and it represented a tiny echo of those atrocities of the Holocaust. It was attempted murder. I tried to recall the faces I'd seen, which had seemed friendly—but you can't tell by faces. I didn't stay more than two days after that. I didn't confront anybody on the set. I didn't do anything. I just left.

*   *   *

Forty Pounds of Trouble, which Norman Jewison directed, was a remake of the old Damon Runyon story "Little Miss Marker," which had already been made into a movie twice.* It didn't affect my career much one way or the other, but it produced one great letter that I kept and had framed. It was actually sent to Milton Rackmil, the president of Universal, who passed it along to me. It was from Robert D. McCay, managing director of the National Association of Underwear and Allied Products in New York, dated April 1, 1963:

> I am writing . . . regarding the failure of Tony Curtis to wear an undershirt in a number of scenes in [*Forty Pounds of Trouble*]. I think you will agree that it is the consensus of opinion among civilized people that the wearing of clothing not only serves to set mankind apart from the beasts of the fields, but also promotes comfort, cleanliness and health.
>
> In view of the wide and continuing distribution of your pictures and the force of example exerted by performers such as Mr. Curtis on the young and impressionable, you can readily see that great actual and potential loss could accrue to underwear manufacturers, whose sales suffer as a result.
>
> Underwear manufacturers and their employees in the 24 states in which our member mills are located are also movie-goers. . . . If sales decline through scenes such as mentioned above, no matter how unintentional, then the motion picture industry will lose them as customers and everybody loses. I trust we may count on your cooperation in the future to the mutual benefit of both our industries.

The unpredictable little ripple effects of my movies never ceased to amaze and delight me.

———————————◆———————————

Captain Newman, M.D. (1963) was directed by David Miller, whose recent *Midnight Lace* (1960) and *Lonely Are the Brave* (1962) were highly regarded. It is set in 1944 in the psychiatric unit of an army air-base hospital, where Dr. Gregory Peck is the officer in charge. (Dr. Cary Grant was sought, but was

*In 1934, with Adolphe Menjou and Shirley Temple, and in 1949 as *Sorrowful Jones,* with Bob Hope and Lucille Ball. TC would make yet another version, the fourth, seventeen years later with Walter Matthau.

unavailable for the role.) TC is Corporal Laibowitz, a Jersey City hustler not unlike the one he played in *Operation Petticoat*, from which this film borrows liberally.

His true talent lies in obtaining contraband, but his job is that of orderly in the psych ward, and he has his hands full with the dangerously insane Colonel Eddie Albert. TC has the first of the film's two most powerful scenes: He is dispatched to tackle the knife-wielding Albert in a violent wrestling match in the shower room. The other famous sequence is the psychodramatic freak-out of shell-shocked GI Bobby Darin, which earned the teen-idol singer a Best Supporting Actor nomination.* Nurse Angie Dickinson and Dr. Peck have some classic pre–women's liberation dialogue:

DICKINSON: When this is over, I want to get out and make some babies.
PECK: I imagine you'd be pretty good at that.
DICKINSON: It's the sort of thing I could learn.

—B.P.

Captain Newman, M.D., was kind of an awkward film. The producer was Bob Arthur, a man I didn't particularly care for. He either didn't like me or didn't believe in me. I felt a lot of antagonism from him. One reason, I think, was because Arthur wanted me to play Laibowitz overtly Jewish, like Jackie Mason. I wasn't going to "play Jewish," although I gave it some touches in that direction.

David Miller was a very fine man and an underrated director. In that shower scene, Eddie Albert made no effort to hold back at all. Usually in shots like that, you make it *look* like you're going wild, but you hold something back. Eddie didn't. It has a shocking, desperate quality to it. That struggle was completely real—but he couldn't get out of my hands.

I hated Bobby Darin's performance, though. It was over the top. But everybody carried on about it because he was a rock star and had just started doing pictures. On the set one day, I got a laugh out of Greg Peck when I

---

*Darin (1936–1973) lost that year's Oscar to Melvyn Douglas for *Hud*. He was married to Sandra Dee from 1960 to 1967 and died at age thirty-seven following a heart operation.

congratulated him on finally getting the chance to work with his boyhood idol, Bobby Darin.

After the movie was finished, I got a call from Greg. He was such a nice man, and still is. But he wasn't exactly a comedian, and people came down hard on him about being stiff and kind of wooden in that film. Gregory either didn't know or didn't give a shit what they thought. So he called me up after we finished *Captain Newman, M.D.*, to say how much he'd liked working with me in it, and—in that very serious and sincere way of his— that he thought we'd make a good comedy team again sometime. Fortunately nobody took him up on it.

The big thing around that time was "all-star" movies. Kirk Douglas bought the rights to a mystery called *The List of Adrian Messenger* (1963) and got John Huston to direct. Kirk was the killer, but the gimmick was the guest stars who were suspects—me, Frank Sinatra, Robert Mitchum, Burt Lancaster—all in heavy makeup and special face masks that Bud Westmore designed. After the regular "The End" credit, they ran the film back and unveiled us: Frank was the gypsy, Burt was the old woman who keeps trying to stop the fox hunts, and I was the Italian organ-grinder. The picture went on a little long, and I think people figured out the mystery sooner than they were supposed to, but it was fairly enjoyable. I thought the best line in the script was the one they stole from Oscar Wilde and gave Burt, about fox hunting: "the unspeakable in search of the uneatable."

Paris When It Sizzles (1964), directed by Richard Quine, sets up William Holden as a screenwriter who can't get his story right and keeps trying to reinvent it, with the secretarial and romantic assistance of Audrey Hepburn in acting out his fantasies. Quine was striving for a kind of Cary Grant light comedy, but Holden wasn't up to it, and Hepburn seems embarrassed. Several of the film's precious few funny moments belong to TC as a hip Hollywood heartthrob named Maurice, who breaks into the film-within-a-film twice, when least expected. He's really a spoofed-up version of TC himself—a cool cat in tight red sweater and white pants, tossing off vintage sixties jargon from his motorbike: "Like, *bonjour*, baby! Groovy! But I'm gonna have to split." Noël Coward and Marlene Dietrich had cameos. TC received no billing or credit at all, for reasons he explains below. Just as well, perhaps. George Axelrod had written *The Seven Year Itch* and *Will Success Spoil Rock Hunter?*, but the Muse failed him this time around. The picture couldn't overcome his script or Bill Holden's deficiency at comedy. It was shelved for two years and a fiasco when finally released.

—B.P.

For years after that, when anybody asked how to account for a budget increase, the joke was, "Charge it off to the profits of *Paris When It Sizzles*." The way my part came about in that was curious. I was in London with Christine and I got a call from Dick Quine.* Bill Holden's liver was really in bad shape. He couldn't drink anymore, and when he did, it would knock him out for days. But he'd gone out drinking somewhere in Paris one night, and now he couldn't work for maybe a week. Paramount was ready to close the production down anyway, because it was over budget and over schedule. They heard about Holden and told Quine, "You don't shoot, we shut down."

So Dick called me and said, "Tony, please come and do three or four days for us. They said they'll let us run if you'll do that." I said okay and flew to Paris, and they put us up at the George Cinq and gave us some cash. Axelrod and Quine frantically wrote a couple of new scenes for me, and while Bill Holden was out sick, I worked with Audrey at the studio. I did about five or six days, and then finally Bill came back to work. I did it because they needed to fill that time. They had to come up with something, and what they came up with was me. At the end, they wrote me a note: "To Whom It May Concern: Let it be known that Tony Curtis has our talents for a screenplay and a director, and any help he needs to put together a movie in the future." I still have that letter, signed by Dick Quine and George Axelrod. Naturally it never got redeemed.

*Richard Quine (1920–1989) was a child prodigy actor-singer-dancer who made his screen debut at age twelve and appeared in many films with the great juvenile stars of the thirties and forties before becoming a director in adulthood. Among his hits were *My Sister Eileen* (1955) and *Bell, Book and Candle* (1958). In 1943 he married actress Susan Peters, who was shot and paralyzed in a hunting accident a year later. She wrote a magazine column and did some stage work and one film in a wheelchair after that. They divorced in 1948 and she died in 1952. Quine took his own life on June 10, 1989.

Portrait of the director as a young man: Richard Quine and Jackie Cooper in *Dinky* (1935)

We went back to London, and I met Noël Coward there briefly. There wasn't much to talk about in terms of *Paris When It Sizzles*. He was in his middle sixties then, his career wasn't going too well, and he wasn't ready, willing, or able to fall back on television. He seemed distracted, and then he drifted away.

My third daughter was born on July 19, 1964. We called her Alexandra Theodora Dido Curtis—a great name. Christine was going to stay home, but then she changed her mind and decided to take the leading-lady part opposite me in *Wild and Wonderful* (1964). Universal should have kept the original title, which was *Monsieur Cognac*—the name of the horny French poodle that liked to get drunk. From that I had to go straight into *Goodbye Charlie* (1964), which was another George Axelrod story. It was about a guy who gets murdered and then reincarnated as Debbie Reynolds. Bizarre story, although there have been a number of pictures with the same idea just recently. Vincente Minnelli directed it, but it's unlike any of his other films.

Except for Stanley Kubrick, I think Minnelli was the most demanding director I ever worked with. He was obsessed with details, tiny little details. Everything had to match. He was always fidgeting with the set. He always wanted everything to look very real and rich. All his pictures had that opulent look to them. He was a really fine man, liked me very much, and we had a wonderful relationship. But he and Ellen Burstyn, who was then working under the name Ellen McRae, kicked the shit out of each other in that movie. They hated each other, for some reason. I couldn't quite understand it. On the other hand, he and Debbie Reynolds got along fine, even though he was always fussing at Debbie to do things a little differently. One day Debbie came on the set and said, "Good morning, everybody." Then she looked over and said, "How was that for you, Vincent?"

That was the end of Axelrod scripts for a while, but I was back right away with Dick Quine. People thought later that Dick borrowed his style from Blake Edwards, because they were best friends and there was a certain similarity in their styles. But Quine directed first. He had a zany sense of humor, even when it didn't always work.

In those "Anthony's Almanacs" I used to send out to my friends, I wrote a play called *Dr. Quinelove, or, How to Stop Worrying and Forget About Acting*, by Anthony I.A.L. Curtis. It was around the time of *Dr. Strangelove*, of course. Some of it goes:

"Richard Quine is a man who has conquered two mediums—and we

216

don't mean those two old gypsy fortune-tellers who bought drinks for him at Le Bistro. . . .

"Time: Pesach of 1964. Place: Living room of a Benedict Canyon house. A sickening overabundance of modern art (all copies) hangs sloppily around the room. . . . Front doorbell rings. Quine rises, walks S.R., throws open the door, and gazes in admiration at a vision of masculine splendor— a man so handsome it is almost painful (at least for Quine). He has a cape and a black and white check poplin topcoat that disappears at his narrow waistline. His white cashmere scarf floats rakishly about. His hair, the purest raven black, is full and healthy. His eyes, Paddock Pool Blue, are bright, alert, sparkling, and radiate a keen intellect, tempered with human under-standing. He is, of course, Tony Curtis. (Note: Director should find some business for Quine to do so that audience has a few moments to drink in the magnificence of the man who has just entered.)"

It went on in that vein.

Anyway, the big rage then was Helen Gurley Brown's book *Sex and the Single Girl,* which sold more than three million copies. Warners paid something like $200,000 for the film rights, and Dick Quine was dying to direct it.

Direct *what?* There wasn't really a story in it. Everybody just knew the title itself would be a big draw, even if the movie had absolutely nothing to do with the book. They looked around, and this was right after the book *Catch-22,* so they got Joseph Heller to cowrite the script. They figured if anybody could do something with it, Joe could. I met him and liked him; a fine man and a brilliant writer. Such a strange concept, though, to take that title and that real-life woman Helen Gurley Brown and turn it into a script that didn't have anything to do with the book—or with anything else.

Sex and the Single Girl (1964), directed by Richard Quine, stars TC as the editor of *Stop,* which proudly claims to be the world's sleaziest magazine. They've just done a nasty job on Natalie Wood in which the worst allegation—for her reputation as sexologist Brown—is that she's "a twenty-three-year-old virgin." TC now vows to prove or disprove that charge for an even more sensa-tional follow-up. Henry Fonda and Lauren Bacall are the unlikely comic support as TC's bickersome neighbors, whose marital prob-lems he uses in order to get himself onto Natalie's couch.

Posing as Fonda, TC confesses to being "inadequate"—recycling the *Some Like It Hot* device whereby a feminine object of pursuit must help him gain sexual confidence. The TC-Wood make-out scenes really *are* hot, especially after the third or fourth martini he pours into her. She is quite convincingly and realistically drunk. (Was she really? TC replies: "No. We never did that in movies. Maybe Marilyn did, but nobody else. You can't get drunk and then work on a scene. Movie drunk has got nothing to do with reality drunk.")

The in-jokes fly fast and thick. After they fall off a dock and return to Wood's apartment to dry off, TC emerges from her bathroom in a woman's robe: "I'm thinking I look like Jack Lemmon in that movie where he dresses up like a girl."

The good chemistry between them is undisturbed by the script's astoundingly sexist dialogue ("I gotta find a way to get to that broad!"), which puts the lie to the "liberated" cachet of Brown's book. In the end Wood confesses, "I don't want to be a single girl," and happily gives up her practice to become TC's wife.

Fonda and Bacall, among other uncomfortable things, are required to do the Twist (to the music of Count Basie). But Bacall's deadpan-dry delivery gets funnier, even as the slapstick gets sillier, complete with car-chase highway hijinx. Despite—or because of—all that, audiences flocked to *Sex and the Single Girl*, which was naughty and topical enough to be the number-fifteen top-grossing film (four million dollars) of the year.

—B.P.

On *Sex and the Single Girl*, I had a lucrative financial deal plus an ownership. Joe Schoenfeld, Natalie's agent, came to me and said, "Why don't you give Natalie a piece of the action? She's only making $65,000." I said, "Joe, I can't do that. It's not up to me. Talk to my agent." Of course he didn't, because he knew what the answer would be from Swifty Lazar.

Everything in those days related to the power and personality of the agents. Each of them had his own vibration. There was one famous agent, Louie Shur, who always kept five or six fur coats in his closet. He'd be going

TC seeking sexual therapy from Natalie Wood as Helen Gurley Brown in *Sex and the Single Girl* (1964)

with a girl and he'd tell her to take her pick of those fur coats, until the relationship was over, and then he'd take it back.

In my case, Lew Wasserman was great—the greatest. I trusted him and every piece of advice he ever gave me implicitly. A couple of years earlier, in 1961, I signed a contract to do a movie called *Lady L* for MGM. I was to get $500,000 plus a percentage. Julian Blaustein was going to produce and George Cukor was going to direct. Cukor wanted Sophia Loren, but the studio wanted Gina Lollobrigida. They signed Gina. The script, by Robert Anderson, was very amusing. Blaustein liked it, but Cukor didn't. So Cukor rewrote it, and Blaustein started to rewrite it another way, and pretty soon they had two different scripts. Besides which, Cukor still wanted Sophia Loren and was pissed off about Gina Lollobrigida.

The start date arrived. I went to Lew Wasserman and said, "Lew, the picture is supposed to start on Monday, but they still haven't called me." Lew said, "Show up on Monday." So I showed up that Monday. And every Monday. There were no sets, nothing. Sol Siegel was running MGM then, and I went into his office the fourth week and said, "Listen, can't we get this picture started?" He said, "What the fuck are you worried about? You're getting paid." With that, I took the pitcher of water that was on the desk and turned it upside down.

So I got paid $50,000 a week for ten weeks and never made the movie. I was prevented by contract from working anywhere else. But thanks to Lew Wasserman, those paychecks kept coming in, and I kept cashing them.* After Lew went to MCA, I was represented by Irving "Swifty" Lazar. Swifty was legendary, and still is. He was given the nickname by Humphrey Bogart, who was impressed by the way he outsmarted his competitors and always beat them to the punch. In his earliest days as an agent, he wasn't even booking bands, he was booking *trios,* and booking them into Mafia clubs: "If they didn't do business, not only would you not get paid, you'd get hit on the head the next day," he used to say. I kept a record of Swifty's sayings. He once told me a good agent should work fourteen hours a day: "If you call his home at eight P.M., and he answers the phone, fire him. He's not putting in enough time for you." Another time he said, "Since I'm rich, it's my ambition to die poor." He always had a consummate belief in his own abilities. He used to say, "Anyone with talent who isn't with me is either a victim of circumstance, prejudice, poor judgment, or is shorter than I am." Swifty stands five feet two inches.

He was an authority on everything, but especially on the subject of why there were so many Jews in the movie business. "No other business would have us," he said. "When I was a kid there were very few companies you could get connected with. I finished law school in Chicago and tried to get work with a nice private firm, but they wouldn't take a Jew. Then I wanted to be attorney general and I went to Washington, but I knew I was doomed the first week. I went from one agency to another. As soon as they saw the name Irving Lazar, they pointed me down the hall to nowhere. But the picture business was different. The goyim didn't fight over the picture business, because it wasn't altogether reputable and there was no way of telling exactly what kind of business it would turn out to be."

Swifty always dressed immaculately, which—if you didn't know him—helped conceal the fact that he was the smartest, toughest motherfucker this side of the Pecos. He knew where all the bodies were buried in Hollywood and New York, and who was buried with them. No one was smarter

---

Lady L was finally shelved by MGM after eight months. Four years later, in 1965, it was produced by Carlo Ponti, rewritten and directed by Peter Ustinov. Paul Newman and Sophia Loren starred, with David Niven in support, but not even that powerhouse combination could save it from box-office disaster.

or tougher than Swifty, and no one could tell a joke better, especially a Jewish joke.

"Okay," he'd say, "these two old chairs were rocking in their Jews. One says to the other, 'Where you from?' The other one says, 'Philadelphia.'

" 'How many Jews in Philadelphia?'

" 'Oh, maybe three hundred thousand.'

" 'Is that so? And how many goyim?'

" 'Oh, maybe two million. And you. Where are you from?'

" 'New York.'

" 'A lot of Jews in New York?'

" 'Oh, maybe two million.'

" 'No kidding? And how many goyim?'

" 'About six million.'

" 'Really?' says the other guy. 'You need so many?' "

Swifty was an important player in those days, and I signed with him. He was the one who put together the deal for *The Great Race,* and he changed that deal completely. He got me and everybody else a raise because Jack Warner said he wouldn't make the picture without me. R.J. Wagner and three or four other guys were being considered for my part, but Jack Warner wasn't about to give it to R.J. or John Derek or anybody else. They were just garbage names to him. He wanted TC. So Swifty not only worked out that contract, he also got me more money. And as soon as he did that, he said, "You can't give Tony that raise and not give Jack and Natalie more, too."

Blake Edwards was directing, and early in production he walked off because he didn't like the way Jack Warner was treating him. Warner said, "Fine, I'll close down the movie for now until I find another director." Blake was back on the set the next day, ready to work. But *The Great Race* went on and on and on, way over budget. Warner was constantly on the verge of pulling that picture because it got so exorbitant. It started out at $3 million and ended up at about four times that. Nobody seemed to be able to do anything about it. It just kept rumbling along under its own power. We shot in Salzburg, in Paris, at Versailles—huge cast, finest accommodations everywhere. There was one pool table for the stars and a separate pool table for the feature players. There were tents with mini-casinos in them. Between shots, everybody was gambling. I don't ever remember another movie like that. It was a miniature Vegas.

The Great Race (1965), TC's last film under Blake Edwards's direction, was a twelve-million-dollar mammoth comedy in an era when those now-extinct animals—*It's a Mad, Mad, Mad, Mad World* (1963), *Those Magnificent Men in Their Flying Machines* (1965)—were still extant. It is full of copycat zaniness and painfully heavy-handed slapstick, beginning with a hot-air balloon that lands on the cardboard villains, played by Peter Falk and Jack Lemmon.

TC is "The Great Leslie," a race driver so heroic that his front tooth gleams on cue, with a little help from Danny Lee's special effects. Natalie Wood is the aspiring "first woman reporter" whom Leslie tries to seduce. She sports a smart new outfit every five minutes, even when stranded on an iceberg, and later spends a great deal of time in her teddy underwear. But every charming scene between Wood and TC is followed by more uncharming slapstick.

Relations among the costars were strained: "Natalie is too career minded," said TC then. "There was a time when she was warm and friendly. Today she seems more wrapped up in herself." When Edwards was asked if he planned a wrap party, he replied, "Sure. It'll be quite an occasion. Natalie and Tony are going to set each other on fire." A billing dispute between TC and Lemmon was resolved only when Warners agreed to make two sets of credits and to alternate their names in all its publicity releases.

TC does some classy bare-chested fencing (with foils as well as sabers) and manages to avoid getting his pristine white suit soiled during the grand-finale pie fight. But the end result was a dull, 163-minute marathon instead of a great race. The year was 1965; the Vietnam War was shifting into high gear. Film, television, and the whole world were changing. Where was Blake Edwards's head?

—B.P.

That picture is clumsy. It's not well balanced or funny. It doesn't stand up today because there was absolutely no sense of reality. But that's the way they wanted it. Blake never tried to tone down Jack's performance. Jack was tighter with Blake than I was. Jack was my buddy, certainly, and Blake was too, in a way. But I knew fucking well he wanted some other guy who would have been less threatening to him. My character needed a solid, pure kind of line. I could have played it at another tempo, but I didn't want to.

If *The Great Race* had been made at its original price, it would have been a huge success. But they were only doing two shots a day—one in the morning, one in the afternoon—and the costs kept escalating. It did well commercially, but the fortune they spent on it was unprecedented, and there was no way any company could make that back.

Jerry Lewis always wore white socks with dark suits. And no underwear. When I was doing *Boeing-Boeing* with him, if the camera was just on me, he would drop cigarette ashes on my jacket in the middle of a scene, or reach down and quietly unzip my fly. He did everything he could to help me concentrate: step on my feet, mug at me during a serious take. I enjoyed every minute of it. There I was, working with Jerry Lewis, the greatest comedian of our time—and I ate him up alive. It was wonderful, and I thought it was a charming movie.

Boeing-Boeing (1965) was directed by John Rich, a *Dick Van Dyke Show* director who made less than half a dozen films before returning to TV and winning two successive Emmys for *All in the Family*. The much-ballyhooed novelty of *Boeing-Boeing* was that comedian Jerry Lewis was playing a straight part for the first time. Paramount arbitrated the billing problem between Lewis and TC with a variation on Warner Bros.'s *Great Race* remedy: Their two names got equal *circular* billing, rotating around an airplane propeller at the outset.

The surprise of the screenplay lay not in the story itself—a farcical yarn in which TC tries to juggle his romances with three different stewardesses—but in the fact that it was written by Edward Anhalt. Anhalt, a decidedly serious writer, had won a joint Academy Award with his wife, Edna, for *Panic in the Streets* (1950) and, the year before *Boeing-Boeing*, a solo Oscar for his screenplay of *Becket* (1964). Among his other important film scripts were *The Member of the Wedding* (1953), *The Young Lions* (1958), and, later, TC's *The Boston Strangler* (1968).

Boeing-Boeing is sexist to the point of misogyny: TC is violently jealous of all three girls. "They all have the idea of getting married, right?" Lewis asks. "Of course," replies TC. "How else do you think polygamy works?" That philosophy provides fine fodder for TC's grumpy housekeeper, Thelma Ritter. Her job is to keep his girlfriends from finding out about one another, but she winds up an accomplice to everything and nearly stealing the picture.

It is a classic mid-sixties sex farce, complete with the multiple red doors and sight gags of a Georges Feydeau play. Jerry Lewis is restrained indeed, except for certain trademark mannerisms and schtick leading up to the weak ending. Not until his brilliant performance seventeen years later in *King of Comedy* (1982) would he take on another straight role. *The London Times* called Lewis and TC "gods of dissimilar races" and said they made "an astonishingly effective comedy team."

—B.P.

In 1966 I sold my Bel Air house and bought oilman Bill Keck's villa in Holmby Hills. It was a beautiful Mediterranean-style place on four acres, with eighteen rooms and an Olympic-size indoor pool inlaid with Byzantine tile. It had a six-car garage for my 1934 Rolls-Royce, 1937 Bentley, 1935 Duesenberg, 1965 Excalibur SS, and new 1966 Lincoln Continental. Outside in the drive area were a Mustang and several other Fords. Surprising, in view of the fact that Christine didn't drive.

Our daughter Allegra was born in Los Angeles on July 12, 1966. She was a beautiful little girl who became even more extraordinarily beautiful later. But her mother and I weren't getting along, for complicated reasons, and we got divorced about a year later.

These days Christine and I are not in touch at all. It's hard for me to be in touch with my ex-wives, especially unfaithful ones. With some of my ex-girlfriends, I can—but the wives, almost impossible. Janet is the only one, because time has eased those pains. I don't even know where Christine lives these days. She was into designing and inventing. There was never a film career for her in the United States, although she did work for a while in Germany on a few other films.

TC and Jerry Lewis overwhelmed by blondes in *Boeing-Boeing* (1965)

I have six children, and at one period all of them were under eighteen and needed child-support payments at the same time. That was over $6,000 a month—a lot back then—and I had to just grind out movies, taking anything I could to maintain them.

I never missed a payment.

———◆———

Arrivederci, Baby! (1966), written and directed by Ken Hughes, was a very black comedy starring TC as a professional ladykiller along several lines. In England, where much of it was filmed, the picture was called *Drop Dead, Darling*. At its opening, we find TC in bed with Nancy Kwan, but soon he's transported to a childhood flashback in the orphanage where he grew up. Wearing short pants and his hair combed down over his forehead, a very precocious TC and the other boys are being inspected, like used cars, by prospective parents. Anna Quayle takes him home to her bosom in more ways than one. She is a dedicated harpist, the adopted TC is her captive audience, and one night it occurs to him to help her really join the angels by electrocuting her as she plays.

So much for the long and diabolically funny flashback. Back to the future, TC has his eye on the beautiful young Italian widow Rosanna Schiaffino, who sleeps

TC and the corpse share a macabre moment in *Arrivederci, Baby* (1966)

with him without even knowing it. But his other eye—the financial one—is on Zsa Zsa Gabor, whom he marries, and whose diamonds he examines and appraises even while they're making love. Zsa Zsa is a nonstop talker and, even if she weren't rich, would have to go. While dedicating a new space capsule, she gets locked in the satellite and conveniently launched into orbit.

Our modern-day Bluebeard gets increasingly adept at his craft and eventually adds Rosanna Schiaffino to his long list of brides. But she turns out to be playing the same game, and the movie degenerates along with their murderous marital relationship.

The first scene in *Arrivederci, Baby!* contained the last film appearance of beloved character actor Mischa Auer (1905–1967), playing an ancient groom who has a heart attack trying to get his clothes off in a hurry to hop atop sexy bride Schiaffino. "He was quite infirm by that time, thin and emaciated," TC recalls, "but what a wonderful actor."

—B.P.

226

I played another soldier-hustler type in *Not with My Wife You Don't* (1966). Norman Panama directed it more or less like the Bob Hope–Bing Crosby "road" movies he used to write. The oddest thing about that picture was casting George C. Scott in it. George is very intense. He never pretended to be a comedian. This was one of his rare comedies, and I was constantly on his case. I didn't give him a chance to breathe. I always made sure my lines were on top of his. As soon as I got an idea what he was saying or asking me in a line, I'd answer without waiting until the end. That way we created an overlap, and he had no choice but to keep up with me. He didn't have an opportunity to psych me out in long pauses, the way he did so well in dramas. The tempo had to be kept up. George is a charming man. He wanted to direct a movie with me. I said, "Well, let's find one," but as so often happens, we never did.

Those mid-sixties comedies were getting more and more offbeat. You never knew what kind of script was coming next or how it was going to be

TC, Virna Lisi, and George C. Scott in *Not with My Wife You Don't!* (1966)

directed, let alone how it was going to be accepted. The formulas were changing. I got interested in *Don't Make Waves* (1967) because the book, *Muscle Beach*, was funny and because Alexander Mackendrick was the director. We hadn't worked together since *Sweet Smell of Success*. He'd done an excellent job for me and everyone else in that.

Erich von Stroheim, Jr., was the assistant director on *Don't Make Waves*. He and Mackendrick hated each other. I think what Erich junior didn't appreciate was the similarity between Mackendrick and his father. They both ran a very tight film company. No talking, no nothing on the set. I remember thinking Erich junior must have been like his old man—so adamant and unyielding. He died a year or so later from a massive heart attack. I think that experience with Erich junior was one of the things that soured Mackendrick on the business. He is still alive and I hope well, but *Don't Make Waves* was the last movie he ever made.

I was a college professor in that film and Claudia Cardinale was the love interest, but a lot of attention went to the second female lead, a surfer girl named "Malibu," who accidentally knocks me out with her surfboard: Sharon Tate. I've thought a lot about Sharon in the years since then, and about what happened to her. Was it the times? Certainly Charles Manson was an evil creation of the times. Her tragedy seemed a harbinger of other tragedies to come.

Sharon was such a beautiful young woman. Though there was a feeling between us, she and I didn't get involved. She was married to Roman Polanski, and I was going through another marriage breakup at the time, and she sensed that. She reached out to me, but she was not a verbal person and neither was I. She and Roman had been married only a little while when she was murdered.

I think it's important to emphasize that she and Roman were not particularly into any drugs at all. There were no drugs, no orgies, nothing awful. She and her friends just happened to be in Manson's way. It could have been me and my friends or anybody else in Hollywood. I was at a dinner party with Joyce Haber, the gossip columnist, just a few nights after the murder, and in front of a dozen people at the table she said something to the effect that they deserved it. Haber and those other gossip columnists were particularly nasty about the Sharon Tate story. They took it upon themselves to suggest that drugs were the reason for the murder, which may have been true for the murderers, but certainly not for Sharon.

For some reason, this was my period of Italian leading ladies. After Virna Lisi and Rosanna Schiaffino and Claudia Cardinale came Monica Vitti.

Sharon Tate checking on TC's medical and sexual condition in *Don't Make Waves* (1967)

The movie was *The Chastity Belt*, and the director had big problems, one of which was that you could never shoot Monica any way except front face. She had a big nose and would never turn in profile. She was also very difficult to get along with. She started having an affair with the cameraman, and they almost kicked her off the picture, but I said, "No, let her stay." The way she rewarded me was, when the picture was over, she said, "I'm going to have to get top billing in Italy." I said, "Are you kidding?" In those days I had top billing all over the world, *everywhere,* but she insisted that in Italy it say "Tony Curtis and Monica Vitti (in alphabetical order)"!*

*   *   *

*The Chastity Belt (1967), directed by Pasquale Festa Campanile, did not have the smoothest distribution history. Because of its bawdy title and story (an eleventh-century knight attempting to seduce a gamekeeper's locked-up daughter), it got an *X* rating in England. Overlong at 110 minutes, it was chopped to 73. Among the unfortunate title substitutes used here and abroad was *A Funny Thing Happened on the Way to the Crusades.*

Those were tough years in my life, from the standpoint of my family. I couldn't handle the pressures from my mother and father, much as I loved them—especially my father. I was always being pressured to do things for them, and especially for my little brother Bobby. Nicky Blair helped me out with him a lot. He lived just five or six blocks away, and he performed many services for them that I couldn't. Bobby loved him, and Nicky even took him in for a couple of months; gave him a hi-fi and his own room. He would just stay in that room with his music all the time until Nicky would say, "Bobby, we're going to go see your mother or Tony today."

Somewhere along the line Bobby became my responsibility. Ultimately I refused to accept that responsibility. I was not my brother's keeper. But I tried to be for years, until finally I just couldn't maintain that role anymore. Bobby's doctors had given us a revised estimate of his condition. It wasn't good. On February 14, 1967, I wrote a letter to my mother to try to make her understand, and kept a copy of it:

> I don't know if you made any sense out of that report, but rest assured there has been a very important change in Bobby's behavior pattern at this point. I can't impress upon you how very important it is at this particular time, Mother Dear, to stay away from Bobby. I know it's difficult for you and I know there's no one around for companionship for you, but see if you can do something so you're not constantly thinking of him. I'm thrilled at the thought of maybe salvaging this boy's life and perhaps giving him a new lease on life. I don't want you to do anything now to jeopardize it. It's really at the crossroads, so please, please, please, Mother, right now you can save this boy's life or destroy it, and believe me, destroying Bobby is destroying whatever love I could have for you, so think twice. Try to hold on, only five or six weeks.

She didn't follow my advice. She wouldn't stay away from him, and that made things worse. Finally it got so bad that Bobby had to be institutionalized. Janet had done a lot of work for an organization called Share that supposedly looked after emotionally disturbed children. I went to them once, asking their help. I got nothing from them. Nobody on their staff wanted to be bothered with Bobby's case. So finally I went to the state of California, because there was no way I could maintain him. It was $300 to $400 a day. And the state became Robert's guardian.

230

I'd visit him in these different insane asylums, in Camarillo, and two or three other places, like the Devereux Foundation for young people who were emotionally unstable, in Santa Barbara. It was very difficult for me to do that. I'd find myself inside the walls of places full of such unreal sights and sounds. Bobby would say to me, "Are you really my brother? Do you have a mother? Where's mine?" Sometimes he'd tell me guys were trying to murder him in there. Maybe there were. There were moments of clarity, but then they would disappear. That environment came close to driving me crazy, too. At one point I remember visiting him and half-expecting them to say, "Hi, Tony—this is *your* room." I just couldn't expose myself to it anymore, and so I stopped seeing him, because it wasn't doing either of us any good. I have no guilt about it. Yet I still grieve, and I always will, that Bobby's life ended so clumsily, thinking about his lost mother.*

*Robert Schwartz died in California on August 22, 1992, at the age of fifty-two.

CHAPTER ELEVEN

THE LOWER DEPTHS

The total gross of my movies up to then, I figured, was about sixty million dollars. Not bad for a street kid out of New York. But I wasn't happy with the recent pictures. My career was losing momentum. I needed a new challenge. I needed a new kind of movie. *The Boston Strangler* was it.

In December 1967 I heard that Robert Fryer, the producer, was looking everywhere for the man to play the title character. Dozens and dozens of guys were tested—big names, little names, no names. I wanted that part badly, and the director, Dick Fleischer, wanted me too. But Dick Zanuck at Twentieth Century-Fox didn't think I could play it. He thought I was too recognizable.

So one day I took some putty and built myself a big nose. I changed my eyelashes, eyebrows, and hair. I had this Leica 35mm camera, and I took pictures of myself—profiles and front views—and had two dozen eight-by-tens printed up on grainy paper. I gave them to Dick Fleischer, who went into Zanuck's office, threw them on the table, and said, "Here's your strangler." Zanuck said, "Yeah, that guy could be him. I like that look—who is it?" Fleischer said, "Tony!" And that's how I got the part.

When production started in January, they pretty much adopted that look I created for the picture. They changed the shape of my nose, permed and dyed my hair, and added forty pounds of weight to my waist. I wore black army boots two sizes too big. But it wasn't until they put black contact lenses over my blue eyes that Albert DeSalvo, the strangler, came to life. It was the most eerie experience I've ever had. Looking into the mirror, I wasn't there anymore. I was nowhere in sight. Instead that brooding, suspicious, uneasy image of a man was looking back at me. I couldn't wait until the end of the day, when I could take off all that makeup and see that adorable blue-eyed kid again.

In *The Boston Strangler*, you see slivers of a lot of different people. It's a two-hour movie, but for the first forty-five minutes, you don't meet Albert DeSalvo. I didn't even come in until the middle. But when you see him the first time, you're stunned just by his *look* and the intensity. Someone else might have played it another way, but I know I brought a certain intensity to the character that wasn't there in the script.

I'd spent a fortune on shrinks, hypnotists, etc., which helped me in this role. Things occurred to me that weren't explicit in the material. There wasn't a lot of dialogue, just the basics to get you from one moment to the other. Fleischer would say, "Tony, in this scene I'd like to get the feeling of what it must have been like for Albert to be knocking at that woman's door and fantasizing what he's going to do to her."

I had to find a level of playing it that was very introverted and cerebral, inside my head. That performance is very interior. That pantomime scene at the end, when I come into a room and talk to an invisible woman—that was all improvised. I decided to go for the texture of it: I felt her neck and put her down on the ground and imagined ejaculating as I strangled her, rubbing my dick between her tits, seeing her beneath me. Those sick images were in my brain. All that stuff at the end, all that anguish on his face, came from a disorientation about who he was. His wife wouldn't fuck him. She was a fundamentalist. His daughter was clubfooted, and his wife was sure that was because of the bestiality of the sex act. So she shut him out and drove him into the streets, and he got so horny he'd kill anybody, and he did: old, young, black, white, no difference. That's why there was no modus operandi. I tried to find an interior level of playing it like that.

Dick Fleischer made a lot of good decisions in that movie. You'll notice that *The Boston Strangler* contains no music. And casting Henry Fonda as the detective was interesting. I'd made *Sex and the Single Girl* with Hank, but obviously this was a very different experience. He was in that league with Jimmy Stewart, Errol Flynn, Cary Grant, John Wayne, Tyrone Power—but for some reason I didn't find him as appealing as those other guys, who were my idols. He was a good actor but a very aloof person. He didn't give much of himself. It was like he felt he was too good for this profession, that acting was beneath him. During the making of *Strangler*, he and I never got together personally or socially. Never really connected. Maybe that was just as well, considering the two characters we were playing.

After the first preview, Dick Fleischer sent me a three-word cable: "I am vindicated."

Richard Fleischer's direction and Edward Anhalt's script of *The Boston Strangler*, based on Gerold Frank's best-selling novel, were brilliant. The split-screen technique—simultaneously showing women's faces, hands bolting doors, the psychopath walking down corridors—came at precisely the same time *The Thomas Crown Affair* popularized that device. Richard Kline's hand-held camera further heightened the tension by shooting at oddly high and low angles throughout.

TC in the searing title role of *The Boston Strangler* (1968)

In the film's eerie first scene, TC watches the JFK funeral on TV. Soon after he ties Sally Kellerman to her bed with intent to kill, but is thwarted at the last moment and, after a chase, apprehended. During his interrogation by Fonda, a series of close-ups and quick cuts to his injured hand reveal that DeSalvo—or some schizophrenic part of him—is lying. Tears run down his cheeks, and an amazingly long pause is followed by the killer's slow, agonizing look of self-recognition.*

* Albert DeSalvo was stabbed to death in his Walpole, Massachusetts, prison cell on November 26, 1973.

234

Variety called it a "triumph of taste and restraint." *The Boston Strangler* stands as TC's finest hour as a dramatic actor, and by far the best performance by any actor that year. But 1968 was a year of great social and political violence, which made the Motion Picture Academy more nervous than ever. Tony Curtis and *The Boston Strangler* were too hot to handle, or even nominate. The Oscar went to Cliff Robertson for a maudlin, forgettable performance in *Charly*.

—B.P.

———————◆•◆———————

Christine got her divorce in Juárez, Mexico, on April 16, 1968, and got custody of our two girls. Four days later I married Leslie Allen at two in the morning at the Sahara Hotel in Las Vegas. She was a model from Newton, Massachusetts. She was twenty-three. I met her in New York, and when she came to visit me on the *Strangler* set, we fell in love.

There's no explaining things like that. Around that same time, Roman Polanski was doing *Rosemary's Baby* (1968). One day he called me up and said, "Tony, I need somebody to play the actor on the telephone who loses the job because John Cassavetes casts a spell and takes the job away from him. I want to sneak you into the studio, and I'll put you on the phone with Mia Farrow." So that's what we did. Not until it was over did Mia Farrow realize it was me. I didn't get billing. That's the way he wanted to do it. Ever since then, whenever I see Mia, we recall that. She's very nice, but I always thought she was fucking nuts to be with Woody Allen. What a pair. And then I'd think, *Mia and Woody were a strange pair? What about me and Leslie?*

A couple months later I was making *Those Daring Young Men in Their Jaunty Jalopies* (1969), titled *Monte Carlo or Bust* in Europe. Director Ken Annakin had made *Those Magnificent Men in Their Flying Machines* (1965). He was trying to repeat the formula, which was okay with me. I always tried to do my best. Whatever the director wanted, I gave him.

Susan Hampshire was the leading lady. We had a car-crash scene together, and during the rehearsals the brakes didn't work. I kept complaining about it, and they said, "Don't worry, we'll fix it." So during the take, we were coming down a hill, I put the brakes on, and they didn't work. We were headed for a stanchion that was holding one of those big arc lights. If I hit that, it could hit Susan and me, so I veered the car over, leaped out, and went up to Annakin. I was really pissed. He said, "It's probably gremlins—there are always gremlins somewhere." I said, "Fuck you and your gremlins! We could've been killed!" He, John Berry on the *Bad News Bears* sequel I made later, and a lot of other directors, in my opinion, were unconscious about the safety of men, women, or children. They just wanted to get that shot, and they didn't care what happened. That's what it was all about.

It was also about working on a regular basis, which was why TC took the role of yet another soldier–scam artist in *Suppose They Gave a War and Nobody Came* (1969), directed by Hy Averback. TC has the bawdy opening scene in bed between two whores. Seems he's been sent to the army base in this podunk, racist town to improve civilian-soldier relationships. But he's too hypersexed for the job, especially after getting a look at Suzanne Pleshette, who speaks bluntly: "You're stupid, pushy, and obnoxious," she tells him, "but you *are* personable. Even so, I don't like being pushed by middle-aged, paunchy garrison soldiers who think they're Warren Beatty."

Ernest Borgnine as redneck Sheriff "Fat Harve" has some fine confrontations with warrant officer Brian Keith on the subject of community relations. The broader aspects of the comedy fall flat, but the script is alternately daring and philosophical for stretches at a time. When the local minister asks TC to "Give us some insight into what the enlisted men need," he replies, "Broads. They need broads," without missing a beat.

There is a disastrous, hilarious square dance given by the army for the locals, followed by the obligatory chase-scene climax in which thirty-two cars, dozens of jeeps and motorcycles, several helicopters, and two tanks are wrecked. *Suppose They Gave a War* was pure Vietnam-era ambivalence—somewhere between comedy and drama, cynical and amoral, more or less offensive to everyone. But TC was convincing in it and got the credit he deserved.

—B.P.

236

I was supposed to play the lead in *The Night They Raided Minsky's* (1968), but after the rewrites, I decided I didn't like it, and Elliot Gould did it instead. By then I was sick of Hollywood and happy to go to Europe and get out of the United States for a while. The big studio system was on its ass. I came back a few months later and did a nightclub act in Vegas at Caesar's Palace. The only funny line in it was one I wrote about a trained pig who could play the xylophone and count how many fingers you held up and do all sorts of other amazing things. "And if you don't like the act," I said, "you can eat it."

But nightclubs weren't really my field. A movie actor has to make movies, and that's what I kept on doing. *You Can't Win 'Em All* (1970) was an adventure story about the Turkish civil war. It didn't have anything going for it except me and Charles Bronson, who was the most entertaining yet introverted man I ever met, very quiet and unassuming. I learned a lot from Charlie about how to stay in shape. He never lifted a weight. He had one of those thick rubber things that you hook to a car to keep the luggage from falling off, and he was always pulling on it. That's how he kept himself in shape. He was a fine, quiet, laid-back man who always did his work nicely and with a sensitivity to how you were doing yours.

In April 1970 I went to London to discuss a television show with Sir Lew Grade, who was "Mr. Show Business" in England and who wanted to create a new adventure series called *The Friendly Persuaders* with me and Roger Moore—that funny, fine, handsome man who became one of my best friends—as a pair of wealthy playboys. At Heathrow Airport I was arrested for possessing marijuana and fined $120. The yentas back home all leaped on that, of course. It was very unpleasant. But I decided to do the series. A few months later I went back to England with Leslie to shoot it, and I bought a fine house on Chester Square in London.

Along the way, they dropped the "Friendly" and just called it *The Persuaders*. My character was "Danny Wilde," and he was not unlike myself: born and bred in the Bronx, not taken in by bullshit. It worked well, but to sustain that character in a series, there had to be more development, and they didn't have enough American writers on the job. I was saying things like, "Give me the gat!" No American gangster says that. It became a cartoon, like *Batman*—mythical men chasing mythical spies in mythical countries. But I did twenty-four of those fifty-minute *Persuaders* in color—the equivalent of twelve movies—and they were a huge success in Europe. England, France, Spain, Italy, and Germany all named it Best Telecast. I got a "Bambi" for it and the same in England, and the French Tele 7 Jours best actor award of 1971.

I decided to go to Paris to accept that one personally. They took over the Versailles palace for the ceremony. Jeanne Moreau and a lot of other people were getting awards, but I was getting the most important one and was the star attraction. When I drove up in a big Rolls limousine, the guards stood erect, and all the photographers got in line. These guys in livery opened the door and waltzed me in—and there I was in the entry of Versailles. I looked around and instantly thought of Louis XIV. Everybody was so deferential, it was extraordinary. Suddenly, I knew what Louis XIV must have felt like coming home from a hunt. "Hi, mom, I'm home!" Everybody would back off and, before he even finished the phrase, give him whatever he wanted.

I walked through those corridors and out to the back of the palace, looking at those thousand acres of manicured gardens and flowers and maze hedges. Every hundred feet for as far as the eye could see stood a guy with a French horn. As I stepped out, the horns tooted. I was standing there in the forefront. Everybody was behind me. I looked around at this pageantry and said to the majordomo, "I feel like I'm the king." He looked back at me and said, "You *are* the king."

So for sixty seconds or so, I was Louis XIV. I saw it like he saw it. I was smart enough to notice it. I knew exactly where I was standing.

The Persuaders ran two seasons in England, but just one in the United States, 1971–72. I couldn't care less that it failed in America. It wouldn't have if they had given it a better time slot. It was more tongue-in-cheek and less violent than American audiences were used to. But it still could have been a monster hit, because Roger Moore and I were both powerhouse players then, and the success of it was proved all over Europe. In global terms, six hundred million people saw *The Persuaders*. I owned 25 percent and made over $1.5 million on it.

A couple of years later when I was living with my friend Gordon Butler in New York, he came in one night and said, "Kelly Le Brock wants to meet you." Kelly was an English model and a good friend of Gordon's.* So I met

---

* American television viewers may recall Kelly Le Brock's immortal narcissistic Pantene commercial in which she coos, "Don't hate me because I'm beautiful."

this exquisite young woman. I was crazy about her. Later, she married Steven Seagal. She told me a wonderful story.

"When I was a girl of twelve or thirteen, going to a boarding school," she said, "I had a poster of you from *The Persuaders* on my wall. I loved you. I used to look at you and think of you while I lay in bed. I'd go into the bathroom and come back into my room nude. But I would take some toilet paper and wet it and put it over your eyes so you couldn't see what I was doing."

———— ◆ ————

Jamie Lee Curtis: "Toward the end of *The Persuaders* series, my sister Kelly and I flew over to London to spend the whole summer. She was thirteen, I was eleven. My father said, 'You can either fly first-class or fly coach and keep the difference of the money.' So we took the money. And my fucking seat didn't go back. I remember being real pissed about that.

"He had this beautiful flat in a four-story townhouse in Chester Square, where he was living the life of the English lord. He had his two daughters by Christine and a new wife and a new baby boy [Nicholas, born December 13, 1971]. Kelly and Leslie got on very well. My sister was kind of a hippie, and it was the rage then to wear Viva cosmetics and T-shirts, and they dressed

that way and went shopping a lot. I remember being kind of a tomboy and not feeling much a part of anything.

"Then we went to Sardinia. He had his convertible Bentley or Rolls taken from London to Sardinia so we could drive around in it there, but when we arrived at this beautiful house, the first thing I did was put on

Jamie Lee and Kelly Curtis in 1978

239

my bathing suit and run into the ocean. He and I shared a love of swimming. It was just a great summer. It was the first time we spent much time together, and he really wanted us to live with him after that. My sister did, but I decided not to. So it was also the summer I kind of lost him, when he made that overture and I declined. It split the family again, and I didn't see him for a long time after that. It was a big break, and it was after a really lovely time: six weeks in Sardinia with your dad, swimming in the ocean and loving every minute of it.

"Alexandra and Allegra had come from Germany with nothing. They had craters in their teeth from cavities, they hadn't been well taken care of. The two little girls didn't speak a word of English. I remember sitting on top of the roof in Sardinia with one of them, who taught me, *Ich woll das nicht!* ("I don't want that!") He wouldn't let them go back. He was so appalled at who they were and how they were, that he took custody of them.

"By the time Kelly went to live with him at the end of that summer, his family had grown from one baby boy to four children overnight, including two girls who hardly spoke English and a rebellious teenager. Pretty soon after that, Leslie had another baby. So my father went from having one kid to five in his house. It must have been a startling thing for him."

—JAMIE LEE CURTIS to B.P., October 13, 1992

I went back to California in 1972 and sold my old house because I needed a bigger place for all those kids. Nicholas was tiny, and I took custody of Allegra and Alexandra through a court order. Benjamin was born on May 2, 1973, by Caesarean, at Cedars of Lebanon. I was trying to make a life for us all.

I had signed to star in a David Merrick play called *The One Night Stand*, by Bruce Jay Friedman, which was supposed to open in October 1973. Friedman had written *Scuba Duba*, which was a Broadway hit in the sixties, and nothing else that ever was. I was renting Henry Fonda's place on Seventy-fifth Street and Lexington Avenue, which was appealing to me because Seventy-fifth was the street I used to live on as a boy. I rehearsed that play in the summer, but it was a horrible experience. We took it to Detroit and Philadelphia, but a one-night stand was pretty much exactly what it had.

Lepke was about the leader of Murder Incorporated, one of the first American-Israeli coproductions. There had been a couple others, but this was the first major film. Production started in January 1974, and I researched the part thoroughly. I was intrigued by the fact that the only mobster to go to the electric chair was Jewish. I had something to do with changing the script and the characterization. The original concept was that Lepke was just manipulative and shrewd, but I envisioned him differently, and that's the way I played him: aggressive and angry. This was the guy, after all, who included Legs Diamond and Dutch Schultz among his "greatest hits."

Lepke was filmed in Culver City; not in Israel, as a lot of people thought because of the Golan-Globus connection. It was also one of the few movies with Milton Berle in a serious role, as my father-in-law. Golan and Globus raised enough money to make *Lepke* and use the change to make a picture called *The Four Aces* with Jack Palance. It was very successful and cost very little to make, since it was done without union auspices. I didn't think much of Golan and Globus as a production outfit. Menahem Golan still owes me $10,000 for that movie. With interest, that would come to about $4 million.

In *Lepke*, there was a rabbi on the set who acted as technical adviser for the execution. He was reading the kaddish, the prayer of the dead. During the filming, on March 19, 1974, my mother died at Memorial Hospital in Culver City. She was seventy-one and had a heart ailment. I asked that rabbi to help me, and he went with me when I buried her at Hillside Memorial Cemetery. Four days later they buried me in the film. That picture was loaded with those kinds of disturbing coincidences.

Lepke (1974), produced and directed by Menahem Golan, was the Jewish *Godfather*, starring TC in the title role, Anjanette Comer as his woman, and Milton Berle as her father. It's the true story of Brooklyn mobster Louis "Lepke" Buchalter, who was sent to Sing Sing at sixteen, raped there, and then savagely beaten for informing on his molester. Lepke spent most of his youth in jail

TC as Jewish Godfather in the title role of *Lepke* (1974)

and later masterminded sixty gangland slayings, often pulling the trigger himself.

The film is extremely violent. One of Lepke's first acts is to push a deadbeat loan client out a window. "Why'd you do that?" asks a cohort. "Now he's never gonna pay."

"Now *everybody's* gonna pay," Lepke replies.

More violence follows. A girl is stabbed in the neck with an icepick during sex. In a fine semi-improvisational scene TC asks Berle for his daughter's hand in marriage. The ethnic wedding scene features Ken Wannberg's "Godfather on the Roof" music, after which Lepke moves into dope and Walter Winchell dubs his operation "Murder, Inc." After a bloody shoot-out in a movie theater, *Lepke* becomes a cross between *The Godfather, Part Two* and *Bonnie and Clyde*. At Coney Island, his pal Warren Berlinger meets death on a merry-go-round. Lepke turns to Winchell, who promises a deal but double-crosses him. It's a speedy journey from courtroom to last meal: Lepke was executed on March 4, 1944, at age forty-seven.

"The savage realism of the electric chair climax is quite horrifying," wrote *Films Illustrated*. But most reviews were hostile. "We have been reading a lot about the Golan Heights," said *The Hollywood Reporter*. "Consider *Lepke* a Golan low."

—B.P.

About 1974 I was introduced to cocaine. I had seen it earlier but never really bothered with it. It was only during *Lepke* that I found myself using and liking it. It was sold on the set through the wardrobe department. Somebody who was doing the costumes was also selling cocaine, and it seemed like a very laid-back experience. No one knew about its power to devastate, or if they did, they weren't about to tell you. All you knew was it picked up your energy.

At the end of the day, by four or five, instead of taking a whiskey, I'd take a hit of cocaine. Or even during the day, you did a line or two and you wouldn't need to have lunch, which saved time. I'd waltz right through the day, and about five-thirty or six, if we had to work another couple of hours, a couple of lines of cocaine just sailed me through. I was alert, attentive. It had no negative effect on me. That's how I got inducted—me and an awful lot of people around me.

It was stated as absolute fact that it was not addictive. This is what we were told: It was not addictive. And it didn't *feel* addictive. You could stop and say, "I'm not going to use any more," and you wouldn't. It was extraordinary. It took a long while to get hooked, and you kept using it until you became addicted. I found that's what was happening to me. It provoked and aroused me. It had certain aphrodisiac qualities. It made my sexual desire much more intense. So it started to have a very telling effect on my personal life. A year or two after that, I was using it constantly and into freebasing too—smoking it. When that hit me, everything went haywire.

My marriage was falling apart. It wasn't necessarily because of drugs, but the drug use contributed to it. I didn't like my partner's behavior, and so I started to use. That softened you up. After two or three pipefuls, you say, What wife? What infidelity? You forgot your troubles and got happy.

It had a wonderful way of defusing you, shorting out the switches that made you so vulnerable: infidelity, ego, all the things that affected you personally. I didn't like the way I was looking. I'd lose weight and gain weight, never enough to make me obese, but I stopped working out. I was pulling my hair out. I would find myself unhappy at the house, uncomfortable being there, and I would seek out those coke connections. I'd meet a girl who would say, "I know where to get half an ounce," and so I'd find myself in Laurel Canyon at the house of some guy who would sell it to me.

Then I'd go home and stay there. I never went out and about. I would stay in my condominium, and when I got the big house back after my divorce, I would hang out there and smoke most of the day. Then I'd go down Hollywood Boulevard or Sunset to little side streets like Sierra Bonita, Fuller, or Orange, where people in little houses sold cocaine. About seven or eight at night, I'd show up for a little coke party with a group of those people. And I'd pay for it.

For some reason, I never worried about anyone recognizing me or telling the papers. I somehow enjoyed that sense of danger. I was so depressed with my living experience, maybe I was even hoping someone would catch me. Maybe that would have stopped it sooner. But it didn't. Nobody ever reported anything—a few rumors in those garbage magazines, but that was all. I was never bothered by the police. I don't know whether those dealers paid off the police or whether their operations were so small they just never attracted attention.

During the highs, I did a lot of drawings and wrote poems. That was all I was interested in doing. I didn't want to see movies, I didn't listen to music. There were different strata of drug abuse and there still are: The marijuana users seemed fairly innocent. The alcoholics looked down on the marijuana users. The marijuana users wouldn't think of using prescription drugs or pills. The pill pushers looked down on the cocaine and LSD users and potheads. The heavy ones were the heroin shooters. I never shot. I was lucky. I was not in a shooting group.

I did acid on three occasions—small tabs of it. I liked it because it lasted a long time, and it was really a brain freedom. It didn't get ugly for me. It released part of my brain into some abstract thinking. I daresay I would have gotten there eventually anyway, but I was happy for that freedom it gave me in my mind. I didn't realize that it really just stopped your existence, and that it was only for those few high moments that you felt lucid and happy. After that, you were scrounging around: *What can I sell to get what money for what drug?*

I'd find myself in people's apartments with loaded guns on the table and all that paraphernalia lying around—pipes, blowtorches, 150-proof Bacardi rum, ether, ammonia, baking soda—watching them make the brew. How it worked was fascinating. I got to be quite good at it myself. We'd share freebasing recipes with each other in those dens. Black guys, white guys, brown girls, green girls . . .

On the film sets, there was a tacit approval of coke, because it was precision-made for moviemaking. A day's work in a movie involves coming to work at six in the morning and theoretically quitting at five-thirty or six at night. A twelve-hour day? Forget it. It was a fourteen-, sixteen-, eighteen-hour day. You'd break for dinner, then go back to work some more, and the actors would be falling apart. But all of a sudden the actors were agreeable and friendly and energetic. Wait a minute, what the fuck is going on? What miracle drug are they taking? And the workers on the set, too—the crew—and the transportation and production departments. Everybody. On coke, the whole company would zip along and get through the day's work beautifully.

A few of the producers or their spies had to know about it, but they never said a word. Once a movie gets started, nobody stops to ask questions except, "What's the status of that shooting schedule?" They cannot go over schedule. The sole concern is how much money is spent each day. If it costs fifty thousand dollars a day and the picture is five days over, that's a quarter of a million dollars. It becomes huge, because that quarter of a million dollars accrues interest. So anything that increases efficiency is good, and those "efficient" people get hired more and more. But then people start to get irritable; there are more accidents. Sooner or later cocaine started to take its toll. Dozens of people just fell by the wayside.

Judy Garland was a good example, though she was a little earlier. I never discussed drugs with Judy. It was such a personal thing that nobody shared it with anybody unless you were using with somebody. It was basically an anonymous experience. You went out and did it with strangers. You couldn't do it with the people you lived with. You certainly couldn't do it with the people you worked with, because then they would "have" something on you. Everyone behaved as if nobody was using drugs. Nobody admitted to it. Everybody smiled and said, "Hail fellow well met," and as soon as the day was over you'd go into your little cubicle where you could do what you wanted. These things were never tolerated publicly. The movie industry didn't want to know—and didn't want anybody else to know—who was a homosexual, who was a lesbian, who was a drug user, who was Jewish . . . Anything that took you outside of the mainstream was anathema. Mainstream America was a narrow funnel, and there was nothing you could do to change that. It's more or less the same now.

Anything to improve the efficiency of making a movie is tolerated, if not encouraged. You can't blame a production manager for looking the other way. He doesn't want any problems on the set. He wants everything to move along smoothly.

A producer once told me that a certain actor—I'd love to name him, but I can't—was hired for a certain movie, and he insisted on being provided with five grams of cocaine a day. Part of the deal. This producer went to another producer and asked, "What should I do?" He said, "Put it on the transportation bill." That's how you hid it. That's how you could hide a lot of things.

A producer takes his girlfriend to Palm Springs, or a female producer takes her boyfriend to Chicago. She puts it down on the books as "location hunting." We don't know what she was trying to locate—looking for Dick, right? The man is in Acapulco, scouting for beaver. That's the nature of the business. A film is the most fragile entity of all. Film production is like a blotter, it absorbs everything. Once the studio says, "Okay, go ahead and do the movie, and you've got $10 million to do it," the budget absorbs every conceivable charge to get it done.

The producer says, "Listen, I've got to see this actress." What actress? "Well, this English actress who'd be great for the part." Okay, bring her over. No one knows that he's fucking the English actress or that she's fucking the actor who's got the lead. Her first-class airplane ticket and a thousand other things are all absorbed in the production budget, and by the time you're done, you can end up with a picture that grosses $100 million and hasn't broken even yet.

There's a light in the valley at Universal—a little spotlight on a tripod with wheels that's worth around $700,000 now. One light. And not even the original bulb. It keeps burning out, and they have to screw in a new one. How can that light be worth $700,000? Well, it's been used for fifty years in a different movie every week. Every time it's used, the company that owns it puts the full price of that light on your bill. I need twelve lights. Each light costs $90 to rent. That light goes out and earns $90 every day. I

246

want to marry that light. I want a family of lights. Forget about putting your kid in the movies. How about your car or your house? People rent their houses for $4,000 a day for the making of a film. Any one soundstage at Universal has been used by eight hundred movies, more or less, and each one was charged for rental space, maybe $1,500 a week. After sixty years? That stage has generated an income of $20 million, and they haven't even bothered to fix it up.

John Huston made a movie in which he wanted a rose, and the production department agreed that he would have it. This was in Africa—it could have been *The African Queen*—and he refused to shoot until he had it. They were on location that day, and he said, "Where's the rose?" Somebody said, Well, we thought maybe we'd get an orchid. "No, I want a rose." Can we shoot that scene next week? "No, we're going to shoot it now. I want the rose."

So they stopped shooting for a day and a half while they scouted out roses in Paris, flew somebody to pick it up and package it and fly it down in a case. And, of course, they didn't buy just *one* rose. They bought two dozen, so they'd have them on hand. They called it the $40,000 rose, because that's how much it cost by the time they got it.

That happens all the time. I need chewing gum for a scene. They buy twelve bags of it. For what? To be sure they've got it. How many do we use? Three sticks. What happens to the rest of it? It's divvied out to people or stuck away somewhere, in the hope that maybe somebody will write some other script where a guy has to chew gum. But nobody ever does.

Marilyn and me in that boat in *Some Like It Hot*—where did that boat come from? And that jacket and hat I wore? Actually, I stole the jacket and I still have it. The hat I had up to a little while ago. Where did they come from and where did they go? If I hadn't kept that jacket, it would be in the wardrobe department at Goldwyn Studios, making money. Once I was making a picture at Universal, playing a soldier, and they put me in a jacket that belonged to John Payne. They shortened the sleeves, but I still looked exactly like John Payne. It was obviously made for him. I wouldn't wear it. I said, "Make something to fit *me*." But most of the time those clothes are just recycled and used over and over again.

One of Marilyn's dresses in *Some Like It Hot* was just sold at auction for $34,000. It cost $38.40 to make. By the time the seamstress and the cleaner and the packer and everybody else got paid, that dress cost maybe $4,000. The other $30,000 is pure gravy. That's how movies are made, and drugs and booze are built into the budget just like costumes. In the seventies and eighties, more and more actors let it be known, subtly or blatantly, that they wanted drugs in the deal.

I have a theory that AIDS is an offshoot of the cocaine experience. Coke made everybody lovable. People started to do things they never imagined they would do. People who were on the edge fell overboard. A whole slew of beautiful women and good-looking guys were not available to anybody sexually until they got two lines of cocaine. All of a sudden they'd follow you anywhere for a gram of coke. The number of lives that got fucked up during that period is uncountable. All those hopes and dreams and aspirations were snorted up their noses and disappeared just as abruptly as that.

The images are still burned into my brain: A loaded .45 with the trigger cocked, sitting on the table next to a freebase pipe. A girl, shattered and broken, coming in crying, "I've got to get some!" Actors, writers, directors, executives—almost everybody was affected. Yet there was a group of people that this never touched—that higher echelon of producers and the real financiers in control, who never allowed it to interfere with the process of making money.

Personally, I had everything. Or it *seemed* like I had everything, and it looked to other people like I was on top of the world. But I felt like the man in that poem "Richard Cory," by Edwin Arlington Robinson, which I memorized:

> Whenever Richard Cory went down town,
> We people on the pavement looked at him:
> He was a gentleman from soul to crown,
> Clean-favored, and imperially slim.

> And he was always quietly arrayed,
> And he was always human when he talked;
> But still he fluttered pulses when he said,
> "Good morning," and he glittered when he walked.

> And he was rich—yes, richer than a king—
> And admirably schooled in every grace:
> In fine, we thought that he was everything
> To make us wish that we were in his place.

> So on we worked, and waited for the light
> And went without the meat, and cursed the bread;
> And Richard Cory, one calm summer night,
> Went home and put a bullet through his head.

TC haranguing Robert De Niro in a tense scene from the Elia Kazan version of Fitzgerald's *The Last Tycoon* (1976)

I love "admirably schooled in every grace." I can see him horseback riding, I can see him fencing, I can see him learning calligraphy. I can see him sitting in Paris, playing Mozart one afternoon and polo the next. "Admirably schooled in every grace." God, that poem is my bumper sticker.

In those days, though, I was still maintaining. That summer I did a magic show in Las Vegas for four weeks. After that, it was a TV production of *The*

Count of Monte Cristo and then *The Big Ripoff* for NBC, which was a pilot for the *McCoy* series.

The most important project was *The Last Tycoon*, which finally got off the ground in October 1975. It was the Scott Fitzgerald story about Irving Thalberg, and Sam Spiegel had spent years trying to put it together. He got Harold Pinter to write the script and Robert De Niro to play the lead. He originally wanted Mike Nichols to direct but settled for Elia Kazan.

Kazan was involved with the Actors Studio. One of the first things he ever said to me was, "You know, Tony, working with you is really a big surprise. I was told you'd be very difficult." Obviously those motherfuckers in that Strasberg School of Bullshit bum-rapped every actor who didn't go through their system. I taught them all a lesson.

I liked working with De Niro, an interesting man. It all depends on the part: Get a good scene, and what else do you need? Jeanne Moreau and I weren't sure about each other when we first met. We came out of such diverse backgrounds, but it worked out perfectly. I loved working with her. I got Leslie a small part in that picture. When it was over, I had to rush into *Casanova and Co.* (1977)—the less said, the better. They put me in drag, and in some places it was retitled *Some Like It Cool*. Next was *The Manitou* (1977), where some four-hundred-year-old evil spirit decides to reincarnate itself on Susan Strasberg's neck. The director of that, William Girdler, was scouting locations in the Philippines a few months later when he was killed in a helicopter crash.

The most bizarre project of my life was *Sextette* with Mae West. Mae and I got to be friends, although I wasn't prepared for what she was. She was eighty-five then. She had no sense of time. There was nothing in that film that related to what century it was. Those British producers would call me to work and I'd say, "What time is Mae going to be there?" They'd tell me to be there at eleven. But I knew Mae wouldn't really be on the set until one. I researched all my leading ladies so I'd know when to arrive and not have to sit around unnecessarily. That's what I learned from working with Marilyn. It didn't take me long to figure out Mae.

Mae's bodyguard would drive her in at eleven, and at ten after they'd start on her hair. Then they would take her into a kind of bathroom/dressing room for her daily enema, which took another half hour. Then they put wardrobe on her, and maybe by one-fifteen they'd wheel her onto the set. So I left for work when she started her enema. I had spies on the set who told me when the enema was finished; don't ask me how they knew, but they knew. She was quite deaf and a little blind, and she couldn't remember a line. George Hamilton was in the picture, and at one point, after we'd been working about three weeks, George was talking to Ken Hughes, the director, and Mae was standing next to him. George said, "When I come into the scene, I'll just say hello to Mae, then go to the bookshelf, pick out a book, come back, walk around Mae, and then start the dialogue." Ken Hughes turns to Mae and says, "How does that sound to you, Mae?"

"What?"

"How does it sound, what George said?"

She says, "Who's George?"

Mae also couldn't move too well, poor darling, and she wore six-inch wedgies. She was about four feet eleven inches, a tiny little woman, so they put her in these high shoes. You never saw her feet, so you couldn't see those wedgies. She was always encased. When they wanted her to turn around in the scene, since she couldn't hear, a prop man would lie flat on the floor with his arms stretched out around her feet, and turn her around, literally. She was like the battleship *Potemkin*.

She had a hearing aid that was connected to the booth where Ken Hughes sat and smoked. It looked like a telephone booth with glass windows, and it was wired up to her earphone. Waiting for the shot, Ken would smoke, and this booth would get fogged up until you could barely see him. In the middle of my line he would say her line so that she could say it when I finished. But it was a high-frequency radio connection, and it picked up a lot of other stuff. One day during a scene I heard her say "605 Fountain"— the hearing aid was picking up police calls, and she blurted this out—"605 Fountain, proceed with caution!" or whatever the fuck it was. Another time she picked up some helicopter signals and started to report traffic conditions on the Hollywood Freeway.

We had dinner on two occasions at the producer's house, and she would regale us with stories: "Let me tell you, big boy . . . " She wrote all the dialogue for that movie—every line. She wrote one great exchange for me and herself: I played a Russian diplomat, and I say to her, "My darling Marlo, remember the songs I used to sing to you in my native tongue?" She says, "I don't remember the songs, but I remember the native tongue."

Some people said she should never have made *Sextette;* that the producers should have gone out and found a beautiful young woman, called her Mae West II, and let her play it. But Mae wouldn't go for that, and you can't blame her. It was her script, after all. Some people also said it was a little unusual to have an enema before each day's shooting. But after so many years in this profession, I found nothing unusual. Like clockwork, every day at a certain time, Mae had her enema. I don't know how it was administered, I don't know what medical corps came out to do it. All I know is, she had her hair done, her enema, and her makeup, in that order.

Sextette (1978) has a screenplay by Herbert Baker from the play by Mae West. Except for a small part in *Myra Breckinridge* (1970), this was West's first major movie in thirty-five years; only her twelfth, and last, film. She goes out in Edith Head–style as the legendary sex goddess Marlo Manners, in London on the occasion of her sixth marriage. The lucky man is Timothy Dalton, but he can hardly get through the crowd of ex-husbands and lovers around her. Among them is "special guest star" TC as Soviet diplomat Alexei Karansky.

Along the way, West recycles all her trademark lines from previous films ("It's not the men in my life, it's the life in my men"; "When I'm good I'm very good, but when I'm bad I'm better"; "Is that a gun in your pocket, or are you just glad to see me?"). Moving only rarely and at a snaillike pace, she camps and vamps and pats her hair, always accompanied by burlesque music for emphasis.

The film is riddled with song-and-dance routines, or bits and pieces thereof, beginning with "Hooray for Hollywood." These are hilarious to the point of parody, but intentionally or unintentionally? One can't quite tell. Most astounding is the West-Dalton duet of the Captain and Tennille hit, "Love Will Keep Us Together." Mae sings "Baby Face" and Judy Garland's "After You've Gone" to TC, as he lies at her feet with his balalaika. When someone observes that her romance with Alexei was over "just like that," Mae replies, "With Alexei, *everything* was over just like that."

TC as sexy Alexei plays it very broad. He has no other choice.

252

TC and the immortal Mae West in her last film, *Sextette* (1977): "She was beyond direction."

"You remember that vulgah night we spent on the river?"

"What?"

"I mean, that night we spent on the Volga River."

Mae's vintage epigrams include a comparison of marriage to books: "The whole story takes place between the covers." But her best line is delivered in a gym where she is surrounded by musclemen.

"I'm a pole vaulter," says one of the beefy guys.

"Aren't we all," she replies.

Later, in bed with Dalton, she says, "There's nothing between us that can't be straightened out." And when he tells her she has done more for her country than anyone since Paul Revere, she responds, "I'm looking forward to saying the same thing he did: 'The British are coming!' "

Before settling on Dalton as her leading man, West had rejected Christopher Plummer, Peter Ustinov, Vincent Price, and even Paul Newman for being "too old"! Her other costars in *Sextette* were an odd assortment indeed: Dom de Luise as her manager, Ringo Starr as a Hungarian film director, George Hamilton as a gangster, Alice Cooper as a waiter, and Keith Moon as an over-the-top faggy dress designer. There were cameos by Walter Pidgeon, George Raft, Rona Barrett, and Regis Philbin as—who else?—themselves. Barrett and TC had no encounters during the filming. "I never went near her," he says. "Had I known she was in the movie, I never would have done it."

Independent producers Daniel Briggs and Robert Sullivan spent $3 million on the production, of which Mae West received $250,000, plus 20 percent of the gross. The film seemed to boggle the minds of audiences and critics alike. *Time* magazine said it was "so bad, so ferally innocent, that it is good, an instant classic to be treasured by connoisseurs of the genre everywhere." *The Village Voice* called it "one of the most innocently perverse star vehicles ever made."

—B.P.

———————◆•———————

Believe me, there was no sophisticated concept—no way those song-and-dance routines were conscious parodies. *Sextette* was a third-rate movie put together by third-rate people to take advantage of Mae West's cult. Nothing more, nothing less. They scammed around putting the money together. They just barely got that picture together. The only reason they got all the big-name people was because they didn't use us for very long. We came in, delivered our goods for two or three days, and were out of there. The parody effect was something completely unconscious that was read into it later on.

I was sitting in one scene opposite Walter Pidgeon. What a charming, wonderful man he was. He was at one end of a table, I was at the other, and we were watching the antics involved in trying to get Mae to utter some line of dialogue and poor George Hamilton trying to get Mae to remember who he was. Walter and I would giggle when we looked at each other. We got to know each other by that laughter between us.

There was no way to direct Mae. She was beyond direction. She came in and sat down, and that was it. If she moved her lips, you'd better start shooting. You'd dub it later.

———————————— • ————————————

In *The Bad News Bears Go to Japan* (1978), directed by John Berry, TC got top billing—in fact, the *only* billing other than juvenile lead Jackie Earle Haley. Written by Burt Lancaster's son Bill, this was the third adventure of the rag-tag baseball team whose original outing with Walter Matthau and Tatum O'Neal grossed $35 million for Paramount two years earlier.

This time around, the pubescent boys of summer start out with a talk-show appearance on which they demand to go to Japan, against the wishes of their league. TC as Marvin P. Lazar, rumpled and sleazy, hears the interview upon waking up on his office couch, drunk but still drinking after "casting" until 5:00 A.M. His alimony checks are three months' overdue, the loan sharks are going to break his legs, and all his credit cards have been cut in half. In desperate need of a quick influx of cash, he jumps in to negotiate a deal between the Bears and the Japanese.

In Japan, TC bows and scrapes but crudely. He greets a VIP's very proper Japanese wife with, "The old ball and

TC and Erin "Moustafa" Blunt as unlikely soul brothers in *The Bad News Bears Go to Japan* (1978)

chain, huh?" His players immediately get into a fight with the lo-

255

cals. One of the Bears wears a yarmulke. Their little black mascot, Moustafa, constantly shadows TC, fiddling with his love beads and asking about the facts of life. To complicate cross-cultural matters, young Haley falls in love with a Japanese girl.

The funniest scenes involve TC's soul-searching with his rival manager, Tomisaburo Wakayama, and a Japanese talent show of which the *Happy Days* TV theme song in bad English and "Moon River" in bad Japanese are the highlights. TC's culture clashes are nothing compared to his clashes with the Bears, who aren't happy with their share of the take. "What's 4 percent of $30,000? $1,200," says TC. "It won't get you through college, but at least it'll get you a couple of girls while you're in college."

TC and Wakayama end up bonding over booze and planning how to cash in on their kid-based celebrity. "I'd get myself a couple of game shows, then go into the movies," says TC. "I'd use Kubrick first. Him and me, we got the same sensibilities."

—B. P.

With the baseball craze in Japan, that film was expected to do well both at the American and the Japanese box offices, and it did. But why be dishonest about it? It was a clumsy, awkward movie, and I didn't particularly enjoy it.

In 1978 I met Nicolas Gessner, a Hungarian-Canadian director who was shooting a movie about gunrunners in Israel called *It Rained All Day the Night I Left* (1979). I hated the title, but they got Lou Gossett, Jr., and Sally Kellerman, who were both good. We started in October, shooting the interiors in Montreal at Sonolab Studios. Just before Christmas we moved to Israel, about fifteen kilometers from Eilat. Since things were pretty volatile then in the Mideast, the Israeli government provided war-risk insurance for the cast and crew.

My marriage was disintegrating, and my life was splintered. My kids were in L.A. I'd fly in to see them, then fly back to Montreal, and from there on to Israel. I invited my friend Gene Scacove to go to Israel with me, and they gave us two first-class tickets to Tel Aviv. El Al flew 747s that had an upstairs lounge as you went up the spiral stairs—the first-class or ultra-first-class section, depending on the configuration. Since the Israelis didn't carry that many people, the upstairs area of about twenty seats became first-class.

At the airport in New York, they announced a delay because Menachem Begin was booked on the flight, but he was still in Washington finishing business. They had to wait because the prime minister of Israel didn't have a private plane. I was in the lounge waiting, and this diminutive man with an eye patch walked by. He kind of nodded, and I nodded back. He was an energetic kind of a man—I could sense his power and resoluteness just by that little pass in front of me. He walked about fifteen feet beyond me and stopped. Then he turned around slowly, he looked me up and down with that one good eye, and walked back.

"Tony Curtis?"

"Moshe Dayan?"

We shook hands. He said, "The prime minister will be here soon."

Finally they started boarding, but first the Israelis put you in a little room with your luggage and scrutinize you. "Mr. Curtis, has your luggage been out of your sight at all?" No. They look in your eyes suspiciously. I got through with my luggage and on the plane. Gene and I were upstairs in the private section near the prime minister. Menachem Begin and his wife were sitting in front with Shimon Peres's wife and a lot of officers and bodyguards. Gene and I were the only tourists allowed upstairs with them.

It was a nine-hour flight, and about two hours into it an attaché came over and said, "Would you have breakfast with Mr. and Mrs. Begin in the morning?" I said, "I'd like to very much." And in the morning, I sat down and had breakfast with Menachem Begin and his wife at thirty-six-thousand feet. We didn't eat *trayf*, either. Strictly kosher.

When we landed, Shimon Peres was there to meet his wife and he said to me, "Please, if you need anything, call." Every weekend, any time I had time off, I flew anywhere I wanted in the country. I paid my own way, but I sat up with the pilots in their barricaded area. Once I wanted to fly up to Jerusalem for a weekend, but the only flight scheduled was to Tel Aviv. I said, "I really wanted to go to Jerusalem, and I only have a couple days." The pilot looked and said, "I think we're going to stop in Jerusalem first." And we did. They were really accommodating. I was scheduled to visit Golda Meir, but she died just a few weeks before we finished the film.

I liked Sally Kellerman from the time I'd worked with her in *The Boston Strangler*. She's a charming woman. Lou Gossett was wonderful right from the beginning. He arrived with a foot locker containing all his possessions, like he was joining the Marine Corps. I thought, *God, what a good way to travel.*

This was the first Canadian-Israeli coproduction, and we traveled all over Israel to shoot. Gessner brought his key people from Canada—all the drivers and union members—and when they got there, they didn't realize it was the desert. They were constantly getting the equipment stuck in the sand, until finally they made a deal with the Israeli teamsters. Those guys were tank commanders and knew exactly how to get in and out of sand.

It was fascinating, though basically I thought the whole operation was thoroughly inept. I brought as much energy to it as I could, but it was a very difficult period for me. I was still on drugs and trying to deal with a lot of other things. I was thrilled when it was over.

C·H·A·P·T·E·R T·W·E·L·V·E

WRECK AND RECOVERY

By 1979 I was most unhappy with Leslie. There was discord. I really didn't like that marriage anymore. Later, after those Andy Warhol diaries came out, I could never forgive her for that quote of hers. She said she couldn't imagine how she could ever have married an actor and a Jew.

I was doing more cocaine and freebasing. I didn't like the way my career was going. I wasn't getting the kinds of parts I wanted, I was looking bad, everything seemed to be slipping away. I couldn't believe that the bright, hot, hungry kid I used to be was unraveling. The laid-back days when I would go over for lunch in the Columbia commissary and check out all the new girls under contract, make dates with them, go down to the beach—those days were over. The world used to be my oyster. There were cherries to pick all over the place. Now I started to dislike the environment I was living in. I lost the joy and pleasure of it. Something was happening to me.

I started to drink a lot more, which wasn't extraordinary, because everybody drank a lot. Dean Martin's whole act was based on being drunk all the time. Dexedrine and Dexamyl were in wide use. In the morning, if I couldn't get up to go to work, I'd take a couple of uppers to get through the day. At noon I wouldn't eat, and by midafternoon, I'd start to come down. A couple of drinks would pick me up and get me to the end of the day. After work, a lot of times, we had to go to parties, and I could never get out of them before eleven-thirty or twelve. I'd take a couple of sleeping pills, which would put me out until seven or eight in the morning. So I was using a lot of substances, and it became increasingly difficult.

I found myself in a lower-depths environment. I felt like an observer for some esoteric journal, watching the madness of people smoking and walking around and letting their brains leap out of their skulls in the freebase experience. There I was, a part of that in the late seventies and early eighties. In a way, it did enlighten me. It made me come closer to the things I was trying to hide from. For a snappy minute, when you hit that freebase pipe, you were free of any earthly bond. It made you euphoric, and you didn't worry about mundane things for a while.

But only for a while. There was always something eating at me. I'd wake up in the morning, and that anxiety would suddenly take over. As I came out of my dreams, I'd think, *Oh God, I've got to be nervous again. I really miss that girl, and I've got money problems.* So I'd take a hit on that pipe and have nothing to worry about. Fuck it all.

It took me a long time to figure out that a major cause and effect of drug abuse is sexual dysfunction. You either come too quick or you don't come at all. I think men and women both suffer profoundly from that dysfunction in one form or another. It's a terrible discomfort—that physical drive that never seems to abate. Good or bad, sex is a distraction from your pain. It eases the other stress in your life. If you can express yourself sexually, those negative things disappear for a couple of minutes. You say to yourself, "Well! That's the way to handle that problem!"

As you get older, you want to use a substance that's going to prolong that orgasmic experience because it's so pleasant. Cocaine, at the beginning, does that. You think it's a miracle drug. *How come it took me so long to discover this?* Twenty years ago, that's the way we thought. Today we understand that abusing it will destroy you, but for twenty seconds it looks as if it's going to solve your problems. Then you've got to use more, and before you know it, that good thing it gave you disappears and bad things take over. At that point, and especially with freebasing, the problem is coming down. Coming down, you feel like two pieces of rusty metal grinding against each other.

To take the edge off coming down, I started drinking whiskey, which of course made me drunk. But it was interesting. You felt the high of the freebase but also the "low" madness of the alcohol. The sleeping pills were another thing, so your whole day became consumed by what dosages you were going to do of what, and who with. It was so degrading, going out into the street searching for drugs in those days. If you were a good actor like me, you could hide the behavior pattern to a large extent. You looked a little nervous, maybe, but you could still pass. In a community like Hollywood, you were just waiting around for that phone to ring anyway. Since it didn't ring that often, and if you had a little money, you could stay high all the time—just sober up enough to go out for a job now and then. But when the time came, maybe you couldn't do it right because you were more strung out than you thought you were.

It was a very diabolical thing, made worse by whatever your own personal demons were. For me it was discovering the infidelity of a woman; that was devastating. I didn't have enough courage to go out and kill anybody, so I took it inward.

The lowest point was when I was doing a play called *I Ought to Be in Pictures* (1980) for Neil Simon and Herb Ross—those mean-spirited men. I was using a lot of coke and having a lot of trouble at home. Between my marriage falling apart and those people treating me like shit, there was no place I could hide. At night I had to do that play and during the day I had to be at that house, and both were anathema to me. The only haven I had was the backseat of my car (the Trans-Am Pontiac, silver, with a black leather interior, T-bar top, four-speed, and overdrive), curled up under a blanket so nobody would discover me and I could get a few hours of sleep. The great Tony Curtis spent a lot of nights that way, sleeping in parking lots or traveling to places like Las Vegas, just to get away for a while.

In Vegas my pal was Dean Shendal. He was one of the best things that ever happened to me. He was out of St. Louis, I was out of New York; two operators. He used to ride in a rodeo—jump off a horse and wrestle a cow to the ground—until six or seven years ago. A fabulous guy. He was a gambler and used to be part-owner of Caesar's Palace, but eventually he sold all his gambling interests. In Las Vegas I'd be strung out, wired, and Dean would give me a back room in his house and say, "Stay as long as you need to." He looked after me. Dean was a very fine friend and came through for me always. He was very kind to me then.

I loved Las Vegas. I still love it. It's a wonderful environment—carefree, gay, bigger than life. It's got a vitality like no other city in the world. In those days, I used show girls like some guys use vitamin pills—two a day—and Vegas was busting out all over with them. There were more tits than chips in that town. The sizes were big, bigger, and biggest. Everybody in Vegas had to have tits, even some of the guys. There was more silicone in them thar hills than in all the new Boeing 707s. No wonder all those chickies were pumping up their chests: It was a great way to make a living. Las Vegas was one big Research and Development Foundation for the Advancement of Knockerinos.

I used to love just walking around, looking at the way that town was growing by leaps and bounds. People were descending on it from every direction. Flights were now going there directly from Chicago, New York, Miami, and London, without going to Los Angeles first. Those club marquees were always lit up, bright and harsh, with the top names in the country. It was fast becoming a very important city that generated an awful lot of bread for an awful lot of people.

Vegas was a great escape for me and everybody else, but I was in bad shape. Just about everybody I knew except Dean washed their hands of me. "He's dead," they said, and they were almost right. That 1979–1980 period was the heaviest time for coke use in this country. The only thing that saved my life were the drug dealers. Why? Because they soaked me for $150 a gram and cut it so severely that the amount of cocaine I got was under 10 percent. If I'd bought the stronger stuff that's being sold today, I'd have been dead. So in a funny way I guess I have to thank those dealers. My life was saved because of the way those motherfuckers cut the coke and ripped me off. They did me a big favor.

It had been many years since TC and Walter Matthau had worked together or even seen each other, and the normally unsentimental Matthau remembers their reunion: "When he greeted me on the set of *Little Miss Marker*, Tony said, 'Walter—friend of my youth.' I thought it was remarkable, and it stayed with me."

Little Miss Marker (1980), directed by Walter Bernstein and produced by Jennings Lang, was another reworking of the Damon Runyon story, with Walter Matthau as Sorrowful Jones, the bookie with a heart of cold. In the opening scene, TC, as a crook named Blackie, fails to get a loan from him and shoots his dog on the way out. Matthau looks at the corpse and, instead of breaking down, tells his secretary: "Call a few places and see what you can get for the fur. Tell 'em it's wolf."

A guy deposits his daughter as a "marker" for a ten dollar bet, and Matthau gets stuck with the kid (Sara Stimson). He is at his grumpy best in trying to deal with her, grudgingly sharing his dry cornflakes and Murphy bed. Julie Andrews plays a socialite horsewoman who has fallen on hard times and agrees to let Blackie turn her mansion into a casino.

Nasty TC, sporting a variety of sinister, oversized hats, takes time out from rigging his roulette wheels to fix the big upcoming race. He is no friend to quadrupeds, as we saw with the dog, and he now plots to do in Julie's beloved horse. She and Matthau as a love team are almost as unlikely as Mae West and Timothy Dalton. They end up in court, fighting over Miss Marker and offering dubious, rival claims of parental fitness. "What do you do for a living?" Judge Lee Grant asks Matthau. "I'm a bookmaker," he replies. "Fiction or nonfiction?" she asks. The only solution, of course, is joint custody—and marriage.

—B.P.

I thought *Little Miss Marker* was a wonderful picture. I had done it before as *Forty Pounds of Trouble*—that was my version of it. This was Walter Matthau's version. We knew a lot about each other. Ever since those days at the Dramatic Workshop, we always had a nice relationship and great affection for one another.

Right after that, I got an Agatha Christie mystery script called *The Mirror Crack'd*. I would have a scene with Elizabeth Taylor in which I took her hand and kissed it. For that little moment, I decided to do *The Mirror Crack'd*—no offense to Kim Novak and Rock Hudson, who were also in it. I found myself making a number of decisions like that in those years. *Sextette*, for example. I wanted to make a movie with Mae West for the experience itself, and also because Cary Grant had made one with her. Cary and I had two important leading ladies in common, Marilyn and Mae. I enjoyed the idea—it was part of my funny little composite batting record—that only Curtis and Grant worked with both Marilyn Monroe and Mae West.

The Mirror Crack'd (1980) was directed by Guy Hamilton, whose specialty was Agent 007 (*Goldfinger* [1964], *Diamonds Are Forever* [1971], *Live and Let Die* [1973], *The Man with the Golden Gun* [1974]). The matronly detective Miss Marple was a little tamer

All-star review: Kim Novak, Rock Hudson, Elizabeth Taylor, and TC in *The Mirror Crack'd* (1980)

than James Bond, and Angela Lansbury was trying to differentiate her version from Margaret Rutherford's great characterization of the 1960s. More intriguing than the whodunit itself is the quartet of suspects: Taylor and Novak as rival stars on the comeback trail, and their husbands, Rock, the director, and TC, the producer. The mystery's solution is oddly borrowed from the real-life tragedy of Gene Tierney, whose daughter (by Oleg Cassini) was born retarded because a fan with German measles broke through a barricade and kissed Tierney during her pregnancy.

In this first Taylor–Hudson reteaming since *Giant* (1956), Liz camps it up—but no more than Kim Novak. All four stars, for that matter, are parodies of their film-biz "types," and good sports about it. Says Liz to her mirror: "Bags, bags, go away, come back fast on Doris Day." (The film's title is borrowed from Alfred, Lord Tennyson: "The mirror crack'd from side to side./'The curse has come upon me,'/ cried The Lady of Shalott.") Novak and Taylor are doing Queen Elizabeth and Mary of Scotland, and Novak reflects sensitively on how she plans to play the execution scene:

"Mary's in rags, looking like shit, and in walks—*me*! I'm gonna wipe that cow right off the screen."

Director Hudson, reviewing his lavishly costumed guards, complains, "They're supposed to be the queen's soldiers, not her ballerinas." When a policeman asks TC if he knows of anyone who might want to harm Taylor, he replies, "Yeah—Hedda Hopper." Later, he picks up the phone and in his tough producer's voice barks, "Gimme the Coast." Silent beat. "Whaddaya mean, '*what* Coast'?"

—B.P.

During *The Mirror Crack'd* in England, Rock and I had dressing rooms side by side. Between shots we would hang out together and reminisce about the early days. I would be doing my sketches and Rock would be knitting—either sweaters or rugs, I don't remember which. I just loved that image of Rock knitting and me drawing, like two *alter kockers*, two elderly Jewish gentlemen, two senior citizens sitting in some retirement home, talking of the good old days.

After that, we weren't in communication much. When he died, a lot of people tried to get me to make some statement or comment about Rock Hudson and Sal Mineo and secret homosexuality in Hollywood. I wouldn't do it then, and I won't now. I'm not interested in that. I really don't know what to say. They were good friends of mine, and we were very fond of each other. I never thought of them as "secret homosexuals." It never entered my mind. It still doesn't.

There was a strange man named Ulli Lommel who used to be a teenage actor in Germany and then worked a lot with Rainer Werner Fassbinder and became a director himself. He came over here and made horror movies, or occult movies, or just weird movies, like *Brainwaves* (1982). I was brained out myself in those days, but I was in it, and so was Keir Dullea. Keir was pretty bizarre, but we got along. He'd made *2001* with Kubrick and then seemed to disappear. I thought he looked like Dick Cavett and even sounded like him. People said, "Keir Dullea, gone tomorrow."

The story, or what little of it I can recall, was about a girl whose boyfriend electrocutes her by dropping her boom box in the bathtub. They saved her brain and gave it to me, because I was a mad neurosurgeon and I had this process by which I implanted it in Suzanna Love. It was a peculiar film, to say the least, but I kind of liked Lommel. I'd never worked with a director like that before. He would only say a word or two, then direct you with his eyes.

I was really sick while I was making that movie, trying to undo my drug problems. It was in the middle of that difficult period. I needed money, and I was doing parts like Iago in a black version of *Othello* (1982) and a "J.R." type of character in *Balboa* (1982), neither of which anybody ever saw, thank God.

The interesting one was *Where Is Parsifal?* (1984), not because of the movie but because Orson Welles was in it. So was my friend Peter Lawford, but it was really Orson I wanted to work with. He and I were very good friends. He once told an associate that he thought I was the finest American screen actor. I used to go to Ma Maison, where he'd also have lunch. He was so huge, he couldn't fit through the front door. He'd come in through the kitchen and sit in a big private booth in the back with his poodle Fifi. When I'd come up, that dog would bark like hell. I'd sit down next to him and say, "Othello—Iago is here!" I'd kiss his hand. The fucking dog would be barking like crazy. Welles would just sit there smiling.

I really miss having an the opportunity to be with him. I wish I could have been around for those Mercury movies he made—what an experience that would have been. I almost had him in *Sweet Smell of Success*. He loved that picture. Originally he was going to play J. J. Hunsecker. What a different movie it would have been. I loved that man. I used to go down on the set and watch him and Janet when they were doing *Touch of Evil* (1958), and she was having such trouble with her arm.*

So I did *Where Is Parsifal?* with Orson in England, for Alexander Salkind. Salkind wanted to give his wife, Berta Dominguez, a chance at writing and appearing in a movie, but he also wanted to keep her busy so he could be elsewhere. So he came up with this picture and hired a French-

---

* Fans of that classic *film noir* Welles picture may know that Janet Leigh had a broken arm throughout the whole shooting. Just before *Touch of Evil* production began, Leigh and TC were making a TV picture called *Carriage from Britain* during which costar Jesse White tripped and fell on top of her during a stunt. Rather than give up *Touch of Evil,* she had her broken arm set at an angle that allowed her to camouflage it with a coat. During the motel scenes for which she was scantily clad, the cast was sawed in half and removed for the shots, then replaced and taped up again afterward.

man named Henri Helman to direct it. It was the only time in history a movie was made so that the producer could get away from his wife.

The title character, which I played, invents some laser machine that can save the world. Orson played a small part as a magician. In real life he had a great flair for magic and used to entertain us with tricks. When the movie was nearly finished, they flew him in for three days work, but somehow he got on the wrong plane and ended up in France. They had to charter a special plane to get him to England because he couldn't fit in a normal first-class seat. No normal car could hold him, either—not even a Rolls or a Bentley—so they had to find a special sort of taxi with big doors to get him in and out.

The movie was shot in an old English mansion called Hamden House, where they made a lot of horror films. Orson was sitting there in a kind of wheelchair behind some curtains, waiting to go on. His ankles were huge. I sat down next to him, and we talked before the shot and looked in each other's eyes. That ten minutes with Orson Welles was the best ten minutes I ever spent. Then we did the scene. I was supposed to explain my invention, but I hated the dialogue they gave me, so I made it all up: "This is based on Einstein's theory of relativity, and relatives are always screwing up the relative relativity of your life. . . ." Something like that. Orson thought it was terribly funny.

I was so drunk and disorderly and unhappy then. Orson and Peter Lawford were too—all us outcasts in the same picture, all of us unhappy. Orson was sixty-nine when he died in 1985, because of the weight. "I was born to be fat," he used to say. There's something strangely comforting about being fat. It eliminates all the other living experiences. All you're worried about is when your next meal is. Job problems, family problems—all secondary or nonexistent. You've just got to feed that one monster, your body. You haven't got time for anything except eating. By the time you've finished eating and digested and gone to the toilet, it's time to start eating again. You don't really have to spend much time living.

Where Is Parsifal? opened and closed in about four days. I made a lot of films like that during my user days to pay for my drugs.* Nobody's perfect.

---

* Nobody on the production had any complaints about TC. On the contrary, A. D. Tony Sloman said: "Tony Curtis was marvelous to work with on *Where Is Parsifal?* I'd heard he could be difficult. He was charming, and completely professional. Dressed in a white suit and cowboy hat (for post-synching!), he removed his Stetson and gazed at his image on the screen. 'What a finely-shaped head,' he said to no-one in particular."

But I always made sure that Peter paid Paul. I felt if I took care of things financially, I could allow myself the privilege of buying a nice car, or whatever. I took care of my responsibilities first. But toward the end of that third marriage, things got totally out of hand. A woman named Helen Breitman was my secretary. She and Joe Warren, my main assistant, handled things for me, and they were both wonderful people. They used to call me "Sire." One night when I was freebasing and so despondent and miserable, Helen was so caring. She was in my life for a long time, and then one day Leslie just unceremoniously fired her for some reason.

The drug experience was getting worse. I remember this black dude named Calvin. I went over to his place one night, and he had twenty-eight grams of coke on the table and was mixing it with baby laxative and dextrose. He told me to turn around and close my eyes, then he laid out two big lines and challenged me to tell which was the pure stuff and which was the mix. I did the lines, then I guessed wrong, and he said, "You don't know *what* the fuck you're snortin', white boy!"

Cocaine is a devastating drug. It makes stupid men think they're smart and smart men think they're stupid. It convolutes your whole sense of being. I knew it was going to overwhelm me, and I didn't want to die in my own spittle somewhere. I didn't want to end up ignominiously dead in some hallway or car, not having the money to maintain. That's what prompted my recovery.

The decision to go to the Betty Ford Center in Rancho Mirage, California, was extremely difficult. My friend Eli Blumenfeld said, "You've got to do something, Tony. You can't go on this way." I said, "You're right." Eli is a very fine man and a great friend through thick and thin. I admire him a lot for his brains, his stamina, his morality, and his sense of who he is. He stuck with me more than anybody else. He was the one that really extended himself. He was responsible for getting me into the Betty Ford Center and for organizing me to be able to go there. He drove me down himself. It took an "intervention" to do it. But I did it. I went.

Eli Blumenfeld: "It was obvious to look at him that if something didn't happen, it was going to be the end of Tony Curtis. He and

I had a series of discussions and he agreed to go into the Betty Ford Center. But shortly after he finished his term, so to speak, he went back to the old ways. It was unsuccessful for many reasons, and after another year or so, it was obvious to me that Tony would not last more than a few more months. His life was virtually over. I met with Drew Anderson at the BFC and told him this was not acceptable, that something had to be done. There had to be some way to get Tony into the center, control him,

TC's friend and lawyer, Eli Blumenfeld

and make sure that this could never happen again.

"We talked about some methods that were not widely in use then. Drew Anderson said there was one called 'intervention.' A year later, in 1985, I went to a program at The Buckley School where they were discussing drug-counseling strategies, and when I mentioned intervention, they said they hadn't heard of it. That's how new the concept was. We talked a lot about how it would be handled, because I wanted to make sure it was under controlled circumstances. I wanted to make sure he went right from that room into the center so there wouldn't be any gap. I didn't want him to change his mind.

"We got all the people together and finally sat them down. Jamie and Kelly and Allegra were there, and Drew Anderson and I think Nicky Blair. I don't recall if the boys were there, but just family and a few close friends. Then they brought Tony in, in his traditional white shorts, and it was very traumatic for him. He was extremely surprised—almost in shock—when he saw everyone there. He didn't anticipate that happening. All he was told was that he was going into a room to see Anderson. But that's the way it has to be, because if you're forewarned, you'll never get there. He was startled, and then he became very angry at what was going on. But there was no choice. Not to do it would have been to allow him to drop off the edge. He could have told everyone to go fuck themselves, that he didn't want anything to do with them. He was almost at that point because he thought people were turning on him. But after a while you could see a change in his facial expression and in his eyes as people started expressing their feelings and why they were participating in this. He realized we were doing this because we loved him.

"So he accepted it. He went into the center and fulfilled everything he agreed to in terms of the requirements. He stuck to it tremendously. Tony listened and adhered to the program that was set out for him, but he actually instituted his own. He went to AA or the comparable drug program occasionally, but he had his own: Whenever and wherever he had an opportunity, he would discuss it openly. That was his method. I've seen people get up onstage and say, 'I'm an alcoholic,' but Tony went deeper than that. He had a sense of wanting to help others as well, because it's not easy to get rid of that demon by yourself. Tony was his own support group. It was very effective. The change in his life was amazing from then on. You could see him turn to his work, return to his clarity of thought. It wasn't the same Tony Curtis. Intervention doesn't work for everyone, but it did for him. It had to do with his strength of character."

—Eli Blumenfeld to B.P., March 19, 1993

———— ◆ ————

At the Betty Ford Center I found myself waiting on tables, cleaning up after lunch and dinner—part of their routinization. I was sharing a room with another guy. No blinds on the window. I was unable to sleep, irritable, nervous. There was no effort to ease it for me. They gave some patients tranquilizers to calm them down. Not with me. Absolutely nothing. Cold turkey.

The first week was a test, and I could easily have walked out. But walk out to where? To do what? Everybody was required to keep a diary, and rather than try to recreate the way I felt, here are a few excerpts:

270

March 23, 1984: Left LA abruptly, directly from Cedars Sanitorium, after 3 days of physical and mental anguish and pain. Arrived at the Betty Ford Center in the afternoon. It was a clumsy and difficult day. The first hours here were very trying. Sobbed and wept most of the day. Astounded by the friendly and kindly support of the entire staff and fellow patients.

I am very tired and miserable. . . Had no chance to say goodbye properly and felt sorry for my behavior the days before. Sorry also that I gave in to doing a line of coke before I left. But the past is just that, the past.

Terrible stomach cramps and anxious feelings. I felt I wouldn't be able to sleep at all, which turned out to be true. I have to strip myself of all ego and prideful thoughts and accept all responsibility for my past behavior and actions. Exhausted, stunned and tired . . .

March 24: Still very depressed and sad. Can't believe that it's only been one day. It seems like a lifetime. Can't shake this feeling of doom and depression. Everyone is so supportive and kind. Without those reaching out to me, I feel I could not go on, but I must. I have to reach deep within me to find the energy to stay on it and concentrate. Wish I could sleep. Still no peace.

Meeting my brothers and hearing them speak of themselves is calming and tranquil. So many insights from so many minds and souls. Miss Nicky and Ben and Jamie so much. I need a perspective and insight to this dilemma of mine. Relax, try to relax.

March 25: It is like sitting on a bomb now. I can just barely hold on without my thoughts and feelings diving into the pits of depression. To see family and friends of my brothers and sisters on visitor's day is so bittersweet to me. I wish my love, my family, my friends, were here to see me. Soon, perhaps soon. Have no idea yet what the program is. Quite a mystery . . . Am in a tizzy.

March 26: The program begins. What an experience today has been. I feel myself so wasted by the uncertainty of all about me. . . Some thoughts and feelings are so painful to even think, let alone write. I must work on organizing my thoughts. All must come out if I am to attain my goal, sobriety and some peace and serenity in my living experience. I'm lucky to have this chance to clean out my insides and start life again.

March 27: The program begins to show its face. From the darkness, I begin to see the form it will take. . . I exploded again in spasms of guilt and self-pity, and tears and sobs. I felt better immediately. The hope and ray of light of being helped through this time propels me into another day. A long day. Went to my first AA meeting. People astound me. I have been so sheltered in my life. I must get out more from now on . . . Soon, please, God, soon to have some more peace.

March 28: I'm moving along. What an experience this is. Did my first test this night. Scored well. 121. Chester told me 125 is genius. That pleased me, to think I'm smart. It will help me in my sobriety. I'm glad I've taken this step now . . .

March 29 and 30: The weekend is upon us. Friday's AA meeting was different from the last one I attended. Could see more of the diseased effects of alcohol on the faces of the members. The effects are more subtle than I thought . . . I can't get impatient with myself. I can now, I think, begin to hold tight onto reality. My problem has been hiding from its pain by doping and drinking. Why not hide? Because hiding is not living. No substance or warmth, just movement, no peace or tranquility, just beats.

I rush everything so because I fear the Now. Am taking stock of myself and slowing down. Haven't had to deal with other people as much as I have now at BFC. It's exhausting and trying at times, yet very fulfilling in other ways.

Enjoying these little things are revealing: making my bed, setting tables, being responsible for my own goods. These little things are giants in the order of one's life. Eli is so supportive. I'm lucky to have him as friend and business associate. Signed some escrow papers today. A little richer and happier . . .

April 3: I will not succumb to the temptation [to drop out]. I must shore up all possible cracks as a mason smoothes out his cement. The foundation is the success of the program. I cannot be denied. There are times when I feel deflated and bitter about all that's gone on, yet I know my new life can be clean and solid. The group session today was mind-boggling. Where did all that energy and anger come from? From deep inside? At last, it's all screaming to be free. Let it be, let it be.

April 4: Today came and went without a whimper. Each day is a complete entity of its own with highs and lows. 24 hours is like a lifetime . . . The last few days have been trying for everyone in our group. Each one of my brothers is at a different stage in the program, and from these different plateaus, each sees a different goal. It's unique when all of us, so different in our life stages and styles, find a common ground . . . Safety in numbers. So many of the loves I've felt in my life were so important in their time, yet I don't even recall their faces. Those women are only blurs in my head. I felt so *powerless* to help in any way. I should have done a card trick or told a joke. But it would not have been appropriate. We were all hurting and I was swept up with a feeling of despair. To see Bob suffer so, to know how he felt and how it tortured him, was to see myself in the same light. Those feelings of love, hate, impatience, fear are dizzying and intoxicating at the same time. When the session was over, I was exhausted and could finally sleep without any problems.

April 5 and 6: My second week. What a wonder to have 15 days under my belt without any substances, to be clean and fresh and ready for all challenges. It seems that step one is the major move in the sobriety experience. I really feel, for the first time, a full step in the right direction. Let it continue through the program. I'm so happy and content, and always impatient.

April 7 and 8: The time span of my anxiety-free periods now seems much longer than before. I now have longer times of peace and non-anger than ever before. To think I could have been like this years ago, could have found a way to ease the turmoil inside of me. What an amazing insight to my fears. Forget the past. Just thank God you have discovered now, and love the time you have.

April 9 and 10: When I arrived, I was so tired and felt truly alone and abandoned. Now, by some miracle, the miracle of learning about myself, I can develop friendships without fears of anything. Imagine being liked just for myself. That's what I call good news.

April 9–12: Those days came and went so quickly, a kaleidoscope of feelings and thoughts, all good, with the negative ones disappearing like dust in a wind. This next week will be key. I have new assignments to do, and step two and three this week. Hallelujah, it's going well.

It *was* going well, and it did go well. But it wasn't always smooth, either then or later. There were a lot of emotional ups and downs, especially where women and family were concerned.

My whole life, I have kept notebooks and sketchbooks where I would draw and write down my thoughts. One of my little verse-mottoes was, "Want a home? Write a poem." And I did that a lot. Sometimes I had little silent, poetic dialogues with my lovers in those books:

"Who's losing who? Who's choosing who?" I wrote.

"If I'm losing you, I'm choosing to—who's fooling who?" the girl wrote back. And then I wrote:

"Leave me be. I can see you're gone, and good for me. You're losing me just as a tree loses leaves. When you're gone, I'm free."

Of course, we ended up disappointing each other, the way lovers usually do. "Long as the river, deep as the sea, just don't ask too much of me," I wrote, and she said, "Oh, give me a break." For some reason, that broke my heart, and a break was what she got, along with this poem:

> Love is never wise.
> It never knows its own disguise,
> just discontent and compromise.

There were so many things on my mind in those days, including my two young sons. In one of those journals, I found this to Nicky:

> You be the father, I be the son,
> you be the garden green and I be the chum.
> I'll be the friendship looking for sails,
> deep in the ocean, swimming with whales.
> So time does not bother. You're in my heart.
> When morning be coming, twilight will part.

We both signed it, "Tony and Nicky." He was about seven at the time. We were together somewhere, and I wrote it for him. I don't think he's seen it since then. My marriage to his mother was over, and she was being obstreperous and very negative where the children were concerned. But isn't that how ex-wives are supposed to behave?

This one, in a way, said it all:

> Were I to ask you candidly
> just what you think of me,

274

the kind of chap you think I am,
the kind of guy to be,
my strengths and flaws laid bare
—who'd care?

When I was at the Betty Ford Clinic, one of the things I was asked to do was to draw up a "resentment list" about my mother, which led me deep into the subject of anger—hers and mine. I realized that she was furious at men. Her father beat and abused her mother in the Old Country, as I mentioned earlier, and from then on, she could never forgive any man she ever had anything to do with. As a result, she was resentful and remorseful her whole life.

But I had to deal with my own remorse and resentment—about her. She came to California, bringing my father and brother, long before I could afford it or handle it, putting incredible pressure on me when I wasn't established yet and wasn't even sure I'd stay there. She insisted I put my brother Robert in films, when she knew he was emotionally ill and couldn't possibly handle such a difficult profession. That propelled him further into his mental illness, powerless as he was. She should have spared him that pain by not exposing him to it. Instead she tried to bargain with *me* about him. The idea was that if I got him into films, she would lay off badgering me and blaming me for his illness. Once she gave him $10,000—of my money—knowing full well that Bobby, who was then a ward of the state, would blow it all. In essence, she deliberately gave my $10,000 to the state of California just to spite me.

I also resented a lot of little things—like the way she would take over the screenings of my films, turning them into cookies-and-drinks events, as if those pathetic offerings would make people like the films more. But most of all I resented how cruelly and disdainfully she treated my father, especially in his later years when he was dying from a heart condition and couldn't defend himself. She badgered him with verbal punches, as she used to do to me with physical punches. I tried to ease his pain, but she would find some way to get to him and hurt him.

My mother always complained that she had a terrible life. Nothing seemed to make her happy. I thought my success would change that, but if anything it made it worse, for she claimed that with my success, I had abandoned her. The reality was, she was so disagreeable and mean, I didn't want to be near her. It pained me to see her so crippled. She died unresolved and alone and, I believe, feeling she was no damn good, the poor woman. I loved her so. May she rest in peace and free me of my bonds.

When Drew Anderson at the BFC read these confessions, he wrote: "I've noticed a pattern in your behavior. It appears that when you get hurt or angry, you push people away and don't want to deal with them. I don't think it's people you don't want to deal with, but the feelings of anger and hurt."

And how. Anger to me was an uncontrollable monster. My mother didn't frighten me as much as her anger did, unrelenting and unforgiving. There was no retreating from it. I try now to avoid it in myself by "de-angerizing," if you will. It's losing control that scares me—that loss of control that can lead to violence. That quality is so ugly in me and in other people. I always feared retaliation, and not knowing when to expect it was what worried me—waiting for the other shoe to drop. There is no way to gauge it, and the element of hatred in it was something I avoided handling. Only now am I able to accept the consequences of anger.

Once, at the Betty Ford Center, I was sitting with six or seven other guys in a meeting, and Drew pointed to me and said, "Fellas, take a good look at him. He's the worst fifty-eight-year-old fuck-up you'll ever meet." I loved that. Until then I couldn't have related to that. But my father was fifty-eight when he died, and there I was, a fifty-eight-year-old fuck-up. It made me think.

Way back at Universal in '55 or '56, they were going to do the life story of Hugh Hefner and *Playboy,* and I was going to play Hefner because I was perfect for it and because Hef and I were very close. They hired a novelist named Bernard Wolf to write it—a Russian who had spent two years in Mexico with Leon Trotsky. Wolf wrote the *Playboy* screenplay, and it was great, but Universal ended up refusing to do it because Hefner wanted complete control of final cut, final this, final that.

So they didn't do the movie, but around that time, Wolf went to Nicky Blair and said, "I've got to go up to Big Sur to meet Henry Miller and help him find a house. Can you help me? He doesn't know anybody." Nicky said yes, and they spent three days with Miller in Big Sur and got to be friends. Henry loved Hollywood stories, and for some reason, he especially loved the stories about Tony Curtis. So Nicky introduced him to me at one of his dinner parties, and we hit it off right away. Henry did some paintings for me and I did some for him.

Movie or no movie, Hugh Hefner was always a reliable friend to me. He let me come live with him and stay in a back room at his mansion both before and during that recovery period. People have all sorts of wild ideas about that place, but it was really just his home, even before he was married. There wasn't so much madness going on. That room he gave me was quiet, and I had it all to myself. Sometimes we played pool—a game requiring great concentration, which was good for me. There were days when I couldn't get out of bed, I ached so badly. I was so inundated with substance abuse, my body kept screaming, "Give me a hit!" Sometimes I stayed in bed all day long, and nights too. On the weekend I'd get up enough energy to clean up a bit, socialize a little, and then head back to that room again.

The sum total of dependency and recovery is a profound thing, and so is the friendship of the people who help you through it—those beacons in the night. In England it was a guy named Danny Gillen, who looked after me and gave me a room. Somebody upstairs gave me Danny, that big, strapping Irishman who wouldn't let anything happen to me. When I came back to New York, Gordon Butler took me in. I will never forget Gordon's fretting about me, and Hef's generosity, and Dean Shendal's kindness, and Eli's caring—my pals. I was in the hands of some very good friends, and they passed me from one to the other, and that's the only way I survived it.

It's been about a decade now since Betty Ford, and here's the interesting thing: I found, for the first time in my life, that I didn't need a heavy love relationship to function. Recovery, if it's real, eliminates that constant, burning need. I don't mean intimacy or the need for companionship. Everybody needs that. But when you treat someone with affection, isn't that a better form of love than falling on your knees screaming, "I can't live without you"? For a long time I couldn't sleep alone or be alone—I always needed another body in my bed to make me feel complete. In many ways I still do, and I am lucky enough to have that now. But in those days, recovery taught me to be able to live by myself.

You don't have to be an alcoholic or former drug user to be a recoverer. Love and hate are also addictions. So are envy, avarice, anger, and frustration. Some people *love* the idea of being frustrated—it's a high. Love itself is a high. Hate is a high. It's only that in-between area, that meditative and peaceful living experience, where you can open your eyes in the morning and just be there. Toward that, I'm dedicated. The Higher Power is nothing more than the joy of living and finding a way of lifting ourselves out of the sorrow that we feel.

A good example in my life today is my relationship with my children. I think I can say it is excellent with all of them. When I was using drugs, I didn't have relationships with anybody, especially the kids. It's a two-way street, of course. If they want a good relationship with me, they have to seek it out. I'm the father. I took care of them financially, I did what I could, I'm still trying to do what I can. If they don't like it, let them get another father.

But they don't seem to want another father, which is fine by me. Jamie told some reporter once, "My father sucks the air out of a room." That made me smile, because it's true. Nobody can work a room like I can. When I go out, I love my looks and my presence. I love the way women look at me. I know the effect I have and I enjoy it. It means something significant to me if she understands that. Last year, she and Kelly flew into Dallas for a lifetime-achievement award I was getting from Cinemax-Showtime, which dedicated a whole month to a retrospective of my pictures that hadn't been seen for years. Those girls will never know what that surprise of their showing up there meant to me.

I'd like to do a film someday with Jamie or Kelly, but I'm sensitive about that. What kind of picture would it be? It can't be just a freak show. A comedy with me in drag, or one of them in drag? Arsenio Hall asked me what role I'd like to play with Jamie, and I told him, "I'd like to play her mother."

From their perspective, it must be intriguing and fairly unique. You can really get a sense of who you are if you can see your parents on-screen when they were twenty-two—to see your father or mother doing *anything* at twenty-two. I'm privileged, and so are they. It's been a wonderful profession for me and my children in that respect.

I don't want to change anything. I don't want to relate to time anymore because it ties you down. All of a sudden you say, "Wait a minute, I'd better start reflecting." I don't want to do that anymore. Last night I went out by myself to Spago's for an early dinner, for my quail. It was delicious. Then I stopped off at Nicky Blair's, saw a couple of guys I knew. They were talking about those movies I made, and they went through the whole list. I thought, *Maybe I've really done something nice in my life.* I kind of liked it. I left there and went home without any bodyguards or bullshit. I don't know what the purpose of the living experience is. I only know to focus on whatever question arises in me right now. As a recovering person, I take each moment at a time. That's the way I do it, because that's the way I *have* to do it.

FINE ART AND FAMILY

It had been a long time since a first-class director came to me with a first-class project. When Nicolas Roeg* brought me *Insignificance* (1985), I read the script and knew immediately I wanted to do it. The title was bad, but what a story! Marilyn Monroe, Joe DiMaggio, Albert Einstein, and Joe Mc-Carthy all end up in the same New York hotel. The names couldn't be used, but it's clear who they are. The dialogue was amazing—love, fame, and the atomic bomb. I'd never read a script like it before. Putting those four anxiety-ridden people together was like mixing up four chemicals that you know are going to explode.

I said to Nick, "You're aware of what it means to put me in this piece, the way you're playing this woman?" He said yes. I said, "Then obviously the connotation is that she is Marilyn, and having the real costar from her best movie takes the irony and the coincidence even further?" He said yes.

I know it's hard for people to imagine, but somewhere on this planet there are two or three people who've never heard of Marilyn Monroe. A few million Africans never had time to see the blond bombshell, and a few hundred million Chinese, and probably a lot of Eskimos and pygmies. Out of five billion people, maybe four billion think "Marilyn" is a deodorant or a

---

*British director Nicolas Roeg began as a lighting expert and cameraman on such films as *Lawrence of Arabia* (1962) before directing some of the most imaginative and visually spellbinding films of the 1970s. Many featured rock stars: *Performance* (1970) with Mick Jagger, *The Man Who Fell to Earth* (1976) with David Bowie, and *Bad Timing/A Sensual Obsession* (1980) with Art Garfunkel. His most powerful and shocking film, *Don't Look Now* (1973), contained perhaps the most erotic love scene ever filmed to that time (between Donald Sutherland and Julie Christie). Roeg's wife, Theresa Russell, often played his female leads.

sandwich. So the point is, where does *Insignificance* stand when you eliminate the personalities and you look at its logic? In order for the material to stand up, it had to go beyond that, and it did.

The same is true for any film, of course. In *Some Like It Hot*, when that guy turns on that English accent, it can't just be Cary Grant; it's a half-assed English accent that has to be within the realm of the way somebody, somewhere, actually talks. A lot of young people nowadays see *Some Like It Hot* before they have any idea who Cary Grant is. There's no connection for them. Even *after* they see Cary, maybe there's still no connection. And that's fine. It has to work on both levels. In the movie, Jack Lemmon says to me, "Where'd you get that accent? Nobody talks like that." That's a funny line, especially since it's taking place in the twenties. He's this guy out of New York City who's just trying not to get murdered, he sees this dishy blonde, he wants to fuck her, and the only way he's going to do it is to masquerade as a millionaire with a way of chopping up his words. That's the level it works on. I never worked it deliberately as "a Cary Grant imitation." It wasn't complicated. It gets complicated later, in terms of the plot, but mostly it's just supposed to be funny, and so much the better if the Cary voice makes it a little funnier for some people.

———————————

The same challenge on a dramatic rather than comic level was faced by TC as "the Senator" (McCarthy), Theresa Russell as "the Actress" (Monroe), Gary Busey as "the Baseball Player" (DiMaggio), and Michael Emil as "the Professor" (Einstein) in *Insignificance*. In director Roeg's dazzling, virtuoso style, the film opens with a re-creation—from below—of the famous *Seven Year Itch* scene in which a blast of air from a subway grate makes Monroe's flimsy white skirt billow up revealingly.

The next scene finds TC in a low-life bar, sweating and snarling. It is his job to articulate the philosophical theme in a brilliantly delivered ramble to the bartender: "You know, according to the laws of probability, every time you drink a glass of water, you drink a little piece of Napoleon's crap—maybe even Mussolini's . . . We're all part of that great fuckin' alimentary canal." As a vicious, Red-baiting politician, he soon corners and threatens the Einstein character: "Are you now or have you ever

TC as Joseph McCarthy and Michael Emil as Albert Einstein in Nicolas Roeg's *Insignificance* (1985)

been? You're the movie-star type, the kind that mud sticks to. You know everything there is to know about neutrons, protons, plutons, croutons . . ." Einstein parries fairly smoothly until the Senator declares that the Commies were just faking their losses in World War II. "Fifteen million Russian dead, a Soviet plot?" asks Einstein incredulously. "They're tricky," TC replies.

The screenplay's tour de force comes in the encounters between Einstein and Monroe.

MM: I understand relativity. Do you believe me?

AE: Yes . . .

MM: Really, you do? You're not just saying that? Are you willing to swear to your God that you believe me?

AE: Well . . . maybe you better prove it. With my God, I don't want to take any chances.

Whereupon, she sets up a group of children's toys, purchased just for this occasion, and demonstrates the theory of relativity with perfect understanding.

The Professor's watch always says 8:19—the time of the dropping of the atomic bomb on Hiroshima. *All* clocks in the film say 8:19. Stopped and broken timepieces pepper the movie. Einstein is obsessed with clocks—with Time—with 8:19 A.M.—and increasingly with the Actress, who makes clear her desire to seduce him, even though the wildly jealous Baseball Player is hot on her heels.

Two simultaneous sex scenes are intercut in a stunning montage sequence, to a jazz arrangement of Mozart's Symphony No. 39: The Actress and the Professor perform a slow-motion striptease for each other, the Baseball Player tears up a Marilyn Monroe calendar in a bar, and—at the end of frantically humping a whore—TC weeps. His sexual frustrations will soon be taken out brutally on the Actress and the Professor both.

Everyone communicates eloquently, but never with each other. "It's all *words*," moans Marilyn to Einstein. "I came to know you, and all I get is *words*." And so he throws the precious manuscript of his life's work out the window, its pages fluttering down into the New York streets and across the world onto Japanese gardens. And with that comes the great explosion he has most dreaded: Marilyn and white dress are blood-soaked, swirling around as in that famous scene over the grate, but this time on fire. The manuscript pages swirl with her, aflame and twirling. It is the Apocalypse, and the images accompanying it are horrifying. Then suddenly in this final chaos, everything is reversed—literally—and restored backward to order. The Actress picks up her purse and peeks around the corner of the Professor's door for a cheery, flippant, "Bye!"

It is one of the most astounding endings ever.

—B.P.

———————•—•———————

Nick Roeg is more of a silent director than a verbal one. I thought his working methods were fascinating. By watching him set up the shot and study the rehearsal and by being sensitive to what he was seeing, you would begin to realize how that scene should be played. Nick would give you physical things to do. He would say, "Why don't you walk to the window at the end of that speech and isolate yourself?"

282

With a word like *isolate,* he would clue you in to what he was thinking as a director. No excess verbiage. Just a few clues that you could act upon with your own imagination or creativity. So working with him was a very collaborative effort. Other directors would say, "You stay there, the camera stays here"—arbitrary orders, cut-and-dried.

With Nick Roeg, the way he listened to the run-throughs and watched the scene first was always the motivating factor in how he directed it. Almost without his saying anything to you, you got an idea of how he wanted you to play it and how *you* wanted to play it and enhance it with some ideas of your own. I found that stimulating. I liked that method very much. I liked that picture very much too. There's no other like it. Nobody comes away from *Insignificance* unscathed.

It's hard to say how many films I made altogether. If I include the twenty-four episodes of *The Persuaders,* which is the equivalent of twelve movies, I would say the list is over one hundred.* Nowadays, of course, most film-making activity is for television. The studios try to make it sound like there's a big difference between the two, but there really isn't.

Over the years, I've done a lot of work for television. I was a con man in *The Ripoff* (1975), a pilot for the *McCoy* series on NBC. It was perfect casting for me. Anyone who survives twenty-five years in Hollywood *must* be a con man. That was one of four, two-hour TV films I made for Universal-TV. *Vega$* (1978) was a pilot for the detective series with Robert Urich, where I was Bernie Roth, the casino owner. *The Users* (1978) was based on Joyce Haber's sleazy novel about Hollywood, with Jaclyn Smith and John Forsythe.

There were many others. But the really good one was *Moviola: The Scarlett O'Hara War* (1980), which John Erman directed and the Wolper people put together. Garson Kanin wrote the book, about David O. Selznick's search for the perfect Scarlett in *Gone With the Wind.*

---

* That figure is almost right on the mark. For the first full Tony Curtis filmography, including both theatrical and television films, as well as TV series and appearances, with full casts and credits, see Appendix A, page 326.

TC received an Emmy Award nomination for his performance as Selznick in *Moviola*. But as far as his friend Tommy Culla was concerned, the most compelling performance was behind the wheel of a car. Culla, who often visited him on the set, recalls:

"He was shooting *Moviola* in Burbank at the ranch and had just finished the sequence where Selznick is introduced to Vivien Leigh for the first time. It was a rough scene. He had been working very late, and it was two-thirty in the morning before he finally got a break. I said, 'You're exhausted, would you like a cup of coffee?' He said yes, and I said, 'Follow me.' So we drove to this all-night coffee shop and pulled in, but there was only one parking space. I motioned for Tony to take it, and he did.

TC as David O. Selznick in *Moviola: The Scarlett O'Hara War* (1980)

"The spot I picked out for myself was really small, and I'm not a good driver. I started to try it, but then I just felt, as an elementary matter of physics, I couldn't get my car in there. So I rolled down the window and said, 'Tony, I'm going to park up on the hill. There's no room to get in there.' He said, 'May I try?' He'd been up all night, but he got out, hopped in my Buick, and in one shot just breezed it right in, like Shoemaker out of the starting gate. An inch to spare on either side. It was breathtaking. God, does he know his cars!"

—TOMMY CULLA to B.P., February 14, 1993

Right after *Insignificance* I did a TV film called *Mafia Princess* (1986). That was a beauty. It was the autobiography of Antoinette Giancana, the daughter of mobster Sam Giancana, played by me. Susan Lucci did a beautiful job as Antoinette, but the problem was—and is—that television movies rarely get the respect and attention they deserve. I felt that about *Murder in Two Acts* (1988) too, an Agatha Christie mystery I did with Peter Ustinov and Emma Samms; a gorgeous girl.

It pisses me off that films like that get ignored when a lot of the time they have much more going for them than a theatrical release, like *Lobster Man from Mars* (1989), for example. The gimmick was stolen from Mel Brooks: I'm this producer who gets bad news from the IRS, and I'm about to jump out the window, when somebody comes up with a surefire flop I can use for a tax write-off: "Stevie Horowitz Productions' *Lobster Man from Mars.*" It's kind of a cross between *The Night of the Living Dead, Airplane, Alien, Ghostbusters,* and *Deep Throat,* without the throat. The worst movie in the world. It gets more and more absurd. All I do is sit in a screening room and watch it, and they cut to my reaction every now and then. The fact is, I never actually saw a single foot of the crazy movie I was supposed to be reacting to.*

I did it because I had to make those child-support payments, and they gave me $100,000. You do what you have to do, right? But you don't necessarily like it. Then something much classier happened. A man named Arnold Schwarzenegger. I was tooling around in my white Buick Reatta (red leather upholstery, limited edition, convertible with the top down) when the car phone rang. "Tony, it's Arnold, where are you?" I said, "I'm on Sunset." He said, "When you get home, call me."

I did, and he told me he was going to direct a movie and wanted me to play one of the leads—a remake of Barbara Stanwyck's *Christmas in Connecticut* for TNT. It was his first time as a director and, as always with him, a smart career move. That snob attitude about TV movies would be an advantage, for once: The big-time yenta critics would probably ignore it. He could learn the ropes without having to be bashed by them.

Arnold is a very persuasive man. I said yes immediately, and it was an honor to work with him. There wasn't a detail that he missed. There were no action scenes or decapitations. This was just a low-key comedy. Dyan Cannon is a cooking-show host who can't cook, and I'm the hyper producer who provides her with a family of obnoxious, fake kids for a heart-

---

* *Lobster Man from Mars* was very "late eighties"—a post–David Lynch science fiction satire. Despite, or because of, Stanley Sheff's heavy-handed direction, it is regarded by many as a cult classic and has turned into a heavy-duty video-rental property.

warming holiday TV special. My favorite line is delivered to the director: "I want that snow to be more *sincere.*"

In one scene, I come storming in and criticize everybody. I had to combine a lot of physical movement and dialogue and make it look spontaneous. Just before Arnold said "Action," he leaned close to me and whispered, "Tony, take no prisoners."

That was his simple direction, and I followed it. When Arnold talks, I listen. You don't argue with Arnold. He's a very amusing and intelligent man, and I enjoyed every minute of making that picture with him.

If you've made it this far, I don't want to bore you with a list of every other movie that I've made or that I've been making since then. I'll just cut to the chase and say that my most recent project was a picture Martin Scorsese produced called *Naked in New York,* with Whoopi Goldberg, Kathleen Turner, and Tim Dalton. It's supposed to be released around the same time as this book. What a movie that's going to be!

I hope.

———————•—————

Jennifer Walsh: You don't know a man until you talk to his personal assistant—in TC's case, Jennifer Walsh:

"Working for Tony Curtis is like being in a hurricane. You never do one project at a time, and Tony doesn't do anything on a small scale. We don't have one art opening, we have eight within a two-week period. You go through the eye of the hurricane, things are calm for a while, and then the hurricane comes again.

"Every morning, I go through the litany of Tony's projects and priorities. You know *when* he's got to be somewhere, but you don't know what's really in store. On a shoot, is he going to be on his feet for twelve hours or sit around twiddling his thumbs? It's crucial for him to know this because he's gotten progressively, aggressively busier in the last two years. Tony seems to be the quintessential guy they're looking for: He can play anything from eighteen to eighty. There's such a joy of life in him, which comes out in his acting. He still has an innocent, almost naïve quality that is astounding. On the other hand, he can meet someone and tell you in two seconds exactly what the guy is all about, with a great deal of cynicism. He's the best judge of character I've ever met.

"I'm extremely protective of Tony. I'm the first line of defense. We were in Las Vegas doing an art show, and Tony had just gotten off a plane from Tokyo and rushed in for a public appearance at Caesar's Palace from noon to five. He was roped in in the middle of the gallery and people were pressing in, shaking his hand. At 5 o'clock, just as we were leaving, a new wave of people flooded in. I didn't want him to be subjected to any more. We had just started the long walk from the gallery back to Caesar's when I saw this mob of a hundred people following us.

"Tony's not pretentious. He has never had a bodyguard, which is amazing. I mean, this man is an icon. He gets hundreds of fan letters a week from all over the world—and they all get answered. A lot of stars don't bother to do that. But he's very old-world. There's not a more gracious guy. So this crowd was following him. I was in high heels, running ahead of them, about four paces behind Tony, trying to hold them off. Finally I catch up to Tony and he turns and looks at me and says, 'Jennifer, what are you so nervous about?' This man is going to be stuck for another two hours signing autographs, and he's asking, 'What's your problem?'

"When I first started working for Tony, we had a little ritual. I have a tendency to be uptight about things like organization. Tony taught me to kick back and relax. We took turns pointing out the most unusual event of the day, whether it was the deer behind his house or just, 'Look how blue the sky is.' The first summer I worked for him, I found a six-foot rattlesnake crawling through his garden toward the front door. I immediately told Tony. 'Where is it?' He practically wants to pet the damn thing. I said, 'It's poisonous!' He's checking it out . It's coiled. I think it's going to jump. I think we should go inside. The gardeners ended up taking it away and Tony was upset: 'They didn't kill it, did they?' I said no, they just threw it back where it belonged. He was so relieved. He has a real respect for living things.

"During *Christmas in Connecticut*, there is a scene where Tony comes running down the stairs in cowboy boots, a shirt, a jacket, and his underwear. It was eleven at night and Arnold says, 'Tony, take off your pants.' Tony just drops his pants on the spot. The crew is saying, 'I can't believe he just did that.' Arnold asked him to. Tony knew exactly what Arnold was after. That scene worked wonderfully.

"Another time, we were on the shoot from hell—a project that will remain nameless. Tony and the crew had been through three very intense weeks, and in the middle of it, the director was fired. They got another *director du jour*. The new director walks in and can't find his ass with two hands. There was a change in scene, and everybody was relaxing. This new director came over and said, 'What are you all sitting on your butts for?'

"Tony looked at this guy and said, 'I don't know where you came from, but we've been through three weeks of hell, and we deserve a five-minute break.' He already had the crew's respect, but when he said that to the director, the crew applauded! You don't think of someone of his stature sticking up for the technicians. It was just an example of how he treats people.

"My own father is dead, but I have asked Tony officially, if and when I get married, to give me away. And he said he will. It's not because he's a movie star, it's because he's TC—the maestro who runs around in his white shorts and the beat-up sweaters with paint all over them.

—Jennifer Walsh to B.P., April 8, 1993

In 1977 I wrote a novel called *Kid Andrew Cody and Julie Sparrow* that drew a lot from my own life. It actually started out as two separate books—one on Andrew Cody and one on Julie Sparrow. But then I shuffled them together like a deck of cards, wrote some additional stuff, and combined them. I did up a diagram, with charts of how their lineages intersected. I took it very seriously. I remember textures, I have a sense of what people are like, and I wanted to put those things into words. I saw all those characters I'd played and all those environments I'd been in as a tremendous background for fiction.

So I asked myself why I couldn't write a book. To me acting and writing—all the arts—were interrelated. But my formal education was minimal, so when I decided to start writing, I picked up a couple of how-to books. I couldn't believe the crap in them, and I threw them in the garbage.

Then Irving Lazar sent me something by Somerset Maugham that hooked me: *A Writer's Notebook*.

A lot of *Kid Andrew Cody* related to my father, the character named Max. It related to what I felt—and to what I felt *he* felt—as a highly sexual man. Some of it was in the realm of, "If the queen had balls, she'd be the king." But parts of it were straight out of his and my lives:

> The Kid saw the anguish in Max's eyes. He couldn't understand why. Was it his mother? Was it that poker game? What made him so sad sometimes? What broke his heart? Max was always trying to find out the reason for his existence. He needed a reason. . . . He wanted someone to love him when he was a kid. But no one did. His parents treated him as if he was going to come every second. Someone to chase around with a big towel to catch any of the seepage. . . . Max still couldn't imagine his father taking a shit or his mother wiping herself, not his family. If only he could accept his joyous weaknesses which were his strengths. Chasing a pair of aces was just as profound as chasing Socrates.

Doubleday published that book, and it did okay. The contract provided for a second one, in 1979, called *Starstruck*. It was a Hollywood story. It had a character named Cliff Granite—which I thought was pretty funny— but Doubleday didn't like it, and there was a lawsuit. I had a lot of trouble with them. They paid me a certain fee, and Irving Lazar of course took his commission out of it. Then I had to go to court in New York City, and during the trial he refused to give me any assistance.

The judge loved me. Judge Sweet was his name. That fucking Doubleday attorney said, "During the time you were writing this book, you were—" He made a drinking gesture. I said, "I'm a recovering alcoholic." I found out later that Judge Sweet understood recovery and had recovering people in his own family. He screamed at that attorney. I never forgot that. Maybe I *should* forget it, but that much recovered, I'm not.

To shorten the story, I got a favorable ruling in the lower court but it was reversed on the appeal, and I had to pay back a lot of money. A little while earlier, in the property settlement with my third wife, whatever her name was, she got half the money I got from Doubleday. How come she didn't have to return that to Doubleday? How come Irving Lazar didn't? That pissed me off.

After that, I decided that I wasn't going to take any shit anymore and that I would not be forced into doing things the way other people thought

I should. Remember that scene in *Mr. Blandings Builds His Dream House* between Myrna Loy and the painting contractor? She tells him something like, "I want the dining room bright yellow—not a canary yellow, but a yellow that looks as though the sun has just come up." He has a pad and goes, "Uh-huh." Then she says, "In the powder room, I would like a rose color— not a deep rose, but a light rose, a little lilac to it. And in the kitchen, I want it white—not a bright white, not a cream . . ." The phone rings. She says, "Excuse me," and goes to answer it. The contractor's painter comes up, and the contractor just points to the three rooms and says, "Yellow, pink, white."

It was a great scene. But I don't want that for myself. I'm not a cast of thousands. I don't want some agency telling me it has to be A, B, or C. I don't want some ancient fucking contract that somebody made up thirty-seven years ago, and all they do is fill in my name. I feel the same way about movie parts as with books. Somebody says, "We've got this cameo—" and I say, "Fuck you. I don't do bits." They say, "But we've got Sylvester Stallone . . ."

I don't care if it's *Mrs.* Sylvester Stallone. There isn't a name anybody can say that will impress me. I've spent too many years being herded by that goat who gets all those sheep into the slaughterhouse. The sheep know something's wrong, but their instinct to follow is so overwhelming that they go along until it's too late. I can be herded too, but nowadays my antennae are up. I've learned to take a different approach.

I put a house up for sale at 800 grand. A guy came in at 730. I said, "Now I want 950." The broker said, "What are you doing?" I said, "Well, he's not coming up with my price, so why can't I change it?" The broker said, "That's not the way you do it." I said, "Maybe that's not the way *you* do it, but that's the way *I'm* doing it." Maybe I learned that from Stanley Kubrick.

It may not be the best way to do business, and I might not strike a lot of deals, but it's a helluva lot more fun. More and more, I feel like my friend Frankie in New York, who was very sweet, but once you crossed him—forget it. He never forgave a thing. No compromises.

When you're vulnerable, you have to compromise. "What is it you want me to do? Okay." You have to put up with it. But I have a very European attitude. Once someone deceives or lies to me, whether it's an agent or a producer or an ex-wife, I never forget it. There are certain things that are unforgivable, nonredeemable, and nonrefundable.

The movie business is no better or worse than any other, and all the pressures and scams involved in it are not unique. It just happens to be the business I know best. If you don't get a part, you take it personally: "God, they don't want me. Maybe I've done something." But it's not that at all. It's just the disinterest and the heartlessness of any profession. You have to be careful of your own personal mind-fuck. You turn it into: "Why do they hate me?" They don't hate you. It's just unthinking. If you're not in with the one that has the leverage, you're not going to make movies, no matter how gifted you are. And you alienate a lot of people on your way up and on your way down.

Take the wives of the producers and agents, for example. Up to a little while ago, all the big agents and producers were men, and everybody threw themselves at the men because they were the ones who had the leverage. The wives sat there quietly watching it all, watching people be polite or rude to them, but if their husbands had leverage, they had leverage with the husbands, and they had their own method of knocking people off. They were able to say, "I don't think so-and-so should be in the movie." Actors could be really shunned and kept from working because of the fact that a wife's nose was out of joint.

There was a park in L. A. where I used to take my children pony riding, back when I was really disgruntled during those early drug days. I would pick up Allegra and Alexandra and take them there; that was all the time I really had to share with them, I was so distracted. It was a pony-ride park, later they tore it down and built what is now the Beverly Center, a giant shopping mall. But it used to be a laid-back kind of corner with sweet little rides for children.

Anyway, there I was one day with my children, and I saw Ruth Koch, Howard Koch's wife. Howard and I met when he was an assistant director on *Beachhead* for the Mirisch company. Then he moved up and became a big producer in town. By then he was also the president of the Motion Picture Academy. I acknowledged Ruth, but I guess I didn't acknowledge her in the way she wanted me to. The next day I got a call from Howard. "Why were you so rude to my wife?" I said, "I don't remember that." He said, "Well, please apologize, and if you do, I'll let you give out one of the Oscars at the Academy Awards presentation."

I didn't apologize, and I didn't hand out any Oscars. But I've held that in my heart all these years. The Koches are very friendly with me now, but I don't see them or a lot of other people lining up to give me a movie. Blake Edwards and Norman Jewison and Robert Mulligan started out with me. I don't see any of those guys making any effort or gesture toward me. It may sound like sour grapes, but I don't care what it sounds like. That's my feeling.

I bought the rights to that Bugsy Siegel story, *We Only Kill Each Other,* a fabulous book. I picked up the option, and Howard Koch was going to produce it for Paramount, and Eddie Anhalt was going to write the screenplay. I was in Italy working on another picture, but we organized it to happen while I was away. In the meantime, Bob Evans took over Paramount, and when I came back, he said, "We're going to shelve the project," for some bullshit reason I don't recall. I never forgave Bob Evans for that.

This was way before Warren Beatty. My concept was much more powerful, with much more Jewishness. Benjamin Siegel was a mean, neurotic kid out of New York City. He became what he was because he was a Jew who had to put up with all of the inequities of being a "Jew boy"—all that same shit that I went through. That was the fabric. I understood that character. I thought about it for years, and I had all the attributes necessary to do it. You couldn't suck out the fabric and make that film with somebody born in Wisconsin. It just wouldn't work, and it didn't.

I resented it. To them, it was just another project. To me, every movie was crucial. That project was pissed away from me because I wasn't able to grab a tenacious enough hold on it. Today that would never happen.

You try not to be bitter. You try to say, "Hail fellow, well met!" But you can't always do it. A lot of men and women in Hollywood are just waiting for the day when their doorbell rings and there's that guy who treated them like shit fifteen years ago, needing a favor. "Oh, hello. Excuse me, I'm busy." You know you're going to do that.

People do that in their personal relationships too. I've done it, and I've had it done to me. What goes around comes around. That girl I stood up or didn't treat properly; four or five years later, all of a sudden she's standing there in front of you, and you get it right in the mouth—or you *wish* you'd get it right in the mouth. Your self-esteem was bruised because she wouldn't go out with you, or vice versa. It's a game all men and women play with each other. I've seen it and I know it. Men play it with men, women play it with women, men and women play it with each other. It's a constant part of the living experience. How come Hemingway and Dostoyevsky never wrote about that subtle war? It's in life, it's in the movie business, it's in every business.

I'm lucky that I had other interests. I'm sitting on a very fine estate.

With no exceptions over the years, I've been very fortunate in my business dealings. I own a big parcel of farmland in Perris Valley, California, that I've been maintaining all these years. Part of the acreage was sold years ago and became an industrial park, a place for small industries. It's called the Curtis Industrial Park, so I've left my mark on southern California.

I'm well-endowed, if you'll excuse the expression. I never went broke. I parlayed all my homes into bigger homes. I've always had a flair for real estate. It had nothing to do with the movie business. Very few actors back then got rich on their film work. Today they can, because picture grosses are so huge, but in those days, hardly ever.

As far as film residuals go, before 1965 actors got nothing. That year, the Screen Actors Guild negotiated a TV residuals arrangement that was not retroactive. But I was part-owner in a lot of my own films from around 1957 on with a percentage of the gross and net profit. I was under contract to Universal, but I was also doing outside pictures. Lew Wasserman made those deals for me, though I don't denigrate my own contribution. There wasn't a bigger player in those days than me. I broke everybody's legs, including Marlon Brando's and Monty Clift's. When I hit, I hit big. They would spend $200,000 on a movie of mine and it would gross $2 million. In those days a movie ticket was 50 cents. Imagine what the take would have been on that $7 ticket of today. Don't imagine, I'll tell you exactly: It would be $28 million.

I think the first picture I owned a piece of was *The Defiant Ones*. I know that on *Some Like It Hot* I got 5 percent of the gross; on movies like *Taras Bulba* and *The Vikings*, 7 percent. I still retain those rights, so I'm always generating some income from them.

I used to own property in Hawaii, but I sold it. For a while I was a part-owner of the Phoenix Suns basketball team, but no more. Contrary to a lot of rumors, I never had any financial involvement in Caesar's Palace in Las Vegas, although I love that place and go there whenever I get the chance. Mostly I hit the blackjack tables. I always set a limit and put that base amount in one pocket and the "gravy" in the other. I go down, then bounce back. A year ago my pal Barry Paris saw me in action there, tucking chips into my shorts, and called it the Bank of Bermuda. I told him that the left Bank of Bermuda Shorts was open for business, but the right Bank of Bermuda Schwartz would never be touched.

I wanted to direct movies. Why didn't I? I never got the encouragement I needed. Lew Wasserman used to urge me to produce films, but I always felt producing was a gimmick—something you did because it was smart tax-wise. I was never interested in it. Directing was more interesting to me, but it ate up so much time. You had to be in production meetings for days and days on end, talking about how much money you were going to spend. I didn't want to do that. I wanted to take fencing lessons . . .

The only part of the film industry I truly loved was acting. They sent you a script. If you liked it, you made the deal. The next thing you knew, you were working on it. You did your eight weeks, and you were out of there. You made a bundle of money, everybody loved you, you were gone. You could do two or three of those a year. As a director, you could do only one. Becoming a director was never a burning desire of mine. I would make a wonderful "instant" director. I can write dialogue instantly and organize a scene. But nobody wants that kind of work. Maybe one day it'll happen. Right now it's not in the cards.

Looking back, I can't imagine my life without the film experience or the drug experience or any other experience, even though I don't pretend to know what the purpose of it all was. It was all an enigma. It happened. To say that it shouldn't have or that it could have been different is like being asked, "If you had to do it all over again, what would you do?" I'd say, "I'd do it all over you." You can't answer that question.

What is the unique quality of George Burns at ninety-seven? In the scheme of things, is there a big difference between sixty-five and ninety-five? It's all the blink of an eye. The beat goes on, the baton passes, and while you've got it, you enjoy it. I love Buckminster Fuller's statement that we have great arrogance to go along with our great ignorance. We fret and fuss and pontificate, while that good-old earth just keeps on going from green to brown and back again. That sky is what it looked like five thousand years ago, but here we are, worried from day to week to month because the wraparound is so brief for us.

I don't see my life as a set of achievements. I just see it as things that I've had to do. That I've had this magnificent film career is a mitzvah for me. All those movies and all those people I worked with in them. Now to have my paintings, my box-making, this writing experience—I love it all, and I still don't understand it. What more do I want? What do I still wanna be when I grow up?

I am constantly, every day of my life, still coming to grips with my inadequacies. I look at a painting: How can I improve it? How can I improve the quality of my living? What drives me to search for that perfection? Is it that nobody's perfect, only I can't accept it? What measuring stick am I using?

I just like the question that arises in me right now: How is this painting going to work out? What colors do I want? I'm thinking of red and blue, but what can be loaded on top of that? I love those paintings. They're not "therapy." You shouldn't do anything in life as therapy. You've got to throw yourself into it completely. Otherwise it's like a line I had in *Sex and the Single Girl*, when Natalie Wood asks what my wife does: "She paints. Her toenails."

I don't paint my toenails. I paint with the same passion and commitment that I make movies. Maybe more. The two things are independent of each other but interwoven. Actually, drawing and painting were my first means of artistic expression, long before I ever got into films. I was making odd designs on the sidewalks in Manhattan and in my schoolbooks from the time I was six. Looking back on it, I think that early language barrier in that Hungarian-immigrant environment was what first motivated me to draw. I could express myself better with pictures than I could verbally. I found painting and sketching a better way to communicate.

I painted in grade school, in high school, in the navy, and in California. At home and away. On my own films and Janet's. I'd visit her on a location somewhere, and while she was working I'd take off with my easel, hike up into the mountains, and paint all day. They'd pick me up on the way back.

I don't ever remember *not* painting.

------------◆------------

TC's bold, vibrant still lifes—acrylic on canvas—and his unique "time boxes" are in major private galleries and collections throughout the world. In 1992 the prestigious Butler Institute of American Art in Ohio mounted the first-ever formal museum exhibition of his paintings and boxes, a show entitled "Tony Curtis: Recent Works." In its catalog, Butler director Dr. Louis Zona wrote:

"The history of art presents numerous examples of creative men and women blessed with the ability to contribute in more than one art form. The sensitivities required for success in one mode of expression can offer foundation for expression in another.

A TC oil painting

"Curtis has carved a unique niche by blending elements of modernism with contemporary concerns. In a sense his works are romantic—classic imagery filtered through his imagination, utilizing cubistic space with expressionistic paint handling and a use of color as vibrant as any work of the Fauvist era. We see in his works the same sensibilities which have drawn audiences through the years to applaud his films—the freedom to explore and extend his talents into new and exciting territories."

The Butler exhibition drew great regional and national attention. TC was lionized for three days of personal appearances, including an outdoor luncheon at the home of art patrons Ciel and Max Draime, whom he adored. The next day, he was called upon to visit another person whom he did not adore—a multimillionaire whose collection was a who's who of canvases by every major American and European name. TC couldn't wait to leave. He had required the use of a brand-new Cadillac Seville, and as we climbed into it, I watched a ritual with which I was becoming familiar: the ceremonial pulling on of his kid driving gloves. Dazzled by the millionaire's art, I asked TC what he thought of it.

"It's a collection of fear," he replied. "Safe choices. No risks."

Brutal, succinct, true.

That social obligation had been tiresome, but there is an antique flea-market extravaganza nearby that has to be checked out for potential box materials. It yields up many treasures, but word of his presence spreads fast and he is soon mobbed by autograph seekers who put an end to his browsing. Back in the safety of the Seville, he is now truly exhausted. And hungry. A Chinese restaurant looks promising; he pulls in and tethers the Seville. We buy a local newspaper to read the reviews of his exhibit.

The Chinese waiter is flabbergasted. "Aren't you—Aren't you—?" He can't quite get out the name. "Aren't you—the famous star of motion pictures?" TC nods with mixed amusement and fatigue. He is always polite, but, at this point, he is spent. He picks at his sweet-and-sour chicken in silence, reading the *Youngstown Vindicator*. I get the sports section. Suddenly he looks up and says, "What does 'mendacious' mean?" He is a man who is not afraid to ask. "Lying," I answer. It is the sum total of our conversation for the whole meal. He nods and goes back to the paper. He does not wish to be disturbed. I want to ask what the review says but think better of it and do what, for me, is the hardest thing in the world: I shut up.

—B.P.

As a kid, I always had a penchant for saving and arranging and rearranging things. I wasn't really consciously aware of it at the time, but there was something about the artistic way you could assemble and disassemble and reassemble a lot of unrelated objects that appealed to me. I'd put them on the floor, on a shelf, in a shoe box: wherever. But I never quite knew what to do with them. They were never permanent, they'd get lost, I'd find other things, and *they'd* get lost too.

It wasn't until years later, in the fifties, that I discovered Joseph Cornell. If anybody helped me "get there" in terms of art—and definitely in terms of boxes—it was Cornell. In painting it was Matisse. But in constructions, it was Cornell who opened up a whole world to me. Now when I make my

Marbles, dice, and a pair of spectacles coexist in TC's classic box construction, *French Impressionists* (1991), on display at the Butler Institute of American Art.

own I move those little objects almost infinitesimally, to please something in my eye and in my brain that says a certain combination is delicate or nice or surprising or right. Right for who? Obviously, myself. If other people like them, that's fine. But that's not my objective. No one else can see them from my point of view. They have to mean something real or unreal or absurd or abstract or quirky to *me*. And without exception, they do.

The consensus among art critics is that TC's paintings are serious and skillful. But it is his box constructions that are most extraordinary and unique: ephemeral boxes, or boxes of ephemera, encased in glass and populated with old letters, photos, keys, dice, marbles, timepieces, vials of liquid—you name it—all carefully ordered with their own esoteric inner logic.

Joseph Cornell (1903–1972) was the founding master of that genre. He and his constructivist art form were largely ignored until the Museum of Modern Art belatedly recognized their genius in the 1940s. Cornell was the king of collection and recollection, his box assemblies the height of enchantment. He lived on Utopia Parkway in Flushing, New York, with his mother and invalid brother Robert, who, due to cerebral palsy, could barely speak or move but whose cheerful imagination inspired Cornell. His boxes began as toys for Robert: a mirrored "thimble forest," for example. But beyond the tragic brother, Cornell had his own deep fascination with games, toys, and small objects—the flotsam and jetsam of life.

Cornell's boxes were like miniature sailors' sea chests salvaged from a wreck. They were souvenirs of an imaginary voyage, moments held captive in a cage. He was interested in "the poetry of ordinary objects," and he haunted the old bookstores and curio shops of Manhattan in search of them. Cornell was associated with the surrealists of the 1930s and, like them, believed that fragmentation was a condition of modern life. In assembling the fragments, he often felt an intense longing to get into the box himself.

In the 1950s Cornell dabbled in experimental films, one of which recorded the demolition of his—and TC's—beloved Third Avenue El. He

Box artist Joseph Cornell (1903–1972) in 1940

died in 1972 at age sixty-nine. After his death, it was discovered that he'd kept elaborate dossiers on movie stars, from Claire Bloom and Jennifer Jones—to Tony Curtis. The artist and the actor had not just boxes but handicapped brothers named Robert in common. In short, TC was profoundly inspired by Cornell the man and by his creations. He was also instrumental, because of his own celebrity, in bringing Cornell's work to the attention of a wider public—and the wider art market—and thus easing Cornell's economic straits in his last years.

—B.P.

————————•————————

I visited Joseph Cornell and his brother on a number of occasions, starting about 1963. Joseph not only made boxes for him, but he rigged up elaborate train sets that Robert could operate by means of a pen or pencil he held in his teeth. It was the most touching, incredible thing to watch. They were the most eccentric people I ever met in my life, and I loved them.

Somehow, thanks to Cornell, I figured out that whatever travail and unhappiness I have now will be gone not too long from now, replaced by something else. I got my hope and my enthusiasm from that, in a strange way. Making boxes kicks my brain into another level, the way it must have for Cornell too. When I'm working on them, I can hear those little things talking to each other inside the glass:

"Hi, I'm a thimble, who are you?"

"I'm a marble, and this guy next to me is a paper clip. But what's that funny object over there?"

"I'm not sure, I think maybe it's a brooch."

"Oh . . . But who's that fuck-face outside, looking at us?"

"Him? That's the guy that put us together."

————————•————————

Art connoisseur Billy Wilder is among those who marvel at TC's art—and physical condition:

"His painting is quite good," Wilder says. "He's a latter-day Matisse, and those boxes he does so very well. And such shape he

300

is in! He still walks through Beverly Hills in his shorts, you know. But I still remember the perspiration that first time when he had to wear a woman's dress. What I would like to know is how his hair is so nice and thick and white. You find out for me. You tell him, 'Billy didn't have the nerve to ask.' "

Over the years, TC periodically discussed the mutual artistic bent with such fellow actor-painter-collectors as Edward G. Robinson, Vincent Price, and Raymond Burr. Unlike some he did not begin painting as a hobby or to pass the time between films. Nevertheless he has often faced the denigrating label of "celebrity artist." That subject in general—and TC's status as a visual and film artist in particular—are matters on which his daughter has strong opinions. Says Jamie Lee Curtis:

"The problem being a 'celebrity artist' or 'celebrity anything' is that it is immediately assumed you can't do it. It's the same with the progeny of actors. The assumption is, 'Oh, there's Tony Curtis and Janet Leigh's daughter trying to be an actress. She can't be any good.' But unlike my dad, most 'noncelebrity' artists haven't been drawing since they were ten and haven't painted two thousand canvases and didn't collect Balthus's *Three Women Bathing* at the age of twenty-five.

"In a lot of ways, he reminds me of Picasso. I'm not saying he's equal to the greatest artist of this century, just that they are both so prolific, and there's a similarity in their relationships with women and in their drawings. With Dad, there's a little Matisse, a little Picasso and, in color choices and brush stroke, a little van Gogh. I'm scared to reference him to other painters because it's still premature

Jamie (1972): TC's serigraph portrait of daughter Jamie Lee Curtis

301

in his art career. But I honestly feel that in fifty or one hundred years, he is going to be known as a great painter.

"Even when he was using drugs, there was a genuine path artistically. You can trace his life, like any other artist's, through the work. You know what's going on in their lives by the drawings. It's dramatic. In my father's case, his work is very alive now because his life is happy.

"He's the only human being I know who can take three plastic forks and spoons on a table and turn them into art. He'd come up with an artistic way of placing them, or of putting that one blue marble in the left corner of a glass. He's a true artist, and not enough people know it. He has struggled to achieve credibility as an artist, and it was the same in film. He was so handsome and successful, he always had to fight past that to show his stuff. He kept saying, 'Hey, guys, you think this is all I can do? I can do this, and I can go do that, and other things too.'

"He has had great success, and it's hard to feel sorry for him. Van Gogh never sold a painting in his lifetime. Part of what makes an artist is being hungry or driven. So maybe it's good that he hasn't been taken more seriously. He's still a young man. He's got twenty-five more years to create.

"He also has an amazing ability to be very articulate with very few words. During one of his crazier times, he wrote a short description of each of his children under their pictures in an album. Under mine he wrote, 'soft and steel.' It was a perfect way to describe me.

"I think his frustration is that he has it all and he's done it all, fair and square, yet he's not fully recognized. I couldn't understand his anger at the film industry when I was younger because I was raised by my mom, who felt very blessed and lucky to have had her opportunities. Dad truly felt he deserved them: He *earned* them. But because he was so handsome and successful, a lot of recognition was denied him.

"I think of Alec Baldwin, who reminds me so much of my dad, with that dark hair and those blue eyes. He's so good-looking, 'he can't possibly be a good actor.' It gets in his way. He could have just stayed an 'action' star, but he said, 'I'm going to play Stanley in *Streetcar* on fucking Broadway, thank you very much.' He

302

had to fight past his good looks to show his stuff. That's what my dad had to do, too.

"There was a time, post–Betty Ford, when I think he felt like a dead man. But once he was sober long enough and knew he could do it, he traveled and perfected hotel living. It was really quite wonderful: a very busy period for him creatively in his painting. Wherever he showed up, the first thing he did was go to the art store, buy an easel, twenty canvases, thirty tubes of acrylic paint, brushes, turpentine, and one of those tall, cylindrical glass things to clean the brushes in. He turned any hotel room into an art studio, much to the dismay of the hotels. He wore those horrible orthopedic sandals. Now he's moved into Birkenstocks. He would go to a department store and buy three pairs of white shorts, three white shirts, a jacket, a pair of pants, and leather gloves. Everything else in his life was in storage.

"Wherever he ended up, he dropped a couple hundred bucks on art supplies and went on to live a Spartan life. He had all his relevant telephone numbers on a manila envelope. 'Jamie'—number, 'Kelly'—number, 'Eli'—number. As he met people, he would write them down on this weathered old manila envelope.

"If it sounds like I think of him more as an artist than as an actor, it's because I absolutely do. In his Carrolwood house, he had a little 'box studio' in the gardener's cottage. Whenever I smell shellac, I think of him and those little architect's drawers filled with dice and keys and stencils, and that sound of spray paint. Almost all my memories of him are as a painter. That flamboyant, gregarious actor was not the guy I liked. What I loved was that man who had this thing he had to do, which was being an artist. I know at times it got very lonely for him, but wherever he was, doing his art, it was always a beautiful environment. I so fell in love with him then. I thought, *My God, what a great way to live!*"

—JAMIE LEE CURTIS TO B.P., October 13, 1992

In those days, after I divorced that third wife, I was shuttling back and forth between my place in Hawaii and the Bel Air Hotel—very nice digs there. I preferred it to the Beverly Hills Hotel because it was less accessible.

My suite was in the back, the maids took care of everything, and I didn't have to worry about the problems of having a house or a condo.

Over the years, I put together one of the best art collections in Hollywood: Picassos, Chagalls, Rouaults, Braques, plus a lot of other artists nobody ever heard of. Janet and I met Karel Appel, the Dutch painter, in 1960, and I commissioned him to do a twenty-by-fifteen-foot mural for the living-room wall of our house on Summit Drive. I rented a studio for him to paint it in, down on Fairfax or La Cienega. It was fabulous—his impressions of America after driving from New York to California. Later on we donated it to the Los Angeles County Museum of Art.

I lost a lot of that collection in divorce settlements, but I held on to some beautiful Chagalls and Mirós and, of course, my 1964 letter from Picasso and other things. My nineteenth-century Maimonides bust and the Buddha that Dick Zanuck gave me after *The Boston Strangler* are still in my living room, and about sixty of my own canvases are strewn around. The house is getting inundated, but I have a new studio outside of town. These days I'm working on a new photo-silkscreen series of the actresses I've known, and I'm exhibiting on a permanent basis at the new Club Tatou Gallery in Beverly Hills. I do my Schwarzenegger-prescribed workouts at the gym and then go right to my studio to paint and work on my boxes.

There is always order in the disorder. My daughter Kelly recently asked me if somebody came in and moved something, would I know it? Instantly. Years ago with drugs, sometimes I'd say, "I don't want to use that now—hide it somewhere, and I'll search for it later." I figured that would delay my use. So the guy would hide it and leave, and two minutes later I'd go in the living room and find it.

I love all my kids, but there's always something about the firstborn, or at least *this* firstborn. Three or four years ago Kelly and I went to Budapest together at the instigation of a Hungarian association that raises funds for the restoration of synagogues in Hungary. A man named Andor Weiss came to me and said, "We want your help. You're the most famous Hungarian in America, and we want you to be our spokesperson." I said I certainly respected the work they were doing, and, to shorten the story, they named it the Emanuel Foundation for Hungarian Culture, in honor of my father, Emanuel Schwartz. I'm the honorary chairman, and Kelly and I are actively involved with it.

Kelly Curtis

Kelly Curtis: "My grandmother and I were very close. As a child, I spent many hours in her home in West Hollywood. She had a garden the size of a small closet, but she managed to grow the biggest zucchini you ever saw. She taught me Hungarian songs and fairy tales, how to cook Hungarian food, and I learned a lot about my family history through her.

"When my father became involved with the Emanuel Foundation, I begged to go along with him to Budapest. It was my first trip there, and it was very moving to be a part of the ground-breaking ceremony for the restoration of the Dohany and Kazinzcy Synagogues and the cornerstone dedication of the Hungarian Holocaust

305

Victims and Heroes Memorial (July 3, 1988). Those events, and our whole trip, brought a lot of attention to the foundation. The Hungarian government even offered to provide matching funds in goods and services. Since the 1956 revolution, there had been no state support of any Jewish cultural efforts. But beyond that, it was also a personal journey for the two of us. I discovered I am very much my father's daughter. He always says that when looking at my hands, he sees the strength of my great grandmother's 'working' hands—he sees our Hungarian roots in me. In Budapest, we met up coincidentally with a man who said he was related to our family. I was skeptical, but he later showed us a letter from my grandfather proving it. He didn't have to: There was a remarkable family resemblance between the cousin and my father.

"We were excited by that experience, and it continued when we went to Mátészalka and were able to walk the streets and visit the house where my grandfather was born. Being allowed into the synagogue where he prayed was a shattering experience, seeing our family's among the names on the wall of the people who didn't return from the Holocaust. It really strengthened our belief in the goals of the foundation, among which is to ensure the legacy of the Hungarians who perished: On the grounds of the Memorial park, people can dedicate a leaf on the inverted-menorah-shaped tree, commemorating the loss of their martyrs and loved ones in the Holocaust. The whole experience brought me and my father together on a much deeper level than ever before. We got to know each other much better.

"I really respect him as a person. He's a survivor. He comes from a very strong race of people, who are passionate and intrepid and who forge their own way. Through his work and his family, my father has come to represent his heritage so well. Survival was the issue for him, and still is, and by discovering that, I came to understand my own stubbornness and fierce dedication to the things I believe in.

"I love becoming the family historian. I want to continue our legacy, and I love sharing that with my father."

—KELLY CURTIS TO B.P., JULY 15, 1993

Kelly has never acquiesced to the practicalities of life. She is an actress, and a good one. That's what her life is dedicated to. She comes from a family where her parents and sister are very successful in that profession, but her motivation isn't from the family, it's from herself. She's very independent. She'll take a job as a waitress to maintain herself, but she won't get involved in the business end of a movie if it doesn't appeal to her. I find that interesting and admire it. Kelly is very compassionate and giving. Of all her sisters and brothers, she reaches out the most to the others. She's the one who keeps tabs on what everyone is doing and maybe chastises them if they're screwing up. On the other hand, she needs as much affection as any of them. Beautiful woman. She has a wonderful marriage to Scott Morfee, who is a writer. They're an exceptional couple.

Jamie has always been very introverted. She seems like she's an extrovert, but she's really an introvert. Brilliant mind—as sharp a mind as I've ever seen. Sees things instantly. One glance and she's got it all. She's impatient. Once she catches the essence, she's out of there. She doesn't need any more input. On the other hand, she's very family oriented. She has a sweet family; her husband, Chris Guest [rock guitarist and cocreator of *This Is Spinal Tap*], and her little girl, Annie. Jamie always yearned for that. She's very gifted, very verbal. Her intelligence gives her freedom.

In my user days, I was drinking a lot around Jamie and taking a lot of pills. We were both using different things. We're not anymore. But in those days, that was one way we interrelated. She didn't ostracize me. She was very nonjudgmental, and still is. She's open and admits her frailties. Very affectionate. All my children were always affectionate. Every one of them needed a good hug now and then, and every one of them knew how to give one in return.

My daughter Allegra is a hair-and-makeup consultant in Florida—a very beautiful woman. All my children are beautiful, and they all have one thing in common: They all have my blue eyes. Allegra was always artistic. She would like to have a career as a dress designer. She works as a model and has done photographs for *Playboy*. She is very sweet, very vulnerable, easily manipulated. Allegra sees life her way, and her way only. She has a sensitive spirit. She doesn't see things abstractly. Fine. Nothing wrong with that.

Her older sister Alexandra is a very smart young woman who runs a theater company in Tampa, managing and directing shows. Alexandra—calm and collected, giving, sweet, compassionate. She was always like that.

Jamie Lee Curtis and TC on the set of *Anything But Love*

Even as a child, there was a womanness about her, a vulnerability. When you met her, you felt safe and secure. She asked nothing from anybody, only gave. And that's the way she is now, the mother of twins, my grand-daughters Dido and Elizabeth, who have inherited their mother's beauty.

Nicholas has always been a very creative person. He's twenty-one—a wonderful artist who makes assemblages and collages. He's also a musician, always searching for himself and for something other than himself. He dropped out of school, turned inward, and became very creative. He strives so hard to express himself, and he is very gifted. But he's chosen two difficult

Allegra Curtis

areas, art and music, where there are no distinct lines. He is very giving and kind and humorous and perceptive about people. A lovely young man. He lives in Dennis, Massachusetts.

His brother Benjamin has a quiet nature. He's going to Marymount College in Palos Verdes and becoming much more gregarious than he used to be. He's very amusing and charming and I enjoy his company a lot. I enjoy all my children. They're all so different. I used to call Benjamin after not seeing or talking to him for months:

"Hi, Ben."

"Hi, Dad."

"How are you?"

"Fine."

Alexandra Curtis Sargent

"Being with him is always a very special occasion—those Sunday rides in the silver Rolls-Royce with the top down in Beverly Hills! We all had to get over the fact that he wasn't the normal middle-class father. He didn't have one himself, and he didn't want to be one. That energy that he has on the screen is so much a part of his real life too. I catch him doing things on screen and say to myself, 'Yes, that's him—that's his intensity.' He never interfered in his children's lives. He's so wonderful with my girls, who are eight now. As a person, he's a very charming gentleman of the old school."

"What's going on?"
"Not much."
"Everything okay?"
"Great."
"How's school?"
"Fine."
"What'd you do last summer?"

Nicholas Curtis

"My dad has led an unbelievable life and never really had a great amount of time to pursue all his family relationships. He has make a great effort at times, but at other times it was impossible for him. I really have a great amount of love and respect for him. He was there in the early years as I was growing up and was a wonderful father. . . . I've been a musician for nine years and done quite a bit of theater for five years and also art. So I'm in awe of him and of the artist he represents. As I get older, I find that my pursuits in life are a lot like his, yet different too. We don't sit down and talk about it, but I think my dad and I have more in common than we both know."

"Went swimming."

"Things are all right?"

"Great."

"Thanks, Ben, for giving me all that information about your life."

"You're welcome, Dad."

"I love you."

"I love you."

Hang up.

Those are my conversations with Ben. He's not so verbal, but for all his detachment there's a great deal of feeling and depth. He is aiming toward law. I'm glad for him. He'll have a good experience in life. He's a fine, honorable person, sweet and caring. They're both wonderful boys.

These are six extraordinary people, my kids.

Benjamin Curtis

"I'm always amazed whenever I see his movies. What an accomplishment. It makes me so proud. *Defiant Ones* is my favorite. *Boston Strangler*—Nick and I watched it with him. As a man, he's a challenging person, which I like. He's got an edge that most people don't have, which is what got him where he is—a unique look, unique personality, unique everything. When we go out on the town, we never try hard to have a good time—just to relax. We don't have to talk all the time. Sometimes we won't say anything for twenty minutes. Just being together is enough. I don't want him to think that I want it easy. He started from zero. I'm not starting from zero, and I know it."

Jamie Lee Curtis: "I finally understand something that I couldn't as a small child: I now have a wonderful relationship with my father because I don't *need* him. All his life, his family, his children, his wives, their lawyers—everybody wanted something from him. He has six children, and all of them *needed* stuff from him, and he provided it. But now it's the *not* needing him that has allowed me just to be his friend and hang out with him.

"I'm not saying he doesn't have that with his other children. My sister had six years with him, so she knew him better, and they have a very special relationship that I envy yet at the same time completely understand. I am a shallow, jaded-ass sort of person, and she is a

312

very deep-rooted person. Except for Kelly, I never really had a deep relationship with my other siblings. Nobody's at fault. It's not an acrimonious situation, it's just three different families. Kelly is one of my closest friends now, but we were not that close growing up. And with my half-brothers and half-sisters, I have no frame of reference. We have no commonality except a piece of sperm.

"The only picture of all my father's children together was taken at my wedding. I begged him. I said, 'What I want for my wedding is all of my siblings and you and my mom in this room.' It was a huge deal, and he was late—but it happened. It was me being the best thing that I am, which is a cheerleader, going, 'Okay, we're doing this right now, come on!' Look at his face in that picture: He's standing there like, 'This is my flock.' It was a hard picture to get. It was the one and only time in my life when all of these people were in the same room.

"I was very young when he and my mother divorced. I don't remember him sitting me down and saying, 'How are you? Are you alive? Who's in there?' He had other wives and children. My mother was there for everything, every birthday, every Christmas,

Jamie Lee Curtis welcoming birthday party guests with open arms (1966)

All six of TC's children, together for the first time, at Jamie's wedding

and he wasn't. I don't have scars from it, but I also don't have that consistency with him. It took a long time to get to the good relationship we have today.

"Something has tortured him all his life, and he has sought relief from it with women, with drugs and alcohol. It's clear to me that it hinged on that triplicate of brothers. You had a twelve-year-old boy and a ten-year-old boy and an overbearing mother who was always saying, 'Look out for your younger brother,' but somehow they got separated and his brother stepped in front of a truck and was killed.

"I don't care who you are, that demon will follow you all your life. You've got a tyrannical mother, and you can imagine, in her grief, the guilt she levied on this boy. So you have a middle brother who is killed, a baby brother who is mentally defective, and the oldest brother, who is artistic and fabulously attractive and turns out to be one of the most popular stars in the history of the movies.

"If you're that boy, you say, 'Why me?' Why is he responsible for his brother's death and his mother's obsessions? I was overwhelmed when I saw that publicity picture of Bobby she made my father and the studio take—that mentality of, 'Put him in a *pikcha*, for Chrissake, what's it gonna hurt? He's your brotha. You're a big stah!' All Tony wanted was to get away—I don't want to be a Jew, I don't want to be your son, I don't want to be his brother. I just want to be an artist and get *away*.

"He had responsibility for his parents *and* his younger brother. Those demons drove him and stalked him, but he's finally escaped from them. I think the fate of those two brothers, compared with his own great success, was the big factor in his life. This was a grown man, a big star, who could have said, 'Mom, shut up,' but he didn't. It generated a lot of anger in him, but without question he did what he had to do and didn't get a lot of credit for it. He had to make a lot of shitty movies to pay off everybody and everything.

"But you know, he's never been happier than when I see him now. He's living the life he's wanted to live. He has six children and has taken care of them all. Other people in his position haven't. What I'm saying is that he is an inspiration to me—a big one. I think that's true too for my sisters and brothers, and I don't know how many people can honestly say that about their fathers."

—JAMIE LEE CURTIS TO B.P., October 13, 1992

"ARE YOU WHO I THINK I AM?"

Once in Las Vegas, I was walking down the sidewalk and this pimply teenage kid saw me and got a big look of recognition on his face. That happens to me all the time, but I never know what the approach will be. In this case, the kid ran up to me, all excited and stammering, and said, "Are you who I think I am?"

I loved him for that. I could identify with him. His line became one of my mottoes. For some reason, when I think of it, I flash back to my childhood when I used to sit with a little shoe-shine box out in front of the St. Regis Hotel on Fifth Avenue and Fifty-fifth Street. Why these associations? I don't know. But they're there. I made up this shoe-shine kit, and my father gave me a little whisk broom to take with me and go shine. I would sit outside the St. Regis on those steps leading up to the entrance and hook a customer now and then, at a nickel a shine. The doorman would eventually kick me away. I had that shoe-shine box for years, and I think I still do, somewhere. Now when I'm in New York, I usually stay at the St. Regis as a guest. But whenever I walk in, I always look to my left, and I always see me and that shoe-shine box on those steps.

Are you who I think I am? Am I who you think you are?

A hundred movies, a thousand paintings, a dozen beautiful women—my life and my cup runneth over. Their cups runneth over too—40D cups—and I love it. I'm really having a good time now. A few months ago

I ran into a guy on an airplane who was carrying a screenplay called *Waiting for Tony Curtis*. It was about some people on a South Seas island where I was supposed to come and shoot a movie, and it was going to be the biggest moment of their lives. I don't know what the status of that script is. I haven't heard. I'm still waiting for Tony Curtis too, like everybody else.

At the beginning of my career, I was mindless. Satisfying my physical needs—eating and having an affair with my leading lady of the moment—those were my major concerns. What time has done is to refine my desires. They're not as opulent as they used to be. By the time you reach fifty or sixty, you begin to see the final curtain and realize that today is not forever and that you'd better reconcile your excesses before you're dead.

I used to be always suspicious of everybody, especially my wives and lovers. Every sensing device I had was alert to trouble. A lot of the time there *was* trouble or if there wasn't, I invented it. I was never quite reconciled to the fact that the world could be good and pleasant. To me there seemed to be a trap in every relationship, in every gesture.

Until I met Lisa Deutsch.

Lisa and I went to Spago's one night for dinner, and I introduced her to someone as my fiancée. That person in turn told Army Archerd, who put it in *Variety,* and from there it was picked up by all the newspapers, magazines, tabloids, TV and radio shows—everybody. I know fame has nothing to do with the meaning of life. You're a famous actor, you're a famous doctor, a famous politician, a famous murderer. Fame in itself is a profession, and some people can't handle it. Certain people, like Garbo, just got undone when those paparazzi descended and the flashbulbs started popping. They couldn't handle what that fame represented. Monty Clift couldn't handle it; it drove him crazy.

I'm cut from a different cloth. I know who the major players are, and I was one of them. So were Marlon and Elvis and Sinatra and Cary Grant, and not a whole lot of others. The profession demands certain things. There's an irony about saying, "I want top billing in a movie and $1 million for two weeks' work. I want all that money and all that billing—but leave me alone." Meanwhile, everyone else is dying for such attention. I have a theory that if directors and writers and producers realized when they started out that they weren't going to get the lion's share of fame, they wouldn't have chosen that profession. A few guys— David O. Selznick and John Huston—knew how to get it. But most of them didn't.

I enjoy the publicity, the paparazzi. This planet is my home. It's that Indonesian's home in Indonesia and that Chinese man's home in China, but it's my home too. I have the privilege of traveling almost anywhere. Certain bullies or religions won't allow you in certain places, but for the most part, I can walk around Bombay or swim in the Arctic Ocean if I want to.

That's why Lisa and I are going to travel a lot. My life is renewing itself. A recent song contains a line, "How can we be lovers if we can't be friends?" I like that, but I like it just as well the other way around: "How can we be friends if we can't be lovers?" I'm learning something altogether new about a woman, thanks to Lisa. I'm starting to see now what my early relationships lacked: a lot of my own input. I couldn't handle that then. I'm lucky that I've been given the privilege of handling it now.

You don't need to be in the vortex of this profession to be happy and complete. But once you've tasted it, it's hard to give it up. I'm not ready to quit by any means. I'm burning out of me those feelings of inadequacy, pain, and anger that I felt for years, especially that mistrust. I was always sure the woman would cuckold me, or at least not like me anymore. I almost encouraged her to go after another guy. If my wife or girlfriend said, "I've got to go to the market," I thought, *Where is she really going? To a little pied-à-terre? The back of a car somewhere?* Those negative thoughts came into every relationship. I knew they were going to do it, and I was going to do it to them before they did it to me first.

Then I found Lisa, the most honorable person I've ever met. In the beginning I would get stressed out and fretful, the way I used to, whenever she went somewhere. She'd say, "We're going to work on that." I love that. We're going to work on making every day stress-free, and we have been. I keep waiting for that other shoe to drop, but there's no other shoe to drop. Any time in your life you can learn about trust.

Tony Curtis and Lisa Deutsch were married in Los Angeles on February 28, 1993. A few weeks later, the bride recounted the courtship and her feelings about the groom:

"I graduated in '91 from the University of West Los Angeles law school, and a year later a friend of mine asked me to go with him to an alumni dinner. It didn't sound very exciting, but he convinced me that I had to make contacts and so I went. It was Sep-

TC–Lisa Deutsch wedding portrait, by Harry Langdon, Jr., February 28, 1993

tember 11, 1992, at the Friars Club. I saw a lot of old school chums. Then I saw Tony Curtis come in with Jamie, Ben, and Kelly. He was getting an honorary juris doctorate. I don't know why he found that compelling or wanted to do it, but for some reason, he did.

319

"Everybody had dinner, and then they introduced Tony, and he told some incredible stories about Hollywood and his life. He was so charming and entertaining and witty. I looked over at my friend and said, 'God, wouldn't it be amazing to sit down and talk with him just for a few hours?'

"Later on there were pictures being taken, and he came over to me and said, 'Would you please take a picture with me?' Those were his first words to me. So they took the picture, and that was that. Judge Michael Harwin was the alumni coordinator, and his wife, Lisa, came up to me later and said, 'Mr. Curtis would like to have your number.' I was trembling. What does this guy want? I said, 'Does he go around picking up girls all over the place?' I was kind of upset. She said, 'No, he's a wonderful guy. If you want to go out with him, do it. If you don't, don't.' So I figured, okay, we'll go out, we'll have a lousy time, and that will be that.

"For some terrible reason, you always think people want something from you. Tony's the same way—but people *do* want things from him.

"The next Monday morning he sent a dozen roses to my home. Every week he sent me another dozen roses. It was very romantic. He called me almost every day, and we just talked and got to know each other. When we actually went on our first date, I wouldn't let him pick me up. I drove to his house because I wanted to have a quick getaway just in case. In L.A. you have to watch your back. If he pulls anything, I'm out of here. He gave me a brief tour of the house, and then we got in his car and started driving to Robata, a Japanese restaurant.

"The moment we got in that car, I relaxed. He was really compassionate and curious and fun. The conversation flowed. It was a wonderful dinner. In my family, for some reason, whenever we go out to dinner, we walk. It's a tradition. So I said, 'Do you mind walking?' We walked up Robertson to Third Street, around Cedars-Sinai, just walking and talking about everything: the cat that ran by, the psychic shop on the corner. Then he drove me back, gave me another little art tour, and I went home. It was a storybook first date. He was a perfect gentleman every step of the way.

"There are so many different aspects of Tony. Sometimes he's a free-spirited, adventurous child, sometimes he's introspective,

320

overanalyzing. But he is so giving and patient and understanding. There's nothing that I can't say to him, nothing we can't discuss, no taboo subjects. I had never seriously considered marriage before, and I know he often said he'd never get married again. But it seemed to make perfect sense for us. We could have lived together, and it would have been okay. It didn't matter to me. I knew I was going to share my life with him. I didn't know two people together could be this happy, this right on. He's so much fun to explore and learn new things and see new things with. He makes everything an adventure. I never know what to expect.

"I didn't even realize he was an artist at first. The first time I came to the house, he showed me some paintings and boxes, but I somehow thought they were things he had collected. I didn't get the fact that he created them himself. I love his work and the way he expresses himself artistically. He thinks everyone has this ability. He says, 'Go into your bathroom and look at how you've laid out things on the counter. That is your artistic expression.' I look at my bathroom and say, 'God, this is a chaos.'

"I was wrong that first day when I said I wanted to sit down and talk to him for a few hours. There's too much. I need a lifetime. I'm looking forward to it."

—LISA DEUTSCH CURTIS TO B.P., March 18, 1993

There is a clear duality in my life. I feel that dual—that duel!—constantly. I carry the weight of my existence between Tony and Bernie, and between their two sets of parents. If the purpose of living is only tomorrow, at the Appomattox of the uterus, something is wrong. It took me a long time to figure out that time and space and material things are just the crudest measures of the living experience. What we see outside is really just a mathematical experience that we're doing inside: What we see or think we see is not necessarily what's *there*. I'm still searching for what really *is* there, and probably always will be.

When I got into movies, I stepped into another level of consciousness and reality. I cannot obliterate that. Those movies are in perpetuity, unless everything gets blown up in a nuclear war. In that case, there'll be no way to run it backward and make it right again, the way Nick Roeg did in *In-*

significance. But maybe just before the planet blows up, it'll be like *Super-man*, when Brando sends off his little child in a rocket with a disk of every movie, book, and work of art ever created. They'll shoot it into the fucking universe, and there I'll be, whether I like it or not—in perpetuity.

Either way, regardless of what planet, I fantasize that some day 1,237 years from now, humans will wonder what people looked like 1,237 years ago, and they'll have a little machine that lets them summon up this dark-haired, blue-eyed guy named Tony Curtis.

"Con-Dor, darling, what do you think he was like?"

"I don't know, Mar-Jel, dear; let's take a look and see."

That concept makes me feel good—that idea of the perpetuity of the films. It's like what Stanton said about Lincoln: "Now he belongs to the ages." I'm not quite Abe Lincoln. But it fascinates and consoles me to think that in 1,237 years somebody here or on Jupiter might still have that little microchip with me and Cary Grant and Francis the Talking Mule on it. I'd love to be there when they sit down to watch it and try to figure it out.

At twenty you say, thank God I didn't get hit by a car, thank God I didn't die from an overdose, thank God I wasn't murdered, thank God I didn't go to jail. At thirty it's thank God I got a job, thank God I'm getting laid, thank God that pain in the ass wasn't something serious, thank God it was him and not me that died, thank God I don't have to support my parents anymore. At forty and fifty and sixty it's some other appropriate thing. Each decade of your life, people die, disappear, like my brother—swallowed up. So many beautiful girls I knew just disappeared and died, and guys too, like Jeff Hunter—all set for stardom, and then died after an accident at forty-three. Each decade takes its toll, and there's no rationality to it. You know, we're not easily put away. Our tenacity, our physical construction is such that it's not that easy to die. It's harder than you imagine. People can go through an awful lot and survive. But then they can also be terminated instantly, for no sensible reason.

It amazes me to think that from the beginning of sound films to when I started in movies was just twenty years. In film history, I made some inroads. I was the first one to play a variety of guys struggling to get out of their background into something better—*Mister Cory, The Great Imposter, Sweet Smell of Success*—young men caught in environments they had to find their own way out of. In the thirties there were young gangsters in the movies, but nobody studied the subtleties of that Indian boy in *The Out-*

sider, who raised the flag on Iwo Jima and wanted a better life. No one explored what a white man and black man chained together would be like on the lam, hating each other. No one explored how a guy on the south side of Chicago could end up owning a big casino and find he still wasn't accepted. Movies weren't made about that stuff.

And they wouldn't have been made if it hadn't been for me, because I represented something to those writers and directors and producers—some kind of tough New York kid trying to pass as somebody else. The all-American, long-haired, greasy kid out of who-knows-where. Those were my contributions as a filmmaker. I can call myself that, even though I don't direct or write, because unofficially I *did* direct and I *did* write—all those scenes where I ad-libbed, improvised, added some dimension or some moment or some *something* that wasn't there before.

I met Elvis Presley a number of times, usually at Paramount or in Las Vegas. He'd say, "Hi, Mr. Curtis!" and I'd say, "Please, call me Tony!" He was always shy with me, and I never knew why for a long time. It didn't occur to me that I was ten years older than he was, and that he'd been aware of me and my movies from the time he was a kid.

I'd catch him looking at me the way we all look at people we admire; a language in itself. Elvis wasn't the most articulate man. Words were not his forte, but he could be incisive. He was doing a movie once where he was riding a motorbike and singing a song, and he said, "I want five backup voices in the song." The producer said, "Elvis, you're riding on a bike. Where would those voices come from?" And he said, "The same place the music comes from." Wasn't that good?

I met one of his bodyguards recently, a guy I knew slightly a long time ago. He said, "You know, Elvis loved you and talked about you so much." To think that the way I thought and spoke about Cary, Elvis thought and spoke about me—and Cary must have thought and spoken about somebody before him.

The baton passes. In the beginning . . . there was so-and-so, then Douglas Fairbanks, then Cary Grant, then Tony Curtis, then Elvis, all the way down. In my early twenties, those guys in their early thirties—Kirk Douglas, Burt Lancaster, Frank Sinatra—were the guys I hung out with. I was their younger brother.

"Who you fuckin'?"

"Oh God, I got a new beautiful girl!"

"Where you goin' tonight?"

"I'm going for drinks at the Club Gala, then early dinner at Lucy's, then the Mocambo to dance . . ."

Hallelujah, what a time! The girls' dresses were between the calf and the knee, and if they had tits, they let you know it. It wasn't really all that promiscuous. It took a bit of wooing—but what a time!

Those people were my brothers and sisters. Cary Grant was my father or big brother. Why? Because I chose him to be, and he accepted. I was his son, or one of them. Elvis was my younger brother. We didn't have to spend time together to know that. We just knew it. For some damn reason he loved those big collars I wore, with the big tie knots. He dyed his hair black like mine. He sat in some crackerbox movie theater in Tupelo, Mississippi, and pulled his hair down in the front like I did. So did those "teddy boys" in England.

You pass that stuff on, you don't "study" it.

I learned film acting on the job. I had to carve it out of an invisible rock. There was nobody there giving me any advice, no coach or manager saying, "We see a great future for you." Nobody saw anything for me. I was like a mirror with no reflection. I was the least likely to succeed. Most people were envious and angry at me because I was so good-looking. All I gave a shit about was how my hair looked and how my jackets fit. Acting? What the fuck is acting? Give me the line. Come in and say what? "I love you." Thank you. It wasn't "To be or not to be," it was just *be*! What do you want me to be? Be the bellboy, be the doctor, be the convict . . . I said okay, I'll try it, and at twenty-three or twenty-four, I did the best a twenty-three- or twenty-four-year-old guy could do, no better or worse.

I didn't have the complexity of a Marlon Brando, because my life had been much more primitive—trying to stay alive in those harsh New York streets, irritable, wary, every tooth in my mouth decayed. I was like an animal and I'd had horrific experiences, being chased through that city, shivering and frightened on a freezing rooftop overlooking First Avenue, not being able to get down or up for hours. Finally, I couldn't wait anymore and made a dash for it. But the fire escape was coated with ice, and I started to slip. I slid about twenty feet before I managed to grab onto a ledge—and wound up hanging from the edge of some building, three stories off the ground.

If I hadn't grabbed on when I did, I'd be dead. My fingers slowed me down just barely enough. I was being chased because I was a Jew, even though I didn't know what the fuck a Jew was. It felt like a movie where the director says, "Now, here you're a Jew, and this guy's chasing you off the roof, but what you don't know is, there's ice on the fire escape, so you're going to drop twenty feet and then grab on just before you fall."

Only I wasn't in a movie. I was twelve, and I was hanging on by that hand in that icy wind, looking down at the wet street and the car lights. Oddly enough, I remember feeling a strange sort of peace and tranquility hanging there. The only way I knew my life was in jeopardy was by my fingers. I knew if they let go, it would be a clear and crisp and cold death. It was very silent. Night had settled down the city. I noticed that. And, oh, yeah, by the way, what the fuck am I doing hanging from this fire escape?

Those were the peculiar moments that turned Bernie Schwartz into Tony Curtis, and vice versa.

TONY CURTIS FILMOGRAPHY

FEATURE FILMS

1. *Criss Cross* (1949). A Universal-International Production (Michael Kraike). Directed by Robert Siodmak. Screenplay by Daniel Fuchs from a novel by Don Tracy. Photography by Franz Planer. Music by Miklos Rozsa. An armored-truck guard becomes involved in a robbery. Cast: Burt Lancaster (Steve Thompson), Yvonne De Carlo (Anna), Dan Duryea (Slim Dundee), Stephen McNally (Pete Ramirez), Richard Long (Slade Thompson), Tom Pedi (Vincent), Alan Napier (Finchley), James [Tony] Curtis (Gigolo).

2. *City Across the River* (1949). A Universal-International Production (Maxwell Shane). Directed by Maxwell Shane. Screenplay by Irving Shulman and Dennis Cooper from the novel *The Amboy Dukes* by Irving Shulman. Photography by Maury Gertsman. Music by Walter Scharf. New York hoodlums commit street crime. Cast: Stephen McNally (Stan Albert), Luis Van Rooten (Joe Cusack), Thelma Ritter (Mrs. Cusack), Peter Fernandez (Frankie Cusack), Al Ramsen, Joshua Shelley (Crazy), Mickey Knox, Richard Jaeckel (Bull), Anthony Curtis (Mitch), Jeff Corey (Lieutenant Macon), Sharon McManus (Alice Cusack), Sue England (Betty), Barbara Whiting (Annie Kane), Richard Benedict (Gaggsy Steens).

3. *The Lady Gambles* (1949). A Universal-International Production (Michael Kraike). Directed by Michael Gordon. Screenplay by Roy Huggins from an adaptation by Halsted Welles of a story by Lewis Meltzer and Oscar Saul. Photography by Russell Metty. Music by Frank Skinner. A woman becomes a compulsive gambler. Cast: Barbara Stanwyck (Joan Boothe), Robert Preston (David Boothe), Stephen McNally (Corrigan), Edith Barrett (Ruth Phillips), John Hoyt (Dr. Rojac), Leif Erickson (Tony), Anthony Curtis (Bellboy).

4. *Johnny Stool Pigeon* (1949). A Universal-International Production (Aaron Rosenberg). Directed by William Castle. Screenplay by Robert L. Richards from a story by Henry Jordan. Photography by Maury Gertsman. Music by Milton Schwarzwald. A convict is sprung from prison to lead police to former gang members. Cast: Howard Duff (George Morton), Dan Duryea (Johnny Evans), Shelley Winters (Terry), Anthony Curtis (Joey Hyatt), John McIntire (Nick Avery), Gary Moore (Sam Harrison), Leif Erickson (Pringle).

5. *Francis* (1950). A Universal-International Production (Robert Arthur). Directed by Arthur Lubin. Screenplay by David Stern from his novel. Photography by Irving Glassberg. Music by Frank Skinner. A mule assists the army. Cast: Donald O'Connor (Peter Stirling), Patricia Medina (Maureen Gelder), ZaSu Pitts (Valerie Humpert), Eduard Franz (Colonel Pepper), Anthony Curtis (Captain Jones).

6. *I Was a Shoplifter* (1950). A Universal-International Production (Leonard Goldstein). Directed by Charles Lamont. Screenplay by Irwin Gielgud. Photography by Irving Glassberg. Music by Milton Schwarzwald. The story of a shoplifting gang. Cast: Scott Brady (Jeff Andrews), Mona Freeman (Faye Burton), Anthony Curtis (Pepe), Charles Drake (Herb Klaxton), Gregg Martell (The Champ), Robert Gist (Barkie Neff), Larry Keating (Harry Dunson), Rock Hudson (Store Detective).

7. *Winchester 73* (1950). A Universal-International Production (Aaron Rosenberg). Directed by Anthony Mann. Screenplay by Robert L. Richards and Borden Chase from a story by Stuart N. Lake. Photography by William Daniels. Music by Frank Skinner. Music directed by Joseph Gershenson. Western surrounding who owns the famed rifle. Cast: James Stewart (Lin McAdam), Stephen McNally (Dutch Henry Brown), Shelley Winters (Lola Manners), Dan Duryea (Waco Johnny Dean), Will Geer (Wyatt Earp), Jay C. Flippen (Sergeant Wilkes), Rock Hudson (Young Bull), Anthony Curtis (Doan).

8. *Sierra* (1950). A Universal-International Production (Michael Kraike). Directed by Alfred E. Green. Screenplay by Edna Anhalt from a novel by Stuart Hardy. Additional dialogue by Milton Gunzburg. Photography by Russell Metty. Music by Walter Scharf. Western about a father and son on the lam. Cast: Wanda Hendrix (Riley Martin), Audie Murphy (Ring Hassard), Dean Jagger (Jeff Hassard), Burl Ives (Lonesome), Richard Rober (Big Mati), Anthony Curtis (Brent Coulter), Houseley Stevenson (Sam Coulter).

9. *Kansas Raiders* (1950). A Universal-International Production (Ted Richmond). Directed by Ray Enright. Screenplay by Robert L. Richards. Photography by Irving Glassberg. Music by Joseph Gershenson. Western. Cast: Audie Murphy (Jesse James), Brian Donlevy (Quantrill), Richard Arlen (Union Captain), Scott Brady (Bill Anderson), Marguerite Chapman (Kate Clarke), Tony Curtis (Kit Dalton), James Best (Cole Younger), Dewey Martin (James Younger), John Kellogg (Red Leg Leader).

10. *The Prince Who Was a Thief* (1951). A Universal-International Production (Leonard Goldstein). Directed by Rudolph Maté. Screenplay by Gerald Drayson Adams and Aeneas MacKenzie from a story by Theodore Dreiser. Photography by Irving Glassberg. Music by Hans Salter. Romantic period drama, set in thirteenth-century Tangiers. Cast: Tony Curtis (Julna), Piper Laurie (Tina), Everett Sloane (Yussef), Peggy Castle (Princess Yashim), Donald Ran-

dolph (Mustapha), Jeff Corey (Mokar), Betty Garde (Mirza), Marvin Miller (Hakar), Nita Bieber (Cahuena), Hayden Rorke (Basra).

11. *Son of Ali Baba* (1952). A Universal-International Production (Leonard Goldstein). Directed by Kurt Neumann. Screenplay by Gerald Drayson Adams. Photography by Maury Gertsman. Music by Joseph Gershenson. A period adventure set in Baghdad. Cast: Tony Curtis (Kashma Babba), Piper Laurie (Azura/Kiki), Victor Jory (Caliph), Morris Ankrum (Ali Baba), Susan Cabot (Tala), William Reynolds (Mustafa), Hugh O'Brien (Hussein), Philip Van Zandt (Kareeb).

12. *Flesh and Fury* (1952). A Universal-International Production (Leonard Goldstein). Directed by Joseph Pevney. Screenplay by Bernard Gordon from a story by William Alland. Photography by Irving Glassberg. Music by Hans J. Salter. The story of a deaf-mute prizefighter. Cast: Tony Curtis (Paul Callan), Mona Freeman (Ann Hollis), Jan Sterling (Sonya Bartow), Wallace Ford (Jack Richardson), Connie Gilchrist (Mrs. Richardson), Katherine Locke (Mrs. Hollis), Harry Shannon (Mike Callan), Harry Guardino (Lou Callan).

13. *No Room for the Groom* (1952). A Universal-International Production (Ted Richmond). Directed by Douglas Sirk. Screenplay by Joseph Hoffman from a story, "My True Love," by Darwin Teilheit. Photography by Clifford Stine. Music by Frank Skinner. A GI tries to spend time with his new bride amid her relatives. Cast: Tony Curtis (Alvah Morrell), Piper Laurie (Lee Kingshead), Spring Byington (Mama Kingshead), Don DeFore (Herman Strouple), Lillian Bronson (Aunt Elsa), Paul McVey (Dr. Trotter) and Steven Chase (Mr. Taylor).

14. *Meet Danny Wilson* (1952). A Universal-International Production (Leonard Goldstein). Directed by Joseph Pevney. Screenplay by Don McGuire. An entertainer gets involved with racketeers. Cast: Frank Sinatra, Raymond Burr, Shelley Winters, Alex Nicol, Rommy Farrell, Vaughan Taylor. Guest appearances by Jeff Chandler and Tony Curtis.

15. *Houdini* (1953). A Paramount Production (George Pal). Directed by George Marshall. Screenplay by Philip Yordan from a story by Harold Kellock. Photography by Ernest Laszlo. Music by Roy Webb. The story of the famed magician. Cast: Tony Curtis (Harry Houdini), Janet Leigh (Bess), Torin Thatcher (Otto), Angela Clarke (Mrs. Weiss), Sig Rumann (Schultz), Connie Gilchrist (Mrs. Schultz), Michael Pate (Dooley).

16. *The All-American* (1953). A Universal-International Production (Aaron Rosenberg). Directed by Jesse Hibbs. Screenplay by D. D. Beauchamp, from an adaptation by Robert Yale Libott of a story by Leonard Freeman. Photography by Maury Gertsman. Music by Joseph Gershenson. Football drama. Cast: Tony Curtis (Nick Bonelli), Mamie Van Doren (Susie Ward), Richard Long (Howard Carter), Gregg Palmer (Hunt Cameron), Paul Cavanagh (Professor Banning), Stuart Whitman (Zip Parker), Jimmy Hunt (Whizzer).

17. **Forbidden** (1953). A Universal-International Production (Ted J. Richmond). Directed by Rudolph Maté. Screenplay by William Sackheim and Gil Doud. Photography by William Daniels. Music by Frank Skinner. Hoodlum drama. Cast: Tony Curtis (Eddie Darrow), Joanne Dru (Christine Lawrence), Lyle Bettger (Justin Keit), Marvin Miller (Cliff Chalmer), Victor Sen Yung (Allan), Peter Mamakos (Sam).

18. **Beachhead** (1954). A United Artists Production (Howard Koch). Directed by Stuart Heisler. Screenplay by Richard Alan Simmons from the novel *I've Got Mine* by Richard G. Hubler. Photography by Gordon Avil. Music by Emil Newman and Arthur Lange. Marines are caught on a Japanese-held island in World War II. Cast: Tony Curtis (Burke), Frank Lovejoy (Sgt. Fletcher), Mary Murphy (Nina), Eduard Franz (Bouchard), Skip Homeier (Reynolds).

19. **Johnny Dark** (1954). A Universal-International Production (William Alland). Directed by George Sherman. Screenplay by Franklin Coen. Photography by Carl Guthrie. Music by Joseph Gershenson. Racing car drama. Cast: Tony Curtis (Johnny Dark), Piper Laurie (Liz Fielding), Paul Kelly (Jim "Scotty" Scott), Ilka Chase (Abbie Binns), Don Taylor (Duke Benson), Ruth Hampton (Miss Border-to-Border), Russell Johnson (Emory), Joseph Sawyer (Svenson), Robert Nichols (Smitty).

20. **The Black Shield of Falworth** (1954). A Universal-International Production (Robert Arthur and Melville Tucker). Directed by Rudolph Maté. Screenplay by Oscar Brodney from the novel *Men of Iron* by Howard Pyle. Photography by Irving Glassberg. Music by Joseph Gershenson. Olde English adventure drama. Cast: Tony Curtis (Myles Falworth), Janet Leigh (Lady Ann), Herbert Marshall (Earl of Mackworth), Ian Keith (King Henry IV), Torin Thatcher (Sir James), Barbara Rush (Meg Falworth), Daniel O'Herlihy (Prince Hal), Craig Hill (Francis Gascoyne), Rhys Williams (Diccon Bowman).

21. **So This Is Paris** (1954). A Universal-International Production (Albert J. Cohen). Directed by Richard Quine. Screenplay by Charles Hoffman from a story by Ray Buffum. Photography by Maury Gertsman. Music by Pony Sherell and Phil Moody. Choreographed by Gene Nelson and Lee Scott. Musical set in Paris. Cast: Tony Curtis (Joe Maxwell), Gloria De Haven (Colette/Janie), Gene Nelson (Al Howard), Corinne Calvet (Suzanne Sorel), Paul Gilbert (Davey Jones), Mara Corday (Yvonne), Allison Hayes (Carmen), Myrna Hansen (Ingrid).

22. **Six Bridges to Cross** (1955). A Universal-International Production (Aaron Rosenberg). Directed by Joseph Pevney. Screenplay by Sidney Boehm from the novel *They Stole $2,500,000 and Got Away with It* by Joseph Dineen. Photography by William Daniels. Music by Joseph Gershenson. Story of the Boston Brinks robbery. Cast: Tony Curtis (Jerry Florea), George Nader (Edward Gallagher), Julie Adams (Ellen Gallagher), Sal Mineo (Jerry, as a Boy), Jay C. Flippen (Vincent Concannon), Jan Merlin (Jan Norris), Richard Castle (Skids Radzievich).

23. **The Purple Mask** (1955). A Universal-International Production (Howard Christie). Directed by Bruce Humberstone. Screenplay by Oscar Brodney from a play by Paul Armont and Jean Monoussi. Photography by Irving Glassberg. Music by Joseph Gershenson. French Revolution costume drama. Cast: Tony Curtis (Rene), Colleen Miller (Laurette), Gene Barry (Captain Lawrence), Dan O'Herlihy (Brisquet), Angela Lansbury (Madame Valentine), George Dolenz (Marcel Cardonal), John Hoyt (Fouche), Paul Cavanagh (Duc De Latour).

24. **The Square Jungle** (1955). A Universal-International Production (Albert Zugsmith). Directed by Jerry Hopper. Screenplay by George Zuckerman. Photography by George Robinson. Music by Heinz Roemheld. Boxing drama. Cast: Tony Curtis (Eddie Quaid/Packy Glennon), Ernest Borgnine (Bernie Brown), Jim Backus (Pat Quaid), Pat Crowley (Julie Walsh), Leigh Snowden (Lorraine Evans), Paul Kelly (Jim McBride), John Day (Al Gorski), David Janssen (Jack Lindsey), John Marley (Tommy Dillon), Joe Louis (Himself).

25. **The Rawhide Years** (1956). A Universal-International Production (Stanely Rubin). Directed by Rudolph Maté. Screenplay by Earl Felton, Robert Presnell, and D. D. Beauchamp from the novel by Norman Fox. Photography by Irving Glassberg. Music by Frank Skinner and Hans Salter. Western in which a gambler tries to clear himself of a murder charge. Cast: Tony Curtis (Ben Matthews), Colleen Miller (Zoe), Arthur Kennedy (Rick Harper), William Demarest (Brand Comfort), William Gargan (Marshal Sommers), Peter Van Eyck (Antoine Boucher), Minor Watson (Matt Comfort), Donald Randolph (Carrico).

26. **Trapeze** (1956). A United Artists Release (produced by Hecht-Lancaster). Screenplay by James R. Webb, adaptation by Liam O'Brian. Directed by Carol Reed. Photograpy by Robert Krasker. Music by Malcolm Arnold. Circus drama. Cast: Burt Lancaster (Mike Ribble), Tony Curtis (Tino Orsini), Gina Lollobrigida (Lola), Katy Jurado (Rosa), Thomas Gomez (Bouglione), Johnny Puleo (Max the Dwarf), Minor Watson (John Ringling North).

27. **Mister Cory** (1957). A Universal-International Production (Robert Arthur). Directed by Blake Edwards. Screenplay by Blake Edwards based on a story by Leo Rosten. Photography by Russell Metty. Music by Joseph Gershenson. A young man becomes a partner in a sophisticated gambling establishment. Cast: Tony Curtis (Mister Cory), Martha Hyer (Abby Vollard), Charles Bickford (Biloxi), Kathryn Grant (Jen Vollard), William Reynolds (Alex Wyncott), Russ Morgan (Ruby Matrobe), Henry Daniell (Earnshaw), Willis Bouchey (Mr. Vollard), Louise Lorimer (Mrs. Vollard).

28. **The Midnight Story** (1957). A Universal-International Production (Robert Arthur). Directed by Joseph Pevney. Screenplay by John Robinson and Edwin Blum. Photography by Russell Metty. Music by Joseph Gershenson. Whodunit set in San Francisco. Cast: Tony Curtis (Joe Martini), Gilbert Roland (Sylvio Malatesta), Marisa Pavan (Anna Malatesta), Jay C. Flippen (Sergeant Jack

Gillen), Argentina Burnetti (Mama Malatesta), Ted DeCorsia (Lieutenant Kilrain), Kathleen Freeman (Rosa Cuneo).

29. *Sweet Smell of Success* (1957). A United Artists Release (Hecht-Hill-Lancaster for Norma-Curtleigh). Directed by Alexander Mackendrick. Screenplay by Clifford Odets and Ernest Lehman from a novella by Ernest Lehman. Photography by James Wong Howe. Music by Elmer Bernstein. New York drama about a ruthless columnist. Burt Lancaster (J. J. Hunsecker), Tony Curtis (Sidney Falco), Susan Harrison (Susan Hunsecker), Martin Milner (Steve Dallas), Sam Levene (Frank D'Angelo), Barbara Nichols (Rita). Chico Hamilton Quintet.

30. *The Vikings* (1958). A United Artists Release (Bryna Productions and Curtleigh). Directed by Richard Fleischer. Photography by Jack Cardiff. Music by Mario Nascimbene. Viking adventure filmed on location in Norway and Brittany. Cast: Kirk Douglas (Einar), Tony Curtis (Eric), Ernest Borgnine (Ragnar), Janet Leigh (Morgana), Alexander Knox (Father Godwin), Frank Thring (Aella). Narrated by Orson Welles.

31. *The Defiant Ones* (1958). A United Artists Production. Directed by Stanley Kramer. Screenplay by Harold Jacob Smith and Nathan E. Douglas. Photography by Sam Leavitt. Music by Ernest Gold. Two convicts are shackled together during their escape in the South. Cast: Tony Curtis (John "Joker" Jackson), Sidney Poitier (Noah Cullen), Theodore Bikel (Sheriff Max Muller), Charles McGraw (Captain Frank Gibbons), Lon Chaney, Jr. (Big Sam), Whit Bissell (Lou Gans), Carl Switzer (Angus).

32. *Kings Go Forth* (1958). A United Artists Release. Produced by Frank Ross. Directed by Delmer Daves. Screenplay by Merle Miller, based on the novel by Joe David Brown. Photography by Daniel L. Fapp. Music by Elmer Bernstein. Romantic triangle involving a half-black woman and two soldiers in World War II France. Cast: Frank Sinatra (Lieutenant Sam Loggins), Tony Curtis (Sergeant Britt Harris), Natalie Wood (Monique Blair), Leora Dana (Mrs. Blair).

33. *The Perfect Furlough* (1958). A Universal-International Production (Robert Arthur). Directed by Blake Edwards. Screenplay by Stanley Shapiro. Photography by Philip Lathrop. Music by Frank Skinner. An army psychologist arranges a glamorous furlough for a soldier. Cast: Tony Curtis (Paul Hodges), Janet Leigh (Vicki Loren), Linda Cristal (Sandra Roca), Keenan Wynn (Harvey Franklin), Elaine Stritch (Liz Baker), Marcel Dalio (Henri), Les Tremayne (Colonel Leland), Jay Novello (Rene), King Donovan (Major Collins), Troy Donahue (Sergeant Nickles).

34. *Some Like It Hot* (1959). A United Artists Release. (Mirisch Company, an Ashton Picture). Directed by Billy Wilder. Screenplay by Billy Wilder and I. A. L. Diamond suggested from a story by R. Thoeren and M. Logan. Photography by Charles Lang, Jr. Music by Adolph Deutsch. Costumes by Orry-Kelly. Two musicians disguise themselves as women to escape after witnessing the St.

Valentine's Day massacre. Cast: Tony Curtis (Joe/Josephine), Marilyn Monroe (Sugar Kane), Jack Lemmon (Jerry/Daphne), George Raft (Spats Columbo), Joe E. Brown (Osgood Fielding).

35. **Operation Petticoat** (1959). A Universal-International Release (Robert Arthur for Granart Productions). Directed by Blake Edwards. Screenplay by Stanley Shapiro and Maurice Richlin. Photography by Russell Harlan. Music by David Rose. Sailors and nurses in close quarters aboard a submarine during World War II. Cast: Cary Grant (Admiral Matt Sherman), Tony Curtis (Lieutenant Nick Holden), Joan O'Brien (Lieutenant Dolores Crandall), Dina Merrill (Lieutenant Barbara Duran), Gene Evans (Molumphrey), Arthur O'Connell (Sam Tostin), Richard Sargent (Stovall).

36. **Who Was That Lady?** (1959). A Columbia Pictures Release (Ansark–George Sidney). Directed by George Sidney. Screenplay by Norman Krasna based on his play. Photography by Harry Stradling. Music by André Previn. Romantic comedy about a college professor posing as an FBI agent. Cast: Tony Curtis (David Wilson), Janet Leigh (Ann Wilson), Dean Martin (Michael Haney), James Whitmore (Harry Powell), John McIntire (Bob Doyle), Barbara Nichols (Gloria Coogle), Larry Keating (Parker), Larry Storch (Orenov), Simon Oakland (Belka), Joi Lansing (Florence Coogle).

37. **The Rat Race** (1960). A Paramount Release (William Perlberg–George Seaton Production). Directed by Robert Mulligan. Screenplay by Garson Kanin from his play. Photography by Robert Burks. Music by Elmer Bernstein. A musician and a dance-hall hostess share a New York apartment together. Cast: Tony Curtis (Pete Hammond, Jr.), Debbie Reynolds (Peggy Brown), Jack Oakie (Mac), Kay Medford (Soda), Don Rickles (Nellie), Joe Bushkin (Frankie), Gerry Mulligan (Gerry), Sam Bukera (Carl).

38. **Spartacus** (1960). A Universal-International Release (Bryna Productions, produced by Edward Lewis). Directed by Stanley Kubrick. Screenplay by Dalton Trumbo from the novel by Howard Fast. Photography by Russell Metty. Music by Alex North. Epic spectacle of slave revolt in the late Roman Empire. Cast: Kirk Douglas (Spartacus), Laurence Olivier (Crassus), Jean Simmons (Varinia), Tony Curtis (Antoninus), Charles Laughton (Gracchus), Peter Ustinov (Batiatus), John Gavin (Julius Caesar), Nina Foch (Helena Glabrus), Herbert Lom (Tigranes), John Ireland (Crixus), Woody Strode (Draba).

39. **The Great Imposter** (1960). A Universal-International Production. Directed by Robert Mulligan. Screenplay by Liam O'Brien from the book by Robert Crichton. Photography by Robert Burks. Music by Henry Mancini. The story of Ferdinand Waldo Demara, Jr., a man who assumed many identities. Cast: Tony Curtis (Ferdinand Waldo Demara, Jr.), Edmund O'Brien (Captain Glover), Karl Malden (Father Devlin), Raymond Massey (Abbott Donner), Gary Merrill (Demara Sr.), Arthur O'Connell (Chandler).

40. *Pepe* (1960). A Columbia Pictures Release (produced by G. S.–Posa Films International). Directed by George Sidney. Photography by Joe MacDonald. Screenplay by Dorothy Kingsley and Claude Binyon from a story by Leonard Spigelgass and Sonya Levien, based on the play *Broadway Magic* by Ladislas Bush-Fekete. Edited by Viola Lawrence and Al Clark. Music by Johnny Green. Costumes by Edith Head. A ranch foreman goes to Hollywood to reclaim his stallion. Cast: Cantinflas, Dan Dailey, Shirley Jones, Carlos Montalban. Guest stars (as themselves): Joey Bishop, Billie Burke, Maurice Chevalier, Charles Coburn, Richard Conte, Bing Crosby, Tony Curtis, Bobby Darin, Sammy Davis, Jr., Jimmy Durante, Jack Entratter, Colonel E. E. Fogelson, Zsa Zsa Gabor, Greer Garson, Hedda Hopper, Peter Lawford, Janet Leigh, Jack Lemmon, Dean Martin, Kim Novak, André Previn, Donna Reed, Debbie Reynolds, Carlos Rivas, Edward G. Robinson, Cesar Romero, Frank Sinatra.

41. *The Outsider* (1961). A Universal-International Production. Directed by Delbert Mann. Screenplay by Stewart Stern from the novel *The Hero of Iwo Jima* by William Bradford Huie. Photography by Joseph La Shelle. Music by Leonard Rosenman. The story of Ira Hamilton Hayes, a Pima Indian, one of the flag raisers on Iwo Jima during World War II. Cast: Tony Curtis (Ira Hamilton Hayes), James Franciscus (Jim Sorenson), Gregory Walcott (Sergeant Kiley), Bruce Bennett (Major General Bridges), Vivian Nathan (Mrs. Nancy Hayes).

42. *Taras Bulba* (1962). (Harold Hecht–Avala Film released by United Artists.) Directed by J. Lee-Thompson. Screenplay by Waldo Salt based on the novel by Nikolai Gogol. Photography by Joe MacDonald. Music by Franz Waxman. Costume drama about Cossacks, filmed on location in Argentina. Cast: Tony Curtis (Andrei Bulba), Yul Brynner (Taras Bulba), Christine Kaufmann (Natalia Dubrov), Sam Wanamaker (Flipenko), George Macready (Governor).

43. *Forty Pounds of Trouble* (1962). A Universal-International/Curtis Enterprises Production (Stan Margulies). Directed by Norman Jewison. Screenplay by Marion Hargrove. Photography by Joe MacDonald. Music by Mort Lindsey. The trials and tribulations of a nightclub manager in Lake Tahoe, based on Damon Runyon's *Little Miss Marker.* Cast: Tony Curtis (Steve McCluskey), Suzanne Pleshette (Chris Lockwood), Claire Wilcox (Penny Piper), Phil Silvers (Bernie Friedman), Stubby Kaye (Cranston), Larry Storch (Floyd), Howard Morris (Julius), Warren Stevens (Swing), Mary Murphy (Liz McCluskey), Kevin McCarthy (Blanchard).

44. *Captain Newman, M. D.* (1963). A Universal-International Production (Brentwood/Reynard). Directed by David Miller. Screenplay by Richard L. Breen and Phoebe and Henry Ephron from the novel by Leo Rosten. Photography by Russell Metty. The story of a psychiatrist on an air base during World War II. Cast: Gregory Peck (Captain Joshua Newman), Tony Curtis (Corporal Jackson Laibowitz), Angie Dickinson (Lieutenant Francie Corum), Eddie Albert (Colonel Norval Algate Bliss), Jane Withers (Lieutenant Gracie Blodgett),

Bobby Darin (Corporal Jim Tompkins), Bethel Leslie (Helene Winston), Robert Duvall (Captain Paul Cabot Winston).

45. *The List of Adrian Messenger* (1963). Universal-International Production. Directed by John Huston. Screenplay by Anthony Veiller from a story by Philip MacDonald. Photography by Joe MacDonald. Music by Jerry Goldsmith. Cast: Kirk Douglas (George Brougham), George C. Scott (Anthony Gethryn), Dana Wynter (Lady Jocelyn), Clive Brook (Marquis of Gleneyre), Gladys Cooper (Mrs. Karoudjian), Herbert Marshall (Sir Wilfrid), with guest appearances by Tony Curtis, Burt Lancaster, Robert Mitchum, Frank Sinatra.

46. *Wild and Wonderful* (1964). A Universal-International Production (Harold Hecht). Directed by Michael Anderson. Screenplay by Larry Markes, Michael Morris, and Waldo Salt from a screen story by Richard M. Powell and David Rapp, from a story by Dorothy Crider. Photography by Joseph La Shelle. Music by Morton Stevens. French film star marries an American musician; her poodle takes a dislike to her new husband. Cast: Tony Curtis (Terry Williams), Christine Kaufmann (Giselle Ponchon), Jules Munshin (Rousseleau), Larry Storch (Rufus Gibbs), Marty Ingels (Doc Bailey), Pierre Olaf (Jacquot).

47. *Goodbye Charlie* (1964). A 20th Century-Fox–Venice production (David Weisbart). Directed by Vincente Minnelli. Screenplay by Harry Kurnitz, based on the play by George Axelrod. Photography by Milton Krasner. Music by André Previn. A gangster comes back to earth as a woman. Cast: Tony Curtis (George Tracy), Debbie Reynolds (Charlie Sorel), Pat Boone (Bruce Minton), Walter Matthau (Sir Leopold Sartori), Martin Gabel (Morton Craft), Ellen McRae [Burstyn] (Frannie).

48. *Sex and the Single Girl* (1964). A Warner Bros. Release (Richard Quine-Reynard Production, produced by William Orr). Directed by Richard Quine. Screenplay by Joseph Heller and David R. Schwartz based on a story by Joseph Hoffmann (from the Helen Gurley Brown best-seller). A psychologist is pursued by a magazine editor. Cast: Tony Curtis (Bob Weston), Natalie Wood (Helen Brown), Henry Fonda (Frank), Lauren Bacall (Sylvia), Mel Ferrer (Rudy), Fran Jeffries (Gretchen), Leslie Parrish (Susan), Edward Everett Horton (Chief).

49. *Paris When It Sizzles* (1964). A Paramount Production (Richard Quine and George Axelrod). Directed by Richard Quine. Screenplay by George Axelrod from an original screenplay by Julien Duvivier and Henri Jeanson. Photography by Charles Jang, Jr. A writer fantasizes different endings for his film story. Cast: William Holden (The Writer), Audrey Hepburn (The Secretary), Noël Coward (Alexander Meyerheim), cameos by Marlene Dietrich, Tony Curtis.

50. *The Great Race* (1965). A Warner Bros. Release (Patricia-Jalem-Reynard Production, produced by Martin Jurow). Directed by Blake Edwards. Screenplay by Arthur Ross from a story by Arthur Ross and Blake Edwards. Photography

by Russell Harlan. Music by Henry Mancini. An international automobile race from New York to Paris. Cast: Jack Lemmon (Professor Fate), Tony Curtis (The Great Leslie), Natalie Wood (Maggie Dubois), Peter Falk (Max), Keenan Wynn (Hezekiah), Arthur O'Connell (Henry Goodbody), Vivian Vance (Hester Goodbody), Dorothy Provine (Lila Olay), Larry Storch (Texas Jack), Ross Martin (Rolfe Von Stuppe).

51. *Boeing-Boeing* (1965). A Paramount Production (Hal Wallis). Directed by John Rich. Screenplay by Edward Anhalt from the play by Marc Camoletti. Photography by Lucien Ballard. Music by Neal Hefti. A journalist carries on several love affairs simultaneously while in Paris. Cast: Tony Curtis (Bernard Lawrence), Jerry Lewis (Robert Reed), Dany Saval (Jacqueline Grieux), Suzanna Leigh (Vicky Hawkins), Christiane Schmidtmer (Lise Bruner), Thelma Ritter (Bertha).

52. *Not with My Wife You Don't!* (1966). A Warner Brothers Release (Fernwood-Reynard Production, produced by Norman Panama). Directed by Norman Panama. Screenplay by Norman Panama, Larry Gelbart, and Peter Barnes from a story by Norman Panama and Melvin Frank. Photography by Charles Lang and Paul Beeson. Music by Johnny Williams. Air-force officers vie for the same woman, who's the wife of one of them. Cast: Tony Curtis (Tom Ferris), Verna Lisi (Julie Ferris), George C. Scott (Tank Martin), Carroll O'Connor (General Parker), Richard Eastham (General Walters), Eddie Ryder (Sergeant Gilroy), George Tyne (Sergeant Dogerty), Ann Doran (Doris Parker).

53. *Arrivederci, Baby!* (1966). Also known as *Drop Dead Darling*. A Paramount Release (Seven Arts Production, produced by Ken Hughes). Directed by Ken Hughes. Screenplay by Ken Hughes. Photography by Denys Coop. Music by Dennis Farnon. A man becomes a black widower in order to inherit money from his wives. Cast: Tony Curtis (Nick), Rosanna Schiaffino (Francesca), Lionel Jeffries (Parker), Nancy Kwan (Baby), Zsa Zsa Gabor (Gigi), Fenella Fielding (Lady Fenella Fawcett), Anna Quayle (Aunt Miriam), Mischa Auer (Rich Italian).

54. *Chamber of Horrors* (1966). Directed by Hy Averback. Mad killer on the loose in a wax museum. Cast: Patrick O'Neal, Cesare Danova, Wilfrid Hyde-White, Patrice Wymore, Suzy Parker, Marie Windsor, Tony Curtis.

55. *Don't Make Waves* (1967). An MGM Release (Filmways-Reynard Production, produced by Martin Ransohof and John Calley). Directed by Alexander Mackendrick. Script by Ira Wallach and George Kirgo, based on the novel *Muscle Beach* by Ira Wallach. Photography by Philip Lathrop. Music by Vic Mizzy. A romantic farce set in southern California. Cast: Tony Curtis (Carlo Cofield), Claudia Cardinale (Laura Califatti), Sharon Tate (Malibu), Robert Webber (Rod Prescott), Joanna Barnes (Diana Prescott), Mort Sahl (Sam Lingonberry), David Draper (Harry Hollard).

56. *The Chastity Belt* (1967). Also titled *On My Way to the Crusades, I Met a Girl Who . . .* A Warner Bros. Release (Fancesco Mazzei for Julia Film Productions). Directed by Pasquale Festa Campanile. Screenplay by Luigi Magni and Larry Gelbart. Photography by Carlo Di Palma. Music by Riz Ortolani. A husband locks his wife in a chastity belt before leaving for the Crusades. Cast: Tony Curtis (Guerrando Da Montone), Monica Vitti (Boccadoro), Hugh Griffith (Sultan of Bari), John Richardson (Drogone), Ivo Garrani (Duke of Pandolfo), Nino Castelnuovo (Marculfo).

57. *The Boston Strangler* (1968). A 20th Century-Fox production. Directed by Richard Fleischer. Screenplay by Edward Anhalt from the book by Gerold Frank. Photography by Richard Kline. The story of Albert De Salvo. Cast: Tony Curtis (Albert De Salvo), Henry Fonda (John S. Bottomly), George Kennedy (Phil Di Natale), Mike Kellin (Julian Soshnick), Hurd Hatfield (Terence Huntley), Murray Hamilton (Frank McAfee), Jeff Corey (John Asgiersson), Sally Kellerman (Dianne Cluny), William Marshall (Edward W. Brooke).

58. *Rosemary's Baby* (1968). A Paramount Picture produced by William Castle. Directed by Roman Polanski. Screenplay by Polanski from the novel by Ira Levin. The devil sires a son. Cast: Mia Farrow, John Cassavetes, Ruth Gordon, Sidney Blackmer, Maurice Evans, Ralph Bellamy, Elisha Cook, Jr., Patsy Kelly, Charles Grodin. Voice cameo by Tony Curtis.

59. *Those Daring Young Men in Their Jaunty Jalopies* (1969). Also known as *Monte Carlo or Bust*. A Paramount Release (Marianne/Mars/De Laurentiis Production, produced by Ken Annakin). Directed by Ken Annakin. Screenplay by Jack Davies and Ken Annakin. Photography by Gabor Pogany. Music by Ron Goodwin. The story of a 1920s car race to Monte Carlo. Cast: Tony Curtis (Chester Schofield), Susan Hampshire (Betty), Terry-Thomas (Sir Cuthbert Ware-Armitage), Eric Sykes (Perkins), Gert Frobe (Willi/Horst), Peter Cook (Dawlish), Dudley Moore (Barrington), Jack Hawkins (Count Levinovitch).

60. *Suppose They Gave a War and Nobody Came* (1969). ABC Pictures Corporation (produced by Fred Engel). Directed by Hy Averback. Screenplay by Don McGuire and Hal Captain. Photography by Burnett Guffey. Music by Jerry Fielding. Cast: Tony Curtis (Lieutenant Shannon Gambroni), Suzanne Pleshette (Ramona), Brian Keith (Nace), Ernest Borgnine (Sheriff Harve), Tom Ewell (Billy Joe Davis), Bradford Dillman (Captain Myerson), Don Ameche (Colonel Flanders).

61. *You Can't Win 'Em All* (1970). A Columbia Pictures Release (SRO Company Production, produced by Gene Corman). Directed by Peter Collinson. Screenplay by Leo Gordon. Photography by Ken Higgins. Music by Bert Kaempfert. A story of war-torn Turkey during the 1920s. Cast: Tony Curtis (Adam Dyer), Charles Bronson (Josh Corey), Michèle Mercier (Aila), Patrick Magee (The General), Grégoire Aslan (Osman Bey).

62. *Lepke* (1974). A Warner Bros. Release (Amerieuro Picture Corp., produced by Menahem Golan). Directed by Menahem Golan. Screenplay by Wesley Lau and Tamar Hobbs. Photography by Andrew Davis. Music by Ken Wannberg. The story of the head of Murder, Inc. Cast: Tony Curtis (Lepke Buchalter), Anjanette Comer (Bernice), Michael Callan (Kane), Warren Berlinger (Gurrah), Milton Berle (Meyer), Vic Tayback (Luciano), Vaughn Meader (Walter Winchell).

63. *The Last Tycoon* (1976). A Paramount Release (Academy Pictures A. G. Production, produced by Sam Spiegel). Directed by Elia Kazan. Screenplay by Harold Pinter from the F. Scott Fitzgerald novel. Photography by Victor Kemper. Music by Maurice Jarre. The story of a Thalberg-type movie producer in the 1930s. Cast: Robert De Niro (Monroe Starr), Tony Curtis (Rodriguez), Robert Mitchum (Pat Brady), Jeanne Moreau (Didi), Jack Nicholson (Brimmer), Donald Pleasance (Boxley), Peter Strauss (Wylie), Ingrid Boulting (Kathleen Moore), Ray Milland (Fleishacker), Dana Andrews (Red Ridingwood), Theresa Russell (Cecilia Brady).

64. *Casanova and Co.* (1977). Also titled *Some Like It Cool*. An Austrian-French-Italian-West German Coproduction. Directed by Franz Antel. Casanova is impersonated by a look-alike. Cast: Tony Curtis (Casanova/Giacomino), Marisa Berenson (Calipha of Shiraz), Sylvia Koscina (Gelsomina), Hugh Griffith (Caliph of Shiraz), Britt Ekland (Countess Trivulzi), Marisa Mell (Duchess Francesca).

65. *The Manitou* (1977). Manitou Productions. Directed by William Girdler. Screenplay by William Girdler, Jon Cedar, and Thomas Pope based on the novel by Graham Mastersom. Photography by Michel Hugo. Music by Lalo Schifrin. An *Alien*-type fetus grows on a young woman's neck. Cast: Tony Curtis (Harry Erskine), Susan Strasberg (Karen Tandy), Michael Ansara (Singing Rock), Ann Sothern (Mrs. Karmann), Burgess Meredith (Dr. Ernest Snow), Stella Stevens (Amelia Crusoe).

66. *Sextette* (1978). Briggs and Sullivan Production. Directed by Ken Hughes. Screenplay by Herbert Baker from a play by Mae West. Photography by James Crabe. Music by Artie Butler. A movie star goes on her honeymoon, only to keep encountering ex-husbands. Cast: Mae West (Marlo Manners), Tony Curtis (Alexei), Ringo Starr (Laslo), Dom de Luise (Dan), Timothy Dalton (Sir Michael Barrington), George Hamilton (Vance), Alice Cooper (Waiter), Keith Moon (Dress Designer), Rona Barrett (Herself), Walter Pidgeon (Chairman), George Raft (Himself).

67. *The Bad News Bears Go to Japan* (1978). A Paramount Production. Directed by John Berry. Screenplay by Bill Lancaster. Photography by Gene Polito and Kozo Okazaki. Music by Paul Chihara. A con man tries to cash in on the kiddie baseball team. Cast: Tony Curtis (Marvin), Jackie Earle Haley (Kelly),

Tomisaburo Wakayama (Coach), George Wyner (Network Director), Lonny Chapman (Gambler).

68. *It Rained All Day the Night I Left* (1979). France-Canada-Israel Coproduction. Directed by Nicolas Gessner. Screenplay by Ted Allan from an original story by Richard Winckler. Photography by Richard Ciupka. Music by Alain Leroux. Two adventurers in the African desert. Cast: Tony Curtis (Robert Talbot), Louis Gossett, Jr. (Leo Garcia), Sally Kellerman (Colonel), John Vernon (George Killian), Lisa Langlois (Sussan), Guy Hoffman (Priest).

69. *Title Shot* (1979). Regenthall Film Productions. Directed by Les Rose. Screenplay by John Saxton from an original idea by Richard Gabourie. Photography by Henri Fiks. Music by Paul James Zaza. A mobster tries to fix a fight. Cast: Tony Curtis (Frank Renzetti), Richard Gabourie (Blake), Susan Hogan (Sylvia), Allan Royal (Dunlop), Robert Delbert (Rufus Taylor), Natsuko Ohama (Terry).

70. *Little Miss Marker* (1980). A Universal-International Production. Directed by Walter Bernstein. Screenplay by Walter Bernstein based on a story by Damon Runyon. Photography by Philip Lathrop. Music by Henry Mancini. The story of a bookie and a little girl left with him as security for a bet. Cast: Walter Matthau (Sorrowful Jones), Julie Andrews (Amanda), Tony Curtis (Blackie), Bob Newhart (Regret), Sara Stimson (The Kid), Lee Grant (The Judge), Brian Dennehy (Herbie), Kenneth McMillan (Brannigan).

71. *The Mirror Crack'd* (1980). Produced by GW Films Ltd. Directed by Guy Hamilton. Screenplay by Jonathan Hales and Barry Sandler based on the novel by Agatha Christie. In the 1950s, a series of murders result when Hollywood stars come to a small British town to make a film. Cast: Angela Lansbury (Miss Marple), Elizabeth Taylor (Marina Gregg), Rock Hudson (Jason Rudd), Kim Novak (Lola Brewster), Tony Curtis (Marty N. Fenn), Edward Fox (Inspector Craddock), Geraldine Chaplin (Ella Zielinsky), Wendy Morgan (Cherry), Charles Gray (Bates), Pierce Brosnan (Actor).

72. *Brainwaves* (1982). Cineamerica Productions. Directed by Ulli Lommel. Screenplay by Ulli Lommel. Photography by Jon Kranhouse and Ulli Lommel. Music by Robert O. Ragland. An accident victim receives the brain of a murdered woman. Cast: Keir Dullea (Julian Bedford), Suzanna Love (Kaylie Bedford), Tony Curtis (Dr. Clavius), Vera Miles (Marian), Percy Rodrigues (Dr. Robinson), Paul Wilson (Dr. Schroder).

73. *Othello: The Black Commando* (1982). AMB Diffusion Eurocine Production. Directed by Max H. Boulois. Screenplay by Max H. Boulois from the play by William Shakespeare. Photography by Domingo Solano. Music by Beethoven. Action film about commandos in Africa and Central America. Cast: Max H. Boulois (Othello), Tony Curtis (Iago), Ramiro Oliveros (Cassio), Joanna Pettet (Desdemona), Naduiska (Gerard Barray).

74. **Balboa** (1982). Entertainment Artists/Production Associates. Directed by James Polakof. Screenplay by James Polakof. Photography by Christopher Lynch. Music by Richard Hieronymus. Episodic soap opera about a scheming real-estate tycoon. Cast: Tony Curtis (Ernie Stoddard), Carol Lynley (Erin Blakely), Jennifer Chase (Kathy Love), Chuck Connors (Alabama Dern), Lupita Ferrer (Rita Carlo), Sonny Bono (Tony Carlo), Catherine Campbell (Cindy Dern), Cassandra Peterson (Angie Stoddard), Henry Jones (Jeffrey Duncan), Steven Kanaly (Sam Cole).

75. **Where Is Parsifal?** (1984). Slenderline Ltd./Terence Young Productions. Directed by Henri Helman. Screenplay by Berta Dominguez. Photography by Norman Langley. Music by Hubert Rostaing and Ivan Julien. An inventor has a party to attract investment in his latest invention. Cast: Tony Curtis (Parsifal Katzenellenbogen), Cassandra Domenica (Elba), Erik Estrada (Henry Board II), Peter Lawford (Montague Chippendale), Ro Moody (Beersbohm), Donald Pleasance (Mackintosh), Orson Welles (Klingsor), Christopher Chaplin (Ivan), Nancy Roberts (Ruth).

76. **Insignificance** (1985). A Zenith Production. Directed by Nicolas Roeg. Written by Terry Johnson. Photography by Peter Hannan. Production design by David Brockhurst. Art direction by Arthur Mack Shafransky. Set direction by Diane Johnstone. Four people who look a lot like Marilyn Monroe, Albert Einstein, Joe DiMaggio and Senator Joseph McCarthy meet in a N.Y.C. hotel room in 1954 to come to grips with Fame and the Atomic Bomb. Cast: Gary Busey (the Baseball Player), Tony Curtis (the Senator), Theresa Russell (the Actress), Michael Emil (the Professor), Will Sampson (the Indian).

77. **King of the City** (1985). An MPR Production, with VTC. Produced, directed, and written by Norman Thaddeus Vane. Photography by Joel King. Music by Jack Conrad, Frank Musker, Michael Sembello, Richard Kerr, Andy Hill, Dominic Bugatti. Choreography by Dennon Rawles. A musical thriller about a bouncer. Cast: Tom Persekian (Cal McFarlane), Michael Parks (Tank), Jamie Barrett (Sissy), Tony Curtis (Hector), Bleu Mackenzie (Tillie), Ron Kohlman (Doctor).

78. **Midnight** (1989). An SVS Films release. Produced, directed, and written by Norman Thaddeus Vane. Photography by David Golia. Music by Michael Wetherwax. A TV horror-film hostess is surrounded by mysterious deaths. Cast: Lynn Redgrave (Midnight/Vera), Tony Curtis (Mr. B), Steven Parrish (Mickey Modine), Frank Gorshin (Ron), Rita Gam (Heidi), Gustav Vintas (Siegfried), Karen Witter (Missy), Wolfman Jack.

79. **Lobster Man from Mars** (1989). An Electric Pictures presentation of a Film-rullen Production. Produced by Eyal Rimmon and Steven S. Greene. Directed by Stanley Sheff. Screenplay by Bob Greenberg. Photography by Gerry Lively. Music by Sasha Matson. Science fiction satire in which producer TC is told he

needs to make a flop film for tax purposes. Cast: Tony Curtis (J. P. Shelldrake), Deborah Foreman (Mary), Patrick Macnee (Professor Piccostomos), Billy Barty (Throckmorton), Anthony Hickox (John), Tommy Sledge (Himself), Dean Jacobsen (Stevie Horowitz), Fred Holiday (Colonel Ankrum), Bobby Pickett (King of Mars/the Astrologer), S. D. Nemeth (the Lobster Man).

80. **Prime Target** (1991). A Hero Films release. Produced, directed, and written by David Heavener. Photography by Peter Wolf. Music by Robert Garrett and David Heavener. A tough cop escorts a Mafia gangster to prison. Cast: David Heavener (John Bloodstone), Tony Curtis (Coppella), Isaac Hayes (Captain Thomkins), Robert Reed (Agent Harrington), Andrew Robinson (Commissioner), Jenilee Harrison (Kathy Bloodstone), Michael Gregory (Agent Robbins), Don Stroud (Manny).

81. **Center of the Web** (1992). Pyramid Distribution Inc., a Winters Group Production. Produced by Ruta K. Aras. Directed and written by David A. Pryor. Photography by Andrew Parke. Music by Greg Turner. Suspense thriller about a hit man and political assassination. Cast: Tony Curtis (Mastermind), Robert Davi (John Phillips), Charlene Tilton (Cathryn Lockwood), Bo Hopkins (the Agent).

82. **The Mummy Lives** (1993). A Klondike Films Release. Produced by Yoram Globus. An Egyptian mummy comes back to life in modern times, all for the love of a woman. Tony Curtis (the Mummy).

83. **Naked in New York** (1993). A Fine Line Release. Produced by Fred Zollo and Martin Scorsese. Directed by Daniel Algrant. Comedy-melodrama in which a new playwright strives to get his play performed in New York. Cast: Whoopi Goldberg (masks of Comedy/Tragedy), Tony Curtis (Carl Fisher, the Producer), Kathleen Turner (the Actress), Timothy Dalton (the Actor), Eric Stoltz (the Writer), Ralph Macchio (the Friend).

TELEVISION APPEARANCES, SERIES, AND FILMS

Cornada (November 10, 1957). "General Electric Theater": TC's television debut as a matador. The title means "thrust with a horn." TC trained with Mexican bullfighter Luis Briones for the role of a hero making a comeback after a near-fatal injury.

Man on a Rock (1958). "Schlitz Playhouse of Stars."

Carriage from Britain (1958). With TC and Janet Leigh, for Revue Television in England.

The Stone (1959). "General Electric Theater."

The Young Juggler (March 29, 1960). "Ford Star Time," NBC. Produced by Curtleigh, this was the story of Saint Barnaby, patron saint of variety acts.

Fade-In (1969). "Bracken's World."

The Persuaders (September 18, 1971, to June 14, 1972) (24-part series). Produced in England by Associated Television Corp. (ATV) and Sir Lew Grade. Adventure series costarring Tony Curtis (Danny Wilde) and Roger Moore (Lord Brett Sinclair).

The Third Girl from the Left (October 16, 1973). "Movie of the Week." Directed by Peter Medak. Script and music by Dory Previn. A chorus girl has misgivings about her impending marriage to a Las Vegas con man. Cast: Kim Novak, Tony Curtis, Michael Brandon, George Furth, Barbi Benton, Louis Guss, Michael Conrad, Anne Ramsey.

The Count of Monte Cristo (January 10, 1975). Produced by Norman Rosemont. Directed by David Greene. Script by Sidney Carroll based on story by Alexandre Dumas. Costume drama. Cast: Richard Chamberlain, Tony Curtis, Trevor Howard, Louis Jourdan, Donald Pleasance, Taryn Power, Kate Nelligan.

The Big Rip-Off (March 11, 1975). NBC. Directed by Dean Hargrove. Cast: Tony Curtis, Brenda Vaccaro, Roscoe Lee Browne, Larry Hagman, John Dehner. Pilot for the NBC Sunday Mystery Movie miniseries in which *McCoy* rotated with *McCloud, Columbo,* and *McMillan and Wife.* Created by Roland Kibbee and Dean Hargrove. TC played McCoy, a con artist with a heart of gold. Roscoe Lee Browne played his associate, Gideon Gibbs.

Vega$ (1978). Produced by Aaron Spelling. Directed by Richard Lang. Script by Michael Mann. Pilot for the TV series about a Las Vegas detective. TC as casino owner Bernie Roth. Cast: Robert Urich, Red Buttons, Will Sampson, June Allyson, Edd Byrnes, Jack Kelly, Greg Morris, Phyllis Davis, Judy Landers.

The Users (1978). Directed by Joseph Hardy. TV movie based on Joyce Haber's novel about a fading Hollywood star. Cast: Tony Curtis, Jaclyn Smith, Joan Fontaine, Red Buttons, George Hamilton, John Forsythe, Darren McGavin, Michelle Phillips.

Moviola: The Scarlett O'Hara War (1980). Directed by John Erman. Based on the novel by Garson Kanin. The story of David Selznick's search for the perfect actress to play the lead in *Gone With the Wind.* Cast: Tony Curtis (David O. Selznick), Sharon Gless, Harold Gould, Bill Macy, George Furth, Edward Winter, Barrie Youngfellow, Clive Revill, Carrie Nye, Morgan Brittany. TC nominated for Emmy Award.

The Million Dollar Face (1981). Directed by Michael O'Herlihy. Based on Lois Wyse's novel *Kiss, Inc.* A pilot about the head of a cosmetics firm, starring TC as Revson, who founded the Revlon Company. Cast: Tony Curtis, David Huffman, Herschel Bernardi, Gayle Hunnicutt, Lee Grant, Polly Bergen, William Daniels, Sylvia Kristel, Roddy McDowall, Murray Matheson.

Inmates: A Love Story (1981). Directed by Guy Green. Love in a coed prison. Cast: Kate Jackson, Perry King, Shirley Jones, Tony Curtis, Pamela Reed, Paul Koslo, Fay Hauser, Penelope Allen.

The Golden Land (1984). British documentary on Jews in America, narrated by Tony Curtis.

Mafia Princess (1986). Directed by Robert Collins. Based on autobiography of Antoinette Giancana, the story of mobster Sam Giancana and his daughter. Cast: Tony Curtis (Sam Giancana), Susan Lucci (Antoinette Giancana), Kathleen Widdoes, Chuck Shamata, Louie DiBianco.

Murder in Two Acts (1988). Peter Ustinov, Tony Curtis, Emma Samms. Based on the detective novel by Agatha Christie.

Thanksgiving Day (1990). Screenplay by Steve Zacharias and Jeff Buhai. Directed by Gino Tanasescu. Patriarch of a wealthy family has a heart attack into a Thanksgiving turkey. Cast: Tony Curtis, Jonathon Brandmeier, Joseph Bologna, Andy Hirsch, Kelly Curtis, Sonny Bono, Morton Downey, Jr.

Joseph Cornell (1991). Omnibus documentary, narrated by Tony Curtis.

Christmas in Connecticut (1992). A Turner Pictures Production. Directed by Arnold Schwarzenegger. Remake of the 1942 Barbara Stanwyck comedy. Cast: Dyan Cannon, Tony Curtis.

PHOTO CREDITS

Tony Curtis Collection:

Schwartz family in New Jersey; Manuel Schwartz as French gentleman; baby Bernard Schwartz; Helen Schwartz holding Bernie; Bernie in Central Park; Schwartz family in the Catskills; Julius Schwartz; TC holding oar; Boy Scout troop; Manuel Schwartz with violin; mother and son in front of tailor shop; Errol Flynn with TC; Bernard Schwartz in navy uniform; navy certification card; Schwartz with Rube Goldberg; quadruple date; Schwartz and friends at nightclub; photo from *The Prince* . . . ; Rock Hudson snapshot; TC in wardrobe test; Schwartz family in Hollywood; Robert Schwartz's Universal publicity photo; TC-signed fan club photo; Martin, Lewis, and TC; TC with cigarette in dressing room; TC with fencing instructor; bearded TC with Kelly; Poitier, TC, and Sammy Davis, Jr.; Hirshfeld drawing; Sinatra and TC; Monroe and TC; Jack Lemmon with Helen Schwartz; TC and Monroe; Helen in Monroe chair; Helen and Manuel with TC in drag; TC with Cary Grant; TC in *Great Impostor*; TC with Carl Sandburg; Quine and Cooper in *Dinky*; Jamie Lee and Kelly; Eli Blumenfeld; TC oil painting; TC box construction; Kelly Curtis; Jamie Lee and TC on set; Allegra Curtis; Alexandra Curtis; Nicholas Curtis; Benjamin Curtis. *In photo insert:* TC on ship rigging; TC in top hat and jeans; TC fishing.

Barry Paris Collection:

City Across the River still; ZaSu Pitts; TC and Sue England; TC and Janet Leigh; Leigh MGM photo; TC and Lancaster photos from *Sweet Smell*; TC and Leigh in *Perfect Furlough* publicity pose; TC reclining on couch for *Some Like It Hot*; TC being drag-fitted; TC saluting in *Petticoat*; TC and Leigh in *Who Was That Lady?*; TC and Christine Kaufmann; TC and Jerry Lewis in *Boeing-Boeing*; TC in *Boston Strangler*; TC as Lepke; TC and De Niro; TC in *Bad News Bears Go to Japan*.
In photo insert: TC with boxing gloves; all TC closeups; TC as Lepke.

PHOTO CREDITS

Photofest:

Winchester '73; The Prince Who Was a Thief; Houdini; Beachhead; Johnny Dark; Trapeze; The Vikings; TC/Poitier; Carl Switzer; Spartacus; Taras Bulba; Sex and the Single Girl; Sextette; The Mirror Crack'd; Insignificance; Moviola.

Leonard Maltin Collection:

Arrivederci, Baby!; Not with My Wife You Don't!; Don't Make Waves.

Jamie Lee Curtis Collection:

TC serigraph portrait of Jamie; Jamie at birthday party; TC's six children.

Smithsonian Institution:

Joseph Cornell photo.

INDEX

Page numbers in *italics* refer to illustrations.

INDEX

INDEX

INDEX